Theaters of the Mind

THEATERS OF THE MIND

Illusion and Truth
on the Psychoanalytic Stage

Joyce McDougall

Basic Books, Inc., Publishers   New York

Library of Congress Cataloging-in-Publication Data

McDougall, Joyce.
  Theaters of the mind.

  Translation of: *Théâtres du Je*.
  Bibliography: p. 289.
  Includes index.
  1. Psychoanalysis—Case studies. 2. Psychology,
pathological—Case studies. 3. Object relations
(Psychoanalysis)—Case studies. I. Title.
RC509.8.M3513 1985   616.89'17'0926   85–47565
ISBN 0–465–08418–4

For Daniel, Joshua, and Oliver

Contents

Foreword

Those familiar with Joyce McDougall's extremely readable and informative *Plea for a Measure of Abnormality* will be pleased to know that this new volume more than fulfills the high expectations raised by its predecessor. Starting from the theoretical frame developed in her earlier book, McDougall now presents a comprehensive view of the five fundamental types of psychopathology: neuroses (including neurotic character pathology); severe character disorders and addictive personalities; perversions (which she calls *neosexualities*); psychoses; and the psychosomatic disorders *(psychosomatosis)*.

Theaters of the Mind is not, however, an impersonal phenomenological textbook on discrete psychopathological entities. It is a broad and rich framework of central conflicts and typical psychodynamic constellations that emerge in the course of psychoanalytic exploration of these different patient populations, couched in a frame of reference that integrates a classical psychoanalytic perspective with contemporary object relations theory.

McDougall's primary interest is in achieving an understanding in depth of her patients' psychopathology as represented by what she calls "theaters of the mind." These theaters consist of fantasied, unconscious, idiosyncratic scenarios that contain desired-for, threatening, and defensively erected relationships of the infantile *I* with significant others. McDougall is less interested in discussing alternative theoretical viewpoints than in pointing to the clinical relevance of particular aspects of various theories; thus she brings theory to life by relating it to immediate clinical situations. In so doing, she convincingly illustrates how an object relations viewpoint is congruent with classical drive theory. She establishes links among the French, British, and American traditions, drawing freely from psychosomaticists such as Marty, De M'Uzan, Sifneos, and Krystal, and from Klein, Bion, and Meltzer, as well as from Arlow, Engel, Lichtenstein, Mahler, and Stoller.

McDougall sees the field of unconscious intrapsychic representations of internalized object relations, including their investment with affects as well as word representatives, as the normal theater of the mind. Throughout the detailed description of the symptoms, the intrapsychic situation, the transference and countertransference developments in each of the five types of psychopathology, she points to universal basic conflicts around the issues of engulfment and separation, recognition of the anatomical differences between the sexes, the oedipal scenario, and the reality of death. Behind the classical scenario of the Oedipus Complex she presents the scenario of a primitive oedipal situation in which father is absent or devalued, mother dominates the scene and invasively controls the mental development of the infant and child, all of which determines primitive fears regarding the nature of the genitals, violent conceptions of sexual relations, and a sense of danger in autonomous assertion.

She elegantly shifts from clinical descriptions to the subtle differences with which basic conflicts are elaborated, elaborations that will determine whether the patient will follow the road to one or another of the dominant types of psychopathology. For example, expanding her theory of the psychodynamics of perversion, spelled out in her earlier work, McDougall pinpoints crucial developments that will lead to a perverse structure and contrasts such developments with others that may lead to a severe character disorder without a specific perversion. McDougall also expands her previous work on psychosomatic conditions; critically reviewing the concepts of alexithymia and operative thinking, she finds that patients with psychosomatosis have, very early in life, renounced the body-image aspect of the self. Such a patient treats his or her body as if it were the extension of a primitive, symbiotic mother whose invasiveness forced the infant to abandon the bodily experience and to cripple affective development.

Theaters of the Mind presents vivid illustrations of how frozen character structures, and even the puzzling operative thinking and object relations of psychosomatic patients, may be transformed, by means of psychoanalytic exploration, into intrapsychic experiences of the previously disavowed or acted-out conflicts. Thus, in the course of a successful psychoanalytic treatment, the adult *I* becomes acquainted and reconciled with the infantile *I*'s as well as with the infantile objects of desire, of frustration, and of terror. McDougall's many clinical illustrations may be brief, but she nevertheless manages to convey to the reader not only the patient's free associations and the developments in the transference, but also the changing nature of her own emotional relation to the patient's communications, her creative use of countertransference reactions to reconstruct those aspects of intrapsychic reality that the patient could not originally tolerate.

Fears of castration reflecting oedipal conflicts, fears of fragmentation connected with identity conflicts and issues of symbiosis, terror of death related to primitive aggression, all acquire clinical reality as immediate, concrete human experiences, as well as serving to anchor theoretical formulations. This direct pulling together of the theoretical and the experiential is one of the most satisfying ingredients of this book. McDougall's central concern for communicating the richness of clinical experiences and her weaving back and forth between clinical experience and theory, in contrast to advancing any particular theoretical view, adds to making *Theaters of the Mind* such an appealing book.

—OTTO F. KERNBERG

Theaters of the Mind

In the interest of protecting the privacy of the patients, all names and identifying details have been altered.

Prologue

The Psychic Theater and the Psychoanalytic Stage

> One always hopes to become someone only to find out in the end that one is several.
>
> *Raymond Devos, French comedian*

"All the world's a stage," and that all the men and women in it are "merely players" expressed Shakespeare's deep conviction that we do not readily escape the roles that are essentially ours. Each of us is drawn into an unfolding life drama in which the plot reveals itself to be uncannily repetitive.

In taking the theater as a metaphor for psychic reality, I am hoping to avoid the standard psychiatric and psychoanalytic classification of clinical entities. Those terms apply to symptoms, not to people. To designate someone as a "neurotic," a "psychotic," a "pervert," or a "psychosomatic" is little more than name-calling and is inadequate to describe anything as complex and subtle as a human personality. It not only fosters the illusion that we have said something pertinent about somebody, but implies that the rest of us are free of the psychic dramas that lie behind the symptoms to which these terms refer.

We all have our neurotic conflicts, our little areas of private folly (at least let us hope so); we are all susceptible to psychosomatic breakdown under stress; and we are all capable of creating perverse fantasies as well as dreaming impossible dreams. Each of

3

us harbors in our inner universe a number of "characters," parts of ourselves that frequently operate in complete contradiction to one another, causing conflict and mental pain to our conscious selves. For we are relatively unacquainted with these hidden players and their roles. Whether we will it or not, our inner characters are constantly seeking a stage on which to play out their tragedies and comedies. Although we rarely assume responsibility for our secret theater productions, the producer is seated in our own minds. Moreover, it is this inner world with its repeating repertory that determines most of what happens to us in the external world.

Who writes the scripts? What are the plots about? And where are they performed?

Language informs us that the scriptwriter is called *I*. Psychoanalysis has taught us that the scenarios were written years ago by a naive and childlike *I* struggling to survive in an adult world whose drama conventions are quite different from the child's. These psychic plays may be performed in the theater of our own minds or that of our bodies or may take place in the external world, sometimes using other people's minds and bodies, or even social institutions, as their stage. We are also capable of shifting our own psychic dramas from one stage to another in times of overwhelming stress. For the *I* is a multifaceted character. Let us listen to a patient, Ben, recounting, whatever thoughts happen to cross his mind, as his analyst has requested:

I'm not sure how to express exactly what I'm feeling. *(This is Ben the analysand, settling down to his session.)*

One thing is sure, I'm thoroughly fed up with my wife and her family. I'd like to throw them all out! *(This is Ben aged about three, at a time when his own family seemed to him unbearable.)*

I can't imagine how Jenny stands them—nor why she imposes them on me. *(Ben the victim now states his claim for compensatory sympathy, but in doing so overlooks the fact that he appears to have chosen a wife who embodies all the troubling aspects of his own family.)*

Yet I really love her; I'd be lost without her. I've only known real happiness since I met her. *(This is Ben, husband and lover, talking.)*

But I still think I might pack up everything and go to Borneo for a few months with Andy; we always got on so well—and he's sick of things, too. *(Here Ben's homosexual adolescent self is putting in a word for his side.)*

Hell! Do I hate my brother-in-law! He thinks he's somebody just because he makes so many thousand a month! *(This is also Ben's unconscious homosexual self, but a competing one who, in childhood, was always filled with admiration and envy of his elder brother. The latter, mom's favorite, ruled the roost.)*

Good God, where am *I* in all this? *(The analysand has returned to the analytic stage and begins to gather up his cast of players.)*

It is evident that the Ben who wants to throw his wife and family out of the house is not the same one who loves his wife so dearly, nor the Ben who also loves Andy and hates his brother-in-law. Which one is *I*?

Free-floating associations, essential to the work of analysis, allow us to discover how many different people within us claim to be *I*. At the same time, it is difficult to hear what several people are saying if they all speak at once—as they do in our unconscious minds. In fact, Ben has pulled five of his *I*'s favorite scenarios out of the archives of his mind in the first few minutes of the session, as do most analysands when they can allow their thoughts to wander freely.

Although being given permission to free associate is a rare opportunity, unthinkable in an ordinary social situation, many patients resist the invitation to "say everything" even within the therapeutic setting. Sometimes patients treat the analytic relationship as though it *were* a social one, becoming apprehensive about the analyst's thoughts and judgments. At other times they are afraid of meeting their thoughts and feelings when faced with little-known or unacceptable aspects of themselves. In addition, some analysands fear the loss of control that is entailed in letting their thoughts wander freely: they are afraid of getting confused or sounding crazy. These reticences are known as *resistance* to the analytic or therapeutic process, and they demand respect until such time as the analysand feels capable of assuming the conflicts and paradoxes that cause resistance.

Another patient, George, starts his session by saying his thoughts are trifling and of no interest to anyone. When the analyst points out that this is difficult to predict since we can never tell where our thoughts will lead us, he reluctantly recounts that he was hurrying out of the house, late as usual, when his wife, Sue, called him back.

George, for goodness' sake don't forget the dry cleaning again!

Dammit! Can't you do that? My office is miles away from the cleaners.

Oh, you're just like my mother. She was always miles away from the cleaners whenever I needed her!

And you're just like mine! Always asking me to do her jobs for her.

At least your mother didn't work all day in a law office and then come home to cook and clean!

George goes on to say how much he has always admired Sue's professional qualifications, so unlike his house-bound and house-proud mother. But for the first time he wonders whether his mind's *I* may have played a trick on him. It now occurs to him that he might have chosen Sue because, in many respects, she resembles his mother so much. He then begins to feel resentful, because she does everything around the house so badly. As the session proceeds, the person inside George who secretly pines for a housewifely mother-substitute, one who would organize his life to perfection, keeps coming on stage. But this is someone George does not want to know, until he realizes with surprise that domestic scenes are becoming more frequent and more bitter. It becomes clear that he must now face these two conflicting parts of himself and put them into better dialogue with each other, since each of them has something important to say.

Little is left to chance in the dramas that make up a human life. Yet we often prefer to believe we are the playthings of fate, obliged to perform unrewarding tasks that present themselves as essential and to fulfill obscure desires that we do not recognize as our own. Unaware of the hidden choices that direct our decisions, we are rarely coherent in accounting for our choice of partners or professions, or for the mixture of success and failure that each choice may bring us. We do not escape the roles that our unconscious selves intend us to play, frequently using people in our lives today as stand-ins to settle problems of the past. It is only when we try to re-create everyday scenes upon the psychoanalytic stage that we often discover to our dismay that we are in full performance yet totally ignorant of who the real characters are or what the story is about.

Who were we when we started that absurd argument with the new neighbor? We've been so busy asking ourselves who the hell he thinks *he* is to park his car where it becomes virtually impossible for us to get into the driveway that we have quite overlooked our role in the ensuing discussion, which ended to everyone's total dissatisfaction. Of course the intrusive newcomer is remarkably like cousin Dave, who came to live with the family when he was eight, taking up half our "driveway" as children. What with his dinky cars and toy soldiers scattered all over the place we no longer even had the playroom to ourselves! It may have been thirty years ago, but Dave is still there among our inner personages, and we are still trying to get him onto any promising stage, using a suitable character to play his role, so that we can at last tell him just what we think of him.

Each secret-theater self is thus engaged in repeatedly playing roles from the past, using techniques discovered in childhood and reproducing, with uncanny precision, the same tragedies and comedies, with the same outcomes and an identical quota of pain and pleasure. What were once attempts at self-cure in the face of mental pain and conflict are now symptoms that the adult *I* produces, following forgotten childhood solutions. The resulting psychic scenarios may be called neuroses or narcissistic disorders, addictions or perversions, psychoses or psychosomatoses but they originate from our childlike *I*'s need to protect itself from psychic suffering.

Let us take a closer look at these repressed scenarios of which symptoms are only vestigial remnants. All drama, tragic or comic, reveals the struggles of men and women, confronted with violent instinctual forces in a world that offers little support in solving conflicts. Swept by storms of love and hate, seeking as much to please and to seduce as to punish and to destroy those closest to us, from childhood on we all have to compromise with two fundamental aspects of external reality: the Forbidden and the Impossible. These form the ineluctable framework from which our personal identity is constructed. Helped or hindered by the demands of the "others," the people who brought us up and the society to which we belong, each of us attempts to find solutions that satisfy the exigencies of our forbidden libidinal longings and our impossible narcissistic desires.

By definition, the Forbidden is potentially realizable. It is theoretically possible, for example, to commit incest or parricide. That such acts may be considered impossible arises from the barrier of repression that makes such guilt-laden wishes unthinkable. The true Impossibles, on the other hand, are connected to inevitable narcissistic wounds that beset the human infant from birth onward, beginning with the wound of being severed from fusional oneness with the mother. These are markedly less accessible to verbal thought and require counterinvestments and compensations of another order.

The psychic repertory of the Forbidden comprises, in the neurotic theater, endless variations on the oedipal theme in both its homosexual and its heterosexual orientation. Instead of enjoying the adult right to sexual and love relations and the normal narcissistic pleasure afforded by work and sublimatory activities, the *I* draws inward in an attempt to hold on to these precious rights. Meanwhile the distressed child hidden in the adult sacrifices pleasure and satisfaction in exchange for compromise solutions that lead to the creation of neurotic symptoms and inhibitions. These compromise solutions, constructed to protect sexuality or to satisfy it in roundabout ways, are camouflaged in an atmosphere of interdiction, anxiety, and guilt.

The Forbidden, as its etymology implies, is always related to what the child has been *told.* Its repertory is therefore composed of highly condensed verbal texts that recount storms and obstacles in the odyssey of desire. The first three "scenes from psychic life" recounted in chapter 2 illustrate the alternating forces of attraction and repulsion of the Forbidden. They preserve, in petrified form, the fruit of childhood sexual theories and fantasies. Such creations, remarkable for their density and overall efficiency, are actually encoded versions of complex plays.

By contrast the theater of the Impossible reveals suffering of a more widespread nature, suffering that frequently makes social and work relationships painfully difficult and leaves people hurt and confused. How do we manage to bind the wounds to our narcissistic integrity caused by external realities—the impossibility of being one with the mother; the failure of the illusion that one can control another's thoughts and actions; the realization that we must accept to be one sex or the other and do not have the power and sexual attributes of both parents; the fact of aging; and finally, the inevitability of death? Most of us manage to make unstable adjustments to these realities, but there is little doubt that in our unconscious fantasies we are all omnipotent, bisexual, externally young, and immortal.

Failure to devise acceptable ways of transforming impossible wishes into substitute satisfactions may create a serious fault-line in the psychic structure, leading to profound narcissistic disturbance. The fragment of analysis of the patient called Angela, whom we shall meet in chapter 10, gives a glimpse into this aspect of psychic perturbation. Should narcissistic defenses and relationships fail, there is a risk of psychotic decompensation. An example of this more serious outcome is the particular disorganization of reality called *delusion*. The scenario of the young would-be murderer, recounted in chapter 2, is a vivid illustration of the tragedy inherent in this particular expression of the Theater of the Impossible. We are no longer witnessing the scenes of the normal-neurotic struggle to protect one's adult rights nor of the narcissistic struggle to maintain one's feeling of self-esteem and personal identity. The psychotic plot turns around the unceasing struggle for the right to exist, against the subject's deep conviction instilled through childhood interpretations, that the right to an independent life, or even to existence itself, was not desired.

When the curtain rises on the psychotic stage, we have the impression that the stage manager has destroyed the setting and instead is allowing the public to witness the disorder behind the scenes. Without the coherent lines of the players through which neurotic scenarios are communicated, we are often puzzled by the story that is presented to us. Psychotic plots, like those of neurotic creation, are made of words and ideas, but the meaning of the words has been reorganized in such a private way that it is difficult to grasp their underlying significance. Delusions, structured like dreams, are nevertheless lived as an implacable reality by the minds that have invented them.

Fortunately, in coming to grips with life's Impossibles, most of us have at our disposal other theaters than that of delusion. There is another stage, on which many impossible and forbidden wishes may find substitute expressions. This stage, lying between the limitless inner universe and the restricting world of external reality, coincides with what Winnicott (1951, 1971) called "transitional space." This potential "space," according to Winnicott, is the intermediate area of experiencing that lies between fantasy and reality. It includes, among many other phenomena, the place of cultural experience and the area of creativity (Ogden 1985). In the time-space continuum of this social area, as Winnicott emphasized, much of what is essential to human life is played out. For many people, however, this intermediate area of experiencing is painfully restricted and may be replete with pathological activities such as the pursuit of addictions of every kind. Scenarios belonging to the Transitional Theater are described in chapter 3.

A special form of addictive pursuit is played out by those who use people as though they were drug substances, resulting in exploitation rather than exchange. Such patients often reveal a tragic disbelief in their right to the indirect libidinal and narcissistic sublimations that the Transitional Theater provides. Unaware that they are using others as stand-ins for objects that are lacking in their inner psychic world, they fear annihilation if the others do not fulfill their expectations. Their scenarios are neither neurotic nor psychotic creations; rather, they borrow ways of thought and action that belong to both. These character symptoms are difficult to stage since they require the cooperation of other peoples' *I* in accepting roles in the subjects' private theater. The drug-like use of others as players in one's secret scenarios is founded upon one postulate of the Impossible, namely, that others exist only as parts of ourselves. At the same time the stage manager is dependent upon the needs and wishes of others and to this extent is forced to submit to the exigencies of the Possible. Blanche's story, recounted in chapter 3, exemplifies one of the many ways in which we may, without knowing it, use another's

I to deal with intolerable feelings. Expressions of hate, anger, guilt, and worthlessness are sought out in the other, who is then punished accordingly.

We come finally to the most dimly lit of the scenarios that belong to the psychic theater: a plot in which the characters manage to put themselves on stage by profoundly altering the body's biological functioning. In these scenes the psyche appears to have given up the struggle, letting the soma stage its own, essentially wordless, show. It is important to distinguish the psychosomatic theater from neurotic scenarios of a hysterical nature that make symbolic use of the body, as well as from those that create a psychotic body-theater in which hypochondriacal delusions or actual mutilation of the body express the psychic themes. Unlike the psychosomatic dramas, these tell stories, and the key words of the plot may be deciphered eventually through the analytic process.*

We must therefore consider the nature of these "stories without words" that make up the repertory of the psychosomatic body-theater. Most individuals recognize intuitively the painful but nevertheless reassuring fact that their neurotic creations, their perverse and addictive activities, and even their psychotic productions contain hidden meanings and therefore belong to them, secretly wished for or needed to weather the storms of life. When we come to the psyche's psychosomatic productions, which do not at first sight appear to be on the side of life, this certitude tends to disappear. One reason for the unheralded performances of psychosomatic drama, for we are rarely forewarned of dramatic physical illness, lies in the fact that the mind has not dealt with a multitude of perceptions, sensations, and affects that normally would clamor for mental representation. These have been radically severed from psychic awareness, and a body-mind split has been created.

In our attempts to reconstruct the obscure plot of the disturbed soma, the characters on the psychoanalytic stage appear as strange creatures, "body-things," primitively eroticized vital

---

*Different body theaters of this kind have been discussed at length elsewhere. See Joyce McDougall, *Plea for a Measure of Abnormality* (New York: International Universities Press, 1980), chaps. 9 to 12.

organs and senses that lurk like mysterious monsters in the wings of the mind's theater. This motley cast has few words at its disposal. Lacking their lines, the actors tend to draw attention to themselves by means of gestures or abrupt physical displacements such as tears or trembling; if they do use words, these serve the needs of energetic discharge rather than those of communication. Each individual psyche hides a number of such archaic personages in the recesses of its mental space, and they tend to come on stage at times when the rest of the psychic repertory is out of commission. Chapters 4 to 8 attempt to conceptualize these strange theatrical productions that are disconnected from the patients' words.

Coming to terms with forbidden and impossible wishes requires in each case a mourning process, but one that brings a recompense for all that is relinquished. The renunciation of the impossible desire for fusion and omnipotent control of others brings in its wake the precious feeling of individual identity. (This frequently serves as a bulwark against grave narcissistic or psychotic breakdown.) The realization that one will never be both sexes or possess either parent sexually is rewarded with the gift of sexual desire and the promise of fulfillment in the future. (Failure to achieve this conviction lays the individual open to neurotic problems or to the obligation to choose homosexual or "neosexual" solutions [chapters 11 and 12] in order to salvage one's sexuality.) There is of course the possibility of psychotic solutions to the difficulty in accepting one's biological gender, such as the choice of transsexualizing one's body, or creating a Schreber-like delusion (Freud, 1911a) that one's sex has been changed by God. Acceptance of the inevitable end of life gives urgent meaning to living and for many people leads to the wish to leave something of one's self behind in the ongoing flow of life —children, works of art, projects of every kind. (Failure in this important domain may lead to a disinvestment of life, with consequent grave depression, autistic withdrawal from the world of others, or an increase in psychosomatic vulnerability.)

Failures in coming to terms with the Forbidden and the Impossible are sometimes due to the far-reaching effects of parents' unconscious problems, as well as inherent fragilities in certain children. If parents' internal dramas drive them to use their children—either their bodies or their minds—to settle scores with the past and repair their own narcissistic images or damaged libidinal relationships, the small megalomaniac is not likely to receive the help required to find solutions to the inevitable traumas of human life. For it is parents who give their children a sense of self, enjoyment in their individuality, masculinity and femininity, and the right to enjoy as fully as possible all aspects of adult life.

The conflicts and characters of the past, as well as our own various child and adult selves, are the essential elements that make up our secret scenarios. We can readily envision the task of the mind's *I* that must meet the demands of all the conflicting inner voices clamoring for attention. The *I* strives constantly to achieve and maintain a measure of libidinal and narcissistic satisfaction in external relationships and activities, while at the same time it tries to make sense of its symptomatic productions and thus assure coherence and continuity. In other words, our psyche seeks to keep the illusion that we really know who we are when we say *I.* This feat requires both imagination and invention, and the *I* is a constant creator. The psychic theater runs twenty-four hours a day!

On the psychoanalytic stage the different theaters and their varied cast of characters slowly emerge. As an analysand begins to have confidence in the analyst's interest and ability to contain the conflicting emotions of love, hate, fear, anger, anxiety, and depression that come to the force, particularly when fantasies about the analyst and the analytic relationship develop, the *I* begins to reveal the different psychic theaters in which its conflicts are expressed. It also allows the inner characters to be recognized by both analyst and patient. Among the throng appear many different aspects of the self, some idealized and others repudiated by the conscious adult *I.* Equally ambivalent dimensions of people from the past also take their place in the analytic discourse, so that their underlying significance can be appreciated.

As the analysis proceeds, wounded and sad aspects of childhood make their appearance, along with joyous and irrational ones, many of them left in the wings years ago. All jostle to be heard, understood, possibly applauded. People from the present day join this crowd, and they too are presented in varying lights; positive and negative feelings about them create temporary confusion until the analysand can see that two important parts of himself or herself are also in question. From the past must come the essential figures of childhood: the parents with their loving and loved dimensions as well as their feared and hated images. Siblings too appear, as both welcomed and unwanted parts of the family constellation. Other family characters, stretching back several generations, come to play their roles in each subject's human drama. The scripts of these internalized characters are remembered or reconstructed in the course of the analysis. Meanwhile the producers and directors must discover the meaning of *their* place in their family history, with the hope that before leaving the psychoanalytic stage they will have come to recognize who they are and what they represented for their parents. Optimally, analysands also become acquainted with their personal life goals and the reasons for past failures to achieve them.

In the psychoanalytic experience, patients hear, in their own free-flowing associations, the forgotten voices of the past and the lost fears and fantasies of childhood. Thus there is created a new stage on which to play the unfolding drama of living. This inchoate experience enables the analysand to engage in a dialogue with the figures of the past. The threads of discourse, broken off in precipitous fashion in childhood, can now be joined once more and their elaboration continued into the present and the future.

As the psychoanalytic adventure continues, the classic characters of the human comedy all take their places on the analytic stage. The many facets of the father, at one moment idealized and at another denigrated, in one scene a seducer, in the next a castrator, at first contradict each other in a confusing series of conflicting memories and fantasies. On the same stage, the complex images of the mother come back to life, refracted, like the father, into several different mothers: adoring and devouring, omniscient and omnipotent, seductive and rejecting, dispenser and withholder of miraculous gifts. By the same token, each *I* reveals unknown facets of *itself:* little Oedipus, neurotic and perverse, tortured by inescapable feelings of guilt, caught in the maze of the Forbidden; the even smaller Narcissus, suffused with shame and inadequacy, fighting for the Impossible.

The analytic stage thus allows the infantile and the adult selves to become better acquainted. The analyst meanwhile becomes a stand-in for any of the people who make up the analysand's internal world. It is essential that the analyst too be able to tolerate the intensity of the analytic relationship in both its loving and its hating aspects, since analysts are also exposed to the risk that their own inner characters and secret scenarios may inadvertently be led into playing roles in the analysands' unfolding adventure, thus deflecting the analytic discourse.

Under optimal conditions the psychoanalytic adventure allows each *I* to bring forth its own Jekyll and Hyde and its own Faust and Mephistopheles, split-off yet vitally necessary parts of every self. Thus love and hate may be reconciled, enabling the subject finally to sign the treaty of many years' silent warfare, which otherwise might lead to exhaustion and death. In other words, while seeking to express themselves verbally, the many *I*s contained within each patient's official *I* listen to each other. Discovering their paradoxes and contradictions, they can henceforth assume their cohesive identity and their mutual enterprise. The analytic discourse, in giving new meaning to the past, enables many patients to resume possession of their abandoned potentialities, to extend their capacity to think and to feel, and to explore such thoughts and feelings without fear.

We might finally question the veracity of the reconstructed texts and resuscitated personages that emerge from the different theaters of the mind, played out upon the analytic stage. Such "truths" are constructed, in dialectical fashion, out of memory and fantasy and provide an inner world in which the *I* of each participant finds more space within which to move, constructing meaning where before there was none. Delivered from the role of hapless victim of the uncontrollable present and the unchanging past, the analysand is no longer endlessly condemned to repeat the old scenarios, to suffer the same old failures, and to meet each new challenge with the old familiar anxiety or despair. "Truth" is the affirmation of the actual and the recognition of one's place in the human, sexual, and social order; it is the acceptance of one's strengths and failings as well as those of others—people of the past and people of the present. For many, the psychotherapeutic experience is the sole way to escape from the compulsive quality of the age-old scenarios that can bring only pain and disappointment with each reenactment.

It is the lot of humankind to be locked in constant conflict with instinctual nature while at the same time endeavoring to take account of the desires and conflicts of others. Thus, many people find solutions that do not require analysis. They use their psychic theaters in ways that deal adequately with the inevitable conflicts of the past, creating healing dreams and actions, rewarding relationships, intense and lasting love, and sometimes sublime works of art that bring as much joy to the creator as to those who behold them. These people already know that, in spite of suffering, life is a creative and continuing adventure at all ages. On the other hand, those who have immobilized and muted many of the plots and players in their internal theater, allowing them no action but to hammer on the walls of the mind, might learn to value the words of Sartre (1965, p. 37): "If you want your characters to live, then liberate them!"

1

Static and Ec-static States: Reflections on the Psychoanalytic Process

Stepping onto the Psychoanalytic Stage

The scenarios are written in an unknown language; the dialogue is inaudible, sometimes reduced to mime; the characters are as yet unnamed. The psychic dramas of the theaters of the mind thus await production on the analytic stage. In the hope of finding meaning and easing pain, two people step out on that stage to bring the drama to life as psychic reality. The analysand has only vague memories for a script, a sense of having been there before but no precise idea of the settings, characters, or actions to be encountered. The analyst already knows, from long years of personal analysis, what the analysand will discover: that we stumble upon these scenes and people, sometimes with utter astonishment, sometimes with a feeling that we have found the missing part of a puzzle, and sometimes with the strength to hear the end of a story or to look at scenes that once seemed fearful to bear.

Analysands taking their first uncertain steps onto this inner stage do so with extreme caution. They are wary of that unknown guide, the analyst. At one moment they believe that the analyst already knows all the scenarios awaiting production; at other times they worry that the analyst will not provide support if the dramas become too strange or too frightening. And indeed this internal world is peopled in a weird and contradictory way. The psychic scenes and the characters in them give themselves away through sudden strange associations, fantasies, slips of the tongue, or dreams, thus sliding through the conscious use of language.

Yet it is these unconscious revelations that often give the analyst a glimpse of what the analysand is seeking, stumblingly, to put on stage.

Listen to this patient speaking of a close friend who has just lost her only son. In the midst of her tears she suddenly thinks of her own younger brother, whom she loves dearly. She begins to worry about his health and the fact that she has been negligent in asking for news of him. "All those digestive problems he's been having . . . my God, I hope he doesn't die of intestinal cancer like Daddy!" She cries once more, this time over her brother's anticipated death, telling me how much she loves him and remembering the good times they had shared in childhood.

At this moment there are two people inside my patient seeking to come on stage. One is the very small girl of the past who, in a state of inexpressible distress, wished death upon this intruder into her family. The joy with which the long-awaited son was greeted had seriously attacked her feeling of identity, raising doubts about her femininity and about whether she was still loved. The other is the adult woman who sincerely loves and admires her brother. The only person speaking at this moment is the adult, but the little girl within her is begging to be allowed to speak her lines and express her feelings. Her conscious adult self cannot admit that she ever harbored feelings of hate for her brother, because she does not yet realize that, even in childhood, her love always triumphed over her hate. The only hint of the scene to come is that my patient feels unaccountably anxious and begins to wonder why she has not written her beloved brother for so long. The time when the timid but affectionate adult within her will accept a dialogue with the small assassin who also inhabits her internal world has not yet come. Only the analyst knows that the woman hates the little girl within her, that the drama will involve understanding her and eventually loving her and forgiving her.

The theater as a metaphor for psychic reality owes its beginnings to Breuer's celebrated patient, Anna O, whose treatment gave Freud many of his first brilliant insights into the workings of the unconscious mind. Fortunately for science, Anna O did not react well to hypnosis, with which Breuer initially attempted to treat her. In a sense it was she who taught her psychiatrist how to conduct her treatment. In recounting to Breuer her perpetual daydreams and other free associations, she referred to her communications as "my private theater." With the discovery that many of her severe hysterical symptoms—deafness, visual disturbances, and muscular paralyses—disappeared after having been "talked away," as Breuer put it, Anna O christened this hitherto unheard-of method of treatment her "talking cure." At other times, since the talking cure appeared to get rid of many thoughts and feelings that encumbered her mind, she referred to it as "chimney sweeping" (Breuer and Freud 1895).

My use of the theater metaphor refers not only to inner psychic reality but also to the psychoanalytic process itself. Here I am indebted to the clinical genius of Melanie Klein. I well remember the horizon that opened before me when I first read her fundamental work, *The Psychoanalysis of Children* (1932). She was the first psychoanalyst to recognize the profound symbolic significance of children's play (which indeed to a child's mind is not playing but working, or "working through" the problems of living) and from there to conceive the idea that analysis of children could be conducted with the use of toys representing many different people and animals. The games, she saw, provide insight into the structure of the child's unconscious mind. Klein claimed that "free" play (which in fact is no more "free" than the associations so labeled in adult analysis) would fulfill the same function as that of verbal communication in psychoanalytic work with adults. The play-scene created by Klein's small patient Peter comes vividly to mind. This three-and-a-half-year-old announced that he had a new brother called Fritz. While recounting this he banged two horses together in various ways. The analyst remarked that this made her think of two people bumping together, to which Peter replied, "No, that's not nice," but added that they are like people who are bumping each other and that "the horses have bumped together too and now they're going to sleep." As might be suspected, this peaceful solution to the primal scene that can produce a little Fritz was not entirely to Peter's liking. Thus we are not surprised to learn that as his game continued he completely covered the horses with miniature bricks and announced proudly, "Now they're quite dead; I've buried them" (p. 41). This game was an acceptable solution to what were undoubtedly overwhelming but inadmissible feelings of pain and narcissistic mortification.

The psychoanalysis of the grown-up children that we are when we call ourselves adults also reveals a playful aspect, a dimension of "as if," "let's suppose that . . . ," or "I'm just playing at . . .." " This psychoanalytic work then moves onto a stage on which all the internal characters and psychic scenarios that have been removed from conscious recall may once again come to life. In this first chapter I hope to give some insight into what occurs within the mind of the analyst while listening to the patient's associations, metaphors, sudden silences, and slips of the tongue, as well as identifying with the moods and feelings that emerge with each new theme. The process of working out and working through that each patient elaborates in "free-floating" associations induces a parallel process of "free-floating" theorizations (Castoriadis-Aulagnier 1975) in the mind of the analyst, who attempts to process and organize the analytic material that forms the body of each session. In my own analytical work, I am aware that my free-floating hypotheses, born of my own as well as my patient's psychic realities, slowly lead me to understand the unique relationship that each analysand establishes with me, and I with each analysand. I try to anticipate the different aspects of each particular relationship, knowing that changing affective experiences will bring about many transformations and many reversals. I come to discover who I am at different times for the patient; there are several mothers, several fathers, and many other "split" people of the past in each person's internal universe. As time goes on, I also become the representative of every patient's personal ideals as well as the incarnation of all that has prevented their realization and that has been a stumbling-block to finding life an exciting, albeit complex and often frustrating, adventure.

The "Work" of Psychoanalysis

The slow process of reconstructing the psychic scenarios hidden in the archives of the mind and recognizing the characters who play the leading roles has a name in psychoanalytic theory. It is called *psychical work* or *the work of elaboration.* Freud talked frequently of the *work (Arbeit)* accomplished by the mind: *dream-work (Traumarbeit),* the *work of mourning (Trauerarbeit), working out (psychische Verarbeitung),* and *working through (Durcharbeitung).* It is the two latter terms with which we are concerned here. Laplanche and Pontalis in their authoritative book, *The Language of Psychoanalysis* (1973), have carefully delineated Freud's distinction between the two forms of elaboration, psychical working out and working through. Working out pertains to the mental apparatus and the concept of its functioning and intrapsychic workings. Working through refers more specifically to the psyche's work in the psychotherapeutic process and to the painstaking constructions involved in the course of psychoanalytic treatment. Laplanche and Pontalis emphasize the evident analogy in the application of the "work" metaphor to the two concepts. To this I would add one further comment, namely, that the psychical working out and working through on the part of analysands has its counterpart in the activity of analysts, since analysts too work upon, elaborate in their own minds, all that is happening between them and their patients.

Analysands are indeed engaged in a demanding task. They are invited to "say everything" that comes to their minds and at the same time to "do nothing." That is, they may not act out upon the associations and awakened emotions that come to mind but instead must elaborate them, work them over as ideas to be explored. The labor required by this unusual request may be thought of as demands that the unconscious, instinctual self makes upon the mental apparatus. These drives and their inevitable conflicts are obliged to find *verbal* expression. The *I* must speak its lines. Once communicated, the lines can be worked through and given new meaning. Analysts, while trying to identify as profoundly as possible with their analysands' inner conflicts, must also be on the alert for their own instinctual promptings and conflicts, since their psychic theaters are just as complex, just as dynamic, as those of their patients. Analysts are continually engaged in the psychological process of working out personal wishes and tensions in the course of the treatment, and therefore they must constantly use their capacities for self-analysis to continue the work of elaboration. In order to grasp what is happening in the minds of their analysands, they must also reflect upon— work through—the thoughts, feelings, and fantasies stirred up in them by their patients' analytical communications. The case history of Karen, discussed later in this chapter, provides a glimpse into this process.

The analyst's work does not end when the session with the analysand is over. In my own practice, the possible significance of a patient's dream, strange illness, or unaccountable accident often hits me suddenly, when I least expect it, when I am no longer "at work." This discovery frequently reveals my own incongruities, unexpected feelings, and odd associations to my patient's words. Thinking about these revelations usually raises more questions than it provides answers, and differs from what analysts engage in when they let their thoughts and feelings float along with those of their patients. Their reflections away from the consulting room seek to put order into the chaos of the human psyche, to find in the inchoate movements perceptible in every analysis further insight into the mysterious nature of the creative process that produces psychic change. This kind of elaboration, while it may sometimes give rise to interpretations in the course of a given analysis, more often leads to questioning the classical psychoanalytic concepts themselves, perhaps to broadening or narrowing their application or to a search for new hypotheses and the beginnings of what may become new concepts. These must then be integrated into the existing body of doctrine or, if they replace earlier metapsychological concepts, must be shown to have greater explanatory power.

Analysts thus have two distinct modes of thinking about their work, one clinical and the other theoretical. What do these modes have in common, and what differentiates them?

From one perspective these two activities—clinical elaboration and theoretical elaboration—may be considered incompatible. Clinical elaboration involves a specific way of listening and trying to get into the patient's experience. The analyst is at liberty to think and to fantasize about the analysand's analytic communications. A preoccupation with theory could only obscure what the analyst is trying to discern of the latent communication behind each patient's analytic discourse. Although what we hear is immeasurably enlarged by all we have learned, and may still learn, from different theoreticians, such learning enriches our clinical work only to the extent that the theories have become an intimate part of our own analytic experience—not only the experience of personal analysis and the confirmation that clinical practice brings, but also the continuing self-analysis in which all analysts must engage. Without the enrichment of self-knowledge, theory is an impediment rather than an aid to what we hear. It may block the emergence of new hypotheses about the psychic reality of, and our specific reactions to, each of our patients. Should that occur, the two psychic theaters, that of the analyst and that of the analysand, may collide instead of completing each other.

Many fine clinicians who think deeply about their patients have no particular desire to "write psychoanalysis" (Smirnoff 1977). For those of us who do write, the activity of setting down what we think and feel about our work can be a flight from the shared solitude of the analytic couple enclosed within the walls of the consulting room. Furthermore, this particular kind of writing helps us to deal with the specific tensions of analytic work. These tensions arise from all that is unknown, perhaps unknowable, about the human psyche, as well as from the inevitable limitation of psychoanalysis to do more than alleviate certain forms of human suffering and the frequent failures to do even that. To highlight the important difference as well as the links between clinical and theoretical forms of psychic elaboration, I will briefly review Freud's initial concept of psychic work and then give an example, drawn from my own clinical practice, to illustrate the way in which clinical elaboration may be transformed into theoretical elaboration by means of a piece of analytical writing.

At the heart of the concept of psychic elaboration, whether expressed in working out or in working through, is the notion of labor: the ineluctable obligation to work that instinctual human nature imposes and the equally implicit demand, in the analytic situation, to work through the thoughts and fantasies prompted by instinctual drives. Each analytic discovery is inevitably met with resistance that requires further psychic work when it implies new insights into aspects of one's life. In this chapter I shall use the more general term *elaboration* to include both the spontaneous functioning of the mind and the repetition and working through of analytic findings. My main concern is to explore the necessity for psychic work that is imposed upon us by drives and conflicts and by the internal dramas to which they give rise.

Static and Ec-static Psychic States

In Freud's conception, the mind's work was always linked to the notions of unpleasure, mental pain, and what he termed *libidinal stasis*, a static or dammed-up state of being that he believed was responsible for the formation of neurotic or psychotic symptoms. He did not hold that this stasis was the sole cause of psychic suffering, nor did he believe that mental stasis had no effects other than pathogenic ones. In fact, in Freudian theory libidinal tension could also find expression in sublimations and in the discovery of objects and activities that bring satisfaction to the person whose psychic structure allows such developments. In other words, since there are an infinite number of ways in which people may resolve, avoid, transform, or otherwise deal with tensions and mental pain, the release of the static libidinal state and the disappearance of the unpleasurable state depend on the direction taken by the psyche in its laboring efforts.

In order to retain the flavor of Freud's original metaphor of stasis, I have chosen the terms *static* and *ec-static* to describe the states of mind in which the work of symptom-formation and its psychic elaboration occurs. The ec-static state is that which puts an end to the earlier stasis or blocked state of mental pain. The nature of the "ecstasy" may range from the physical sphere to the mental and from the pathological to the sublime. The overall aim of the mind's work is of course the maintenance of libidinal *homeostasis,* in both its object-oriented and self-oriented (narcissistic) dimensions.

It was Charcot (1888) who first used the term *elaboration psychique,* from which Freud and Breuer drew their early theoretical inspiration in their research into mental functioning. But in contrast to Charcot, who held that mental work was the *cause* of psychological symptoms, Freud and Breuer proposed that the persistence of symptoms was due to a *lack* of psychic labor. These two positions do not appear to me to be mutually exclusive. The psychic work, in Charcot's conception, that might (in today's terminology) give rise to neurotic or psychotic symptoms or to a perversion or character disorder is the primitive creation or work of a *child's* psyche in its attempt to escape mental pain and/or make sense of incoherent parental communications. Such early infantile inventions tend to close the door, once and for all, to any further elaboration of these attempts at self-cure and therefore in adulthood become full-blown neuroses or psychoses. This premature closure in childhood also prevents the individual from finding more adequate means of dealing with the complexities of adult life. Thus the Freud-Breuer conception expresses the hope that psychotherapeutic work will set in motion new psychic elaboration and lead to the relief of symptoms and the discovery of more satisfactory libidinal and sublimatory activities.

I suggest that the static states of mind that give rise to neuroses and psychoses can have an alternative outcome. Such a blockage may well be present yet leave no mental trace of its existence if, because of a radical split between psyche and soma, the psyche does not register the mental pain or conflict. When this occurs, the individual has no psychic representation of painful affect and the *I* creates no protective solutions. In other words there is no sign of psychic work, and the soma is left to cope alone with the somatic pole of affect. Certain people, in total ignorance of their internal or external stress and its accompanying tensions, are not alerted to the necessity for psychic elaboration of their problems. A patient of mine, for example, who was unaware of her deep emotional dependence on her daughter, had a first attack of ulcerative colitis when her daughter left home to study and a second attack, which nearly cost her life, when her daughter left the country to get married. Such a split between psyche and soma always incurs the risk of increasing psychosomatic vulnerability as the soma, in accordance with its inexorable functioning, attempts to find solutions to unacknowledged stress related to problems that are fundamentally psychological. (Psychosomatic issues are more fully discussed in chapters 4 to 8.)

Stasis can occur in analysts as well as in analysands. Whenever analysts are unable to understand the psychic work that has given rise to neurotic, borderline, perverse, or narcissistic symptoms or that strange lack of psychic elaboration apt to produce psychosomatic symptoms, most of them become aware of a blockage within themselves of the libidinal-narcissistic investment that creates interest and pleasure in their work. The persistent observation that the psychoanalytic process is stagnating or has come to a total halt produces a feeling of stasis. The feeling that they are no longer functioning analytically is unpleasurable and often pushes analysts to reflections of a theoretical order. These in turn frequently lead to an ec-static solution in the form of discussions with colleagues, lectures, symposia, or the writing of analytical papers. In this particular branch of analytical activity the same psychic factors of working out and working through may be observed.

Karen's Story

The following fragment of an analysis will illustrate this situation. The patient in question brought me much food for thought in that her various intense forms of mental elaboration had resulted in the creation not only of successful sublimations but also of inhibitions in her work, complications in her sexual life, and psychosomatic symptoms. Her analytical discourse mobilized in my mind an equally active curiosity and stimulated my own wish to work psychically. The complications she presented, however, led to such a blockage in my understanding of her that I came to write my first psychoanalytic paper, titled "Homosexuality in Women" (McDougall 1964). Although I managed to explore and understand many of my patient's difficulties through a parallel effort to search further into my own psychic reality, a number of important theoretical questions remained unanswered at the end of her analysis. Some of them led to theoretical conceptions many years later, when I again found myself in the same morass of incomprehension.

Karen first sought analytic help some twenty-two years ago, because of serious inhibition in her work. She was a performing artist and had recently experienced a state of uncontrollable panic on stage. This sudden outbreak of psychological disturbance had rapidly brought her professional activity to a near halt. She managed to continue to perform from time to time, but the quality of her work was beginning to suffer. Karen was extremely thin, boyish-looking in an awkward way, and more than carelessly dressed. Her manner was somewhat aggressive. When she spoke, however, her whole face became alive, intense, and almost pretty; she communicated a feeling of tragedy mingled with a passionate attachment to life.

Karen spontaneously offered the following details about her life. Her parents were cultivated people who had achieved considerable success in the social sense (Karen provided this information with a hint of mockery in her voice). Her mother was totally devoted to her children; her father, a Paris doctor, was constantly occupied with his work. "We didn't see much of Dad —and we couldn't get away from Mom." Karen had an identical twin sister (whom I shall call Kati) and two younger sisters. She lived alone in a small studio apartment and had few friends. Most of her time was devoted to her professional interests.

According to the notes I made after this first interview, I had asked only one direct question: did the terrible experience of panic-anxiety occur anywhere other than on stage? My patient replied that she was sometimes seized with panic when she was out in the street, but she was unable to represent mentally what exactly caused her fear. She then added that she frequently suffered from eczema. My first free-floating hypothesis was that Karen presented a grave phobic symptom, probably due to the breakdown in her professional life, which represented the loss of an important sublimatory activity. I surmised that this outbreak might well be the result of unconscious exhibitionistic wishes that were threatening to escape from repression. I wondered vaguely whether her eczema might also contain a hidden exhibitionistic significance linked to forbidden infantile sexual wishes, but I was not able at that time to conceptualize the complex relationship between hysterophobic constructions and psychosomatic symptoms. (The latter will be examined more closely in chapters 4 and 5.)

Two weeks later Karen began her analysis. To my astonishment she literally threw herself onto the couch, jumping from some distance into the middle of it. (This method of entering the "analytic scene," which could be thought of in terms of counterphobic behavior directed toward helping her "jump over" her phobic anxieties, continued for a year, until the couch one day collapsed under the impact. It was only at this point that my attempts at interpreting the meaning of this curious acting out began to take effect.) On this first occasion, having landed like a hand grenade on my couch, she began to cry. Her sobbing continued throughout the whole forty-five minutes of the session. I felt ill at ease, and not knowing what to say, other than making small interrogatory noises, I remained silent.

Karen opened the second session, the following day, by saying, "I should have gone to a male analyst because then it wouldn't have mattered. I wouldn't have this horrible anguish inside me and this feeling of disorientation. I've never cared for any man. The only love I have ever felt, my only sexual desires, are for women." I began to reproach myself for having asked no questions whatsoever about Karen's sexual life; for some reason I had not even asked myself why she had kept this area of her life out of our preliminary interviews. (Later she informed me that if I had questioned her in any way about her sexuality she would probably never have returned to see me.) During this session, I began to revise all my free-floating ideas about Karen's inner struggle with life, a struggle that included an almost-absent father, an over-present mother to be shared with a twin sister, a breakdown in sublimatory expression, neurotic symptomatology, psychosomatic manifestations, and disturbance in sexual identity. The first question that came to my mind concerned the extent to which the experience of twinship in itself might potentially be traumatic. Surely it could carry the risk of disturbing one's sense of sexual as well as of subjective identity? I surmised that on seeing herself for the first time in the mirror, Karen probably exclaimed, "Look, there's Kati!" I believed, naively, that Kati too would be homosexual, but I had no confirmation of this, since in the first months of her analysis. Karen talked very little of her twin. She did, however, speak frequently of her various lovers and of the way in which every relationship ended badly, leaving her in a state of despair.

She also spent many sessions on the anxieties connected with public performances. This symptom gave rise to as much suffering as the constant failures in her love life. I sought in vain for some link between her two sources of pain. There was of course the evident suffering caused by the narcissistic wounds involved in each case, but something deeper was needed to understand the repetitive quality of Karen's lack of accomplishment in both her professional and her private lives. Her transference feelings gave little opportunity for interpretation in that she maintained a highly idealized image of me that she was not ready to question for many months. Its ambivalent dimension was abundantly evident, however, although it could not at that time be analyzed, and I observed that ambivalence played an equally important part in her relations with her mother, her lovers, and her friends. We were all idealized females. Much later I was able to appreciate the reasons why the underlying hatred needed time to come forth, and they in turn enabled me to understand in retrospect my early reluctance to make direct transference interpretations of Karen's deeply hidden ambivalence. I dimly suspected a cannibalistic form of love intermingled with murderous rage.

Almost from the beginning of her analysis, Karen decided to cease all sexual relations, under the impression that doing so would enable her "to concentrate more intensely on her analytic experience." Toward the end of our first year came a session that gave me considerable insight into Karen's love problems, when a primitive and condensed oedipal image and an archaic sexual fantasy came to light. Karen began this session by trying to express her feelings of deep dependence and affection for me and what these feelings meant to her, but she found herself struggling for the right words. As the phrases she sought eluded her, she suddenly jumped up from the couch and sprang toward me, her hands and fingers curled as though she were going to attack me. She fell against my chair and across my knees, her hands tightened as though tetanized. Though later I found myself trembling, I was more afraid for her than for myself in the first few moments. I began to stroke her head as though she were a little child overcome by rage. She slowly relaxed her physical tension and began to sob.

When she seemed completely calm again, I suggested she go back to the couch and try to recount everything she had felt and thought during the last few minutes. Once she had reestablished our customary distance she was able to tell me that she had felt as though she were "possessed by two frightening but entirely contradictory wishes." Her ec-static leap from the couch could now be expressed in words: on the one hand she experienced a wish to eat me, and at the same time she wanted to strangle me. I heard myself reply, without any preliminary thought, that she needed to devour me voraciously as a baby would want to eat its mother, but at the same time she wanted to strangle and tear from inside me the father who prevented her from possessing her mother for herself alone. I felt, as I talked, that I was largely using this long fantasy-interpretation to still my own anxiety. But nothing we say is ever totally coincidental. Karen had often spoken of an obsessive idea that sometimes possessed her, during which she saw herself strangling a man with her bare hands. Her associations to this compulsive thought left no doubt that the intended victim was her father, whom she referred to variously as a "brute," a "pig," and a "shit."

Karen's contracted hands recalled to my mind that her skin allergy had appeared on her hands after her first homosexual experience. The sight of Karen's fingers, drawn up as though in spasm, was to become for me the very image of tetany. I was to see the same spasmophiliac contractions several years later, when I had in analysis two patients who actually suffered from tetany. (Could it be a coincidence that both of them had psychotic mothers?) I observed an attack of tetany during a session of one of these patients, at a moment when he was talking of his extreme dependence on his wife. Faced with the spectacle of his drawn-up hands and arms, I felt an urgent need to render this painful physical communication audible. I told him that at this precise moment his desire was to seize his mother's breast with both hands, but he could not allow this thought to enter his mind because he was terribly afraid at the same time of strangling and destroying that longed-for and disappointing breast-mother and was in fact paralyzed by two contradictory desires. As I spoke his tetanized muscles slowly relaxed. I realized that it was in fact Karen who had first helped me to imagine and understand the primitive battle expressed in this psychosomatic scene. What she had shown me had continued to elaborate itself in my mind from that time on. Obviously the exactitude of such an intervention is open to question and indeed highly dubious. All that can be asserted is that it had become my own fantasy of an archaic sexual scene and as such could be offered to my patient so that he might integrate it into his thoughts and fantasy life. This was important, for his spasmophiliac attack indicated that his capacity to grasp what he was feeling and imagining had come to a halt. It is at such moments that we are moved to daydream for our analysands—and sometimes remember with gratitude our former patients!

Although I had learned an important lesson about primitive fantasies from Karen's leap in the second year of her analysis, I was at that time unable to "hear" what her tortured skin was expressing, unable even to guess at the baby within her seeking for fusional love and at the same time filled with the explosive range that had certainly contributed to the outbreak of eczema.

The question of what caused it continued to occupy my mind, but I found no satisfactory theoretical explanation until some years later, when I had another lesbian patient who also suffered from eczema. Today I would say that Karen's first erotic contact with a female partner had awakened within her feelings too violent and contradictory to be elaborated psychically and that her body therefore had to find an appropriate response through physiological expression. Karen's analysis enabled me later to understand and elaborate the fantasy of an archaic parental relationship contained within the maternal "breast." My study of psychosomatic research has further aided me to work through, from an analytic viewpoint, many of my observations (see chapter 7). I have gained insight into the ways in which the mind, deprived of conscious knowledge of what is happening to the instinctual and affect-charged body, may leave the body vulnerable to somatic explosion.

One Sex for Two

Karen's analysis also brought me my first insight into the deeper significance of homosexual desires and conflicts, which resulted from my erroneous assumption that Karen's twin would also be homosexual. When Karen lamented the loss of her lovers and spoke of her growing conviction that she would never find *l'âme-soeur* ("the soul sister") for whom she constantly longed, I would think to myself that she was searching for her twin. While it was to some extent true that she hoped to find an idealized and in certain ways a mirror image of herself, this was not the role given to her twin in Karen's inner world. One day I drew her attention to the fact that she rarely made any mention of Kati. She then informed me that her sister was happily married with two small children and went on to tell me how much she loved this little family. In short Kati represented, in her sister's mind, the image of a "complete" and happy woman; Karen's thoughts about Kati's family and the happy moments she spent with them were in effect something of an oasis in the desert of her suffering and solitude. I waited in vain for signs of ambivalence, for hate and destructive envy to appear. But the excessive idealization of all the other women in her life and its unconsciously negative counterpart were not permitted to apply to Kati. One day, as I listened to the affectionate and genuine way in which Karen expressed her love for her sister and her family, I became suddenly aware that Kati's feminine life and being were at the same time experienced as *Karen's* sexuality and femininity. I made a note to the effect that "there is only one sex for the two of them." In fact Karen had integrated into her mental image of her sister all her own stifled feminine longings. Consequently she strove to protect this treasure from being attacked or depleted by locking it up in a safe place. The notion that one could thus mortgage, so to speak, one's sexuality, renouncing for an indeterminate time any attempt to use it even in imagination, helped me subsequently to understand the unconscious narcissistic investment that one person can, in fantasy, place in another, so that precious but unavailable aspects of oneself are not lost.

Although, thanks to Karen's analysis, I was able to use this insight to understand that a male homosexual patient's frantic cruising and ceaseless search for the perfect partner was a fantasy attempt to find his own penis and thus repair an extremely damaged image of his own masculinity, my work with Karen seemed to have attained a state of stagnation. A small gain was made when we were able to explore the fantasy that Kati alone embodied the loving and loved aspects of their mother. This step led to the reconstruction of Karen's belief as a young child that she was not safe in her mother's arms, whereas her sister was. Explorations into my own imagination, using Karen's symptoms to guide me, gave rise to further suppositions. Her skin problems, her occasional experiences of depersonalization when in the street, and other symptoms gave insight into the imprecise and indeed archaic image that Karen had of her body as a whole. Her mind's *I* seemed in search not only of her sexuality but also of the limits of her corporeal self.

One Body for Two

Toward the end of our second year's work, I had noted: "Karen does not know the limits of her sex, her mind, or her body. Nothing is contained." This point brought me further insight into the intense attachment to her twin. Fundamentally, in Karen's fantasy, there was only one *body* for the two of them. Many of her problems in relationships with others slowly became analyzable; when her fear of disappearing into the other could be felt and put into words, there were many changes in both the personal and the professional aspects of her life.

Despite the apparent simplicity of this interpretation, it had required many months of struggle on my part, and considerable personal working out as well as working through, to integrate into my thinking all that Karen's analysis taught me. The first important idea was that homosexual relationships are dedicated to recovering magically one's own sex as well as one's sexual identity, and that in spite of the difficulties it arouses, homosexuality can also keep more serious psychic problems at bay. The idea of not truly possessing one's own body, and indeed the question as to whose body it is, had to wait until long after Karen's departure for me to begin to understand the role and significance of such fantasies in narcissistic and psychosomatic states (see chapters 4 to 8).

As for Karen, it became clear that every woman who interested her was at the same time her mother. In regard to the loved and idealized aspects of her internal mother, Karen fell in love with, and desired, substitute mothers with the repressed fantasy that she would thus recover all she had not taken from her mother-as-woman. In regard to the hated aspects of the internal mother, every new partner became an enemy to be destroyed, as well as a threat to her feeling of separate identity in view of her fear-and-longing for total fusion with the other woman. These psychic factors had contributed to the breakup of each past relationship. Since in Karen's internal world her father was experienced as an absent and unworthy object, she could not look to him for protection from the dangers of an overly intimate relationship with her mother. Her early infantile longings for her mother as well as the projected fantasy that her mother wanted to swallow her up, thus getting rid of her and keeping only Kati, found no reassuring paternal barrier in her internal world. Every female relationship that promised life was at the same time the purveyor of death.

Today I would see in this internal drama many further ramifications underlying, for example, Karen's phobic relationship to the physical world. The fantasy of an omnipresent mother gave rise to moments of quasi-psychotic terror; her skin allergies were doubtless a primitive, preverbal kind of protection against the loss of her body limits, as well as a response to her intense desire for fusion with the archaic mother-image of the past. Her mind could not elaborate this profound inner struggle, with the result that her body had been forced to find a solution of its own.

In contrast to these problems, I had encountered no great difficulty in understanding the unconscious significance of Karen's stage fright, and, perhaps in part as a result, her professional inhibitions were among the first of her problems to be resolved. The elaboration of this part of Karen's psychic structure and unconscious fantasy life followed closely the well-known paths of excursion into neurotic symptoms and inhibitions. Through her dreams, daydreams, memories, and associations, Karen brought to our work all the needed elements that allowed us to see, first of all, her terror of being perceived by the public as "phallic," then her equally great fear of appearing "non-phallic," which to her unconscious mind meant castrated. From there we followed a regressive fantasy path in which anal references of various kinds played the same obscuring role as the phallic ones had done.

The next act in Karen's internal drama led to the following scenario: "The public will see that all I have produced is a pile of excrement. Furthermore they will discover that I myself am not worth more than that." In her early sessions she had often said, when talking of her physical self, "I'm just a pile of shit." We were able to put life and value back into these scenarios of forgotten pregenital love, founded on infantile sexual theories in which feces as a valuable and loving gift were confounded with feces as a lethal weapon. Repairing the mental links between Karen's sublimatory professional activity and its instinctual roots came easily and bore fruit. Karen soon began to understand that she had projected onto her public the castrating and persecutory objects that inhabited her inner psychic universe. Behind her fear of looking ridiculous, sexless, and valueless lay an archaic infantile wish to drown the whole world with her childlike products and infantile love.

The careful analysis of all this hitherto unconscious material did not entirely reassure Karen about the danger implicit in her desire to "produce" in public. One day she indulged in one more acting out in the session (and allowed me to understand that acting out is not necessarily negative). Instead of lying on the couch, Karen stationed herself close to the window. She had made the necessary preparations to reproduce for me the traumatic spectacle that had temporarily closed off her creative career. But on this occasion Karen performed as she would like to have done on the fateful day when she had suffered from uncontrollable panic. This production, which moved me almost to tears with its beauty and her talent, lasted the whole session. I had to bring it to a close. We exchanged only two words on that occasion: as she left, Karen said "Thank you," and I replied in turn "Thank you." Some months later Karen gave me two tickets to a performance in which she played a leading part, her first public appearance in four years. The ec-static movement that allowed the static libidinal blockage of her wishes to flow once more was now in place, although we still had much work to do on her damaged feelings of subjective and sexual identity.

The Analyst's Static and Ec-static Experience

Looking back on my mental elaboration of all that occurred in Karen's analysis, I feel that I knew, without knowing, many things that I could conceptualize today. The psychic changes that occurred—the loss of her psychosomatic symptoms, the recovery of her artistic and professional capabilities, and the capacity to make more stable and more loving relationships—I could observe with pleasure, but I was unable to devise a theoretical frame to explain them. It was difficult for me to formulate all that I had understood of female homosexuality. The fact that I had two other homosexual women in treatment at about the same time enriched certain of my basic conceptions, but it also confused my thinking, since the three—each with her unique personality structure—had come to analysis with very different forms of suffering. For example, the patient whom I called Olivia (McDougall 1964), although she had a set of internal oedipal scenarios remarkably similar to those of Karen, was not faced with such frightening psychic monsters. This difference may have contributed to the fact that while Karen needed to keep her homosexual identity, Olivia eventually married and had children.

The many questions that circulated in my mind brought me to the discovery that I was reluctant to arrive at new analytic conceptions. There is a feeling of transgression allied to the very act of thinking a new thought—perhaps of creating anything that has not already been created. Had I not been invited to participate in a book on female sexuality, I might have left my theoretical searchings to slumber peacefully in my mind. Writing that first article also enabled me to discover the immense gap that exists between elaboration such as I knew it in my daily practice, documented in the form of hundreds of illegible notes on my free-floating hypotheses, and that quite different effort to elaborate theoretical conceptions intended for presentation to a sophisticated psychoanalytic public. Moreover, the necessity of integrating what appeared new in my thinking into the classical body of psychoanalytical metapsychology gave me further insight into the underlying libidinal significance of the "child-parent" aspect of scientific research: one may either produce one's own brain-children or leave this activity to the "spiritual fathers."

The fragment of analytic work with Karen and its aftermath in the publication of a theoretical work illustrate the different levels of psychic work that take place within the analyst. Coupling a desire to understand with affective reactions and using to the utmost both the analyst's and the analysand's internal theaters, a constant activity of psychic elaboration evolves in the unconscious minds of both partners to the analytic relationship, so that the analysand's fantasies, metaphors, signs, signifiers, symbols, and conflicts eventually become part of the analyst's own inner world.

To this interchange is added the conscious effort to render communicable all that the analyst has understood of the patient's psychic reality. These insights and their subsequent interpretation come about in unpredictable ways. We are aware of many aspects of our patients' internal theaters long before we are capable of expressing these insights in the form of interpretations. Yet this silent elaborative work is always in progress. The interpretation it eventually produces, sometimes to the surprise of the analyst as well as the analysand, often has far-reaching effects. The analyst thus gives back to the patient the representations, affects, and fantasies that have made up many weeks of analytic communications, but they are returned in a new form, with new meaning, a meaning that is potentially creative rather than destructive.

The particular stasis that gives impetus to theoretical work activity arises from many different sources, of which I have indicated a few. A further aspect that deserves mention is the effect upon analysts of the austerity of the psychoanalytic protocol, which is intended to protect the patient from being invaded by the analyst's problems. This carefully maintained neutrality creates a certain amount of accumulated drive tension in both partners to the psychoanalytic work. While it is the patient's right to express this tension fully in the sessions, the analyst may do so only in the form of interpretative activity. What tension is not used in this way must find expression outside the analytic relationship. If the patient is asked to "say everything and do nothing," the analyst can neither "do" nor "say everything" that comes to mind.

This form of restraint, implicit in the practice of analysis, is coupled with an additional frustration which may also lead analysts to theoretical reflection, namely, the unsatisfied wish *to know more,* to see further into the secret theater of each analysand. In every analysis, discovery reveals further mysteries that will forever remain out of the analyst's grasp. In spite of our avid desire to discover, to understand, and to communicate what we have comprehended, we will always remain in ignorance not only of all that is still unsaid but also of much that has actually taken place in the psychic changes wrought by the psychoanalytic adventure. There is constant solicitation on the part of analysands to make the analyst desert this constraining position: heterosexual, homosexual, aggressive, and narcissistic incitements are proffered continually, and it is the analyst's task to contain these and elaborate them as profoundly as possible, in terms of their unconscious significance, so that the analytic process may continue. Any other response would tend to put a stop to further progress. It is this continuing mental labor of psychic elaboration on the part of both analyst and analysand—this potentially endless exploration of the space that separates two individual psychic realities, two internal theaters, equally complex, equally elusive—that gives to the psychoanalytic adventure its innovative dimension. These psychic worlds, perhaps forever unknowable in their entirety, continue to be creative in both analyst and analysand long after the psychoanalytic partnership comes to an end. It is hoped that this discussion has conveyed something of the processes of working out and working through that prompt analysts to create new theory, which in turn deepens their clinical insight.

2

Scenes from Psychic Life

The Classical Repertory: The Theater of the Forbidden

Phobic, hysterical, and obsessional symptoms are all created by the mind's *I*. However, *I* is not just one but several people. The composite structure called *I* can arrive at those attempts at self-cure that we call symptoms only at the cost of considerable creative effort in which renunciation, anxiety, and suffering all play a role. These masterpieces of the internal theater, created by the infantile *I* with the primitive psychic means at its disposal, tend to take shape in adolescence and then present themselves to the adult *I* as ineluctable facts of life imposed by an external force of unknown source. The fateful words and frightening episodes that the child of the past interpreted—sometimes correctly and sometimes erroneously—as awesome warnings have disappeared from the adult's conscious memory, but in doing so they have taken with them the fantasies, dreams, desires, and mingled feelings of magic and mystery attached to every child's love feelings and sensations of erotic excitement. The aim of the curious psychic compromises that the small child achieves is twofold: to comply with the interdictions of the adult world that seek to restrain unbridled sexual expression and yet to safeguard the possessive and incestuous aims of childhood love. The adult whose mind long ago effaced from conscious memory those portentous childlike decisions now presents a highly symbolic condensed text, a sort of psychic stenogram brought to the analyst in the form of a symptom.

This symptom creation is both painful and incomprehensible to the patient. Although the patient entering analysis is convinced that the psychoanalyst already knows the answer to the enigma of his or her suffering, in fact the distance that lies between the unknown beginnings of the lost scenario and its final form is a span of many years. Many forgotten incidents and discarded dreams have altered the perspective and covered the clues to the creation of the original compromise. And yet the writers of these original scripts generally admit that they are responsible for them and that the secret to their meaning lies hidden within themselves, even when they seek to incriminate others for their suffering and demand that the analyst open the door to which they alone possess the key.

A PHOBIC AND A FETISHISTIC SCENARIO

To illustrate the elliptical nature of these scenarios, I have chosen two examples from what might be considered the "classical" repertory of the psychoanalytic stage: one a neurotic, the other a perverse drama. They are comparable in their psychic function, although the external symptoms appear very different. In both cases the analysands have attempted to preserve some part of their sexual lives from conflicts due to a complicated oedipal organization as well as an overwhelming internal mother-figure. They have found quite different "solutions," and they are equally puzzled by them.

Madame A. talks about an appointment yesterday with her hairdresser, an event that always fills her with trepidation because of the car trip she is obliged to make. Ever since her adolescence, going out of doors has aroused overwhelming anxiety in her. For the last few years her husband has fulfilled, more or less well, the role of counterphobic object in that his presence calms her fears. She also copes by subtly securing the help of her mother or friends. When she wants to go to the hairdresser, she usually succeeds, using many obscure pretexts, in persuading a friend to accompany her and have her hair done at the same time. If she must go alone, she feels compelled to park her car within twenty yards of the beauty shop in such a way that the car is visible from the hairdresser's window. In addition she must also take with her a particular shoulder bag with an exterior pocket in which she places the keys—just in case she feels an urgent need to return to her car. Yesterday she found the right parking place, but the boulevard was completely empty. No friend endowed with protective qualities was there to help her through this catastrophe. Bravely she set out alone, but suddenly in the very middle of the wide boulevard she was seized with panic. Her heart began to pound. She looked in all directions, and finding no one, she precipitately rushed back to her automobile, jumped in, and raced off at high speed for home.

What is happening here? What is this play about? From the onlooker's standpoint, there is an air of a detective movie about the whole scene, but too many elements are missing for us to make sense of it. Indeed, it is a child's story, composed many years ago, when the fantasies that lie behind it were believed to be true.

> Monsieur B., having recalled during the session a painful professional failure, suddenly recounts an imaginary scene. "I see the little girl again; she's wearing a raincoat. There are a number of people around watching her. An older woman who looks like her mother makes her kneel down and roughly pulls back her raincoat; the little girl is naked under the coat. The older woman is going to beat her on her bare behind with a whip. . . ."

He stops suddenly, saying that these fantasies drive him mad. He wants to tell them to me so that we can understand them better, but if he goes on with the story he is afraid he will ejaculate. Here once more is a strangely incoherent and incomplete scenario. The actors are vague, their actions incomprehensible, and the effect of this constricted little drama upon its author is somewhat puzzling to the observer. Yet this scene, with minor variations, has occupied this man's mind for thirty years. It was first "revealed" to him when he was eight years old, its overwhelming physical and emotional impact filling him with shame and incredulity. Again it is a story imagined by a child and destined to become a psychic script dominating the mind of an adult.

We might well question at this point the relationship between a phobic construction and a fetishistic one, since in classical analytic theory neurosis was always considered to be the "negative" of perversion (Freud 1905)—in other words, the same inner conflicts may give rise to a deviant sexual symptom or a neurotic one. What are the similarities between a phobic object and a fetish, and what differentiates them? First let us note the violence with which these psychic scenarios are imposed upon their authors and then the lacunary aspect of the theme in each case. Both authors, who are at the same time actors in their secret theaters, nevertheless feel *acted upon* in unfair ways. As their analyses continued, it became evident that these stories, imbued with the terrifying magic of childhood, had been invented in order to assure the continuity of sexual desire while at the same time avoiding the drastic threats of castration they had interpreted parental interdictions to be in childhood. But in this immutable text nothing can now be questioned. Things are as they are, and the missing actors who might have supplied some clue to the unconscious meaning of the plot have long been silenced. Each patient has continued for years to produce these condensed and repetitive scenes, on an imprecise stage, for an anonymous spectator.

The compulsion to repeat these scenes, which causes suffering, paradoxically at the same time reveals one of the *I*'s fundamental functions, for it demonstrates by its very inexorability the desperate need to maintain, at any cost, the feeling of ego identity. Symptom constructions, like character traits and sublimations, reflect the basic scenarios that make up each subject's psychic repertory and are an integral part of each person's narcissistic and libidinal economy; as such, they are part of the system of psychic survival. Surviving, in this context, means keeping one's sense of self-esteem, as well as one's capacity to love and care for others, on an even keel. We sometimes can maintain this delicate balance only at the price of symptoms. Thus our analysands, whose symptomatology brings mental pain and a restriction on their liberty to live and to love, fight implacably to *keep* their symptoms even while asking the analyst to remove these obstructing forces from their inner worlds.

The theater of neuroses, or rather the neurotic sector of the *I*'s repertory, begins with the oedipal crisis, a double drama with both a homosexual and a heterosexual plot. Every child, in its psychic bisexuality, ardently desires total possession of both parents for itself alone. The desire *to be* the parent of one's own sex and possess the other parent is just as keenly matched by the desire *to be* the parent of the opposite sex and possess the same-sex parent. Children's possessiveness seeks to obtain the powers and privileges of both members of the parental couple. In everyone's unconscious scenarios these specially loved and desired people are represented symbolically by their sex.

If the phallus (as distinct from the penis, in that it is the symbol of unity and fertility that belongs to and joins both sexes) acquires its true significance, the child, boy or girl, finds his or her place and gender identity guaranteed. If instead the penis becomes detached from its symbolic significance many dramatic scenes arise for both sexes. The paternal penis, an idealized and coveted object for all children, plays a different role depending not only on the anatomical sex of the analysand but also on the extent to which it has or has not become the symbol of sexual complementarity. This fundamental signifier (Lacan 1966) also determines the way in which the female genitals are represented in the unconscious.

The vagina, because of its invisibility, poses problems for both boys and girls. As long as the representation of the vagina has not benefited in imagination from its phallic significance (that is, the penis is a genital organ that requires the female genital to complete it and give it its sexual significance, and vice versa), then not only does it run the risk of becoming a detached representation but also a limitless and potentially dangerous one. As an ill-defined and invisible entity, this sexual representation henceforth may be displaced endlessly onto every conceivable external space or object: narrow tunnels, open windows, deserted streets, deep water, earth, air, heights, and depths. The choice, like the representation, is limitless!

When there is no psychic scenario capable of uniting the two sexes in the love act, in which each sex becomes the reason for the existence of the other, then the autonomous penis risks being an object that tears and lacerates in the psychic repertory, while the unlimited vagina separated from its function as a loving and desiring container for the penis becomes an organ that may crush, strangle, and castrate all that it encounters.

Let us now return to our two illustrative scenarios, with their elusive meanings. The whip as a "punishing penis" and the deserted boulevard as a "strangling vagina" are readily detected by the analytic ear. That does not mean that these damaged symbolic objects are easily interpretable in this form, however. Such interpretations would have no impact so long as the characters and crucial events of the past, as well as the affects attached to these significant objects, remained in the shadows and found no spontaneous place on the psychoanalytic stage. The desperate distress of the small child as well as the intensity of infantile wishes must bide their time in order to achieve new meaning in an adult context.

Madame A. had created a neurosis, Monsieur B. a perversion. The phobic object (or place or situation) is, as we know, an object that arouses fear and terror and triggers vigorous action to avoid it. On the other hand, the fetish (which may also be a place or situation) is an object of adoration and excites intense activity in search of it. A period of time is required in psychoanalytic treatment for each object to reveal its ambivalent counterpart. In spite of the divergences it is evident that phobic and fetishist patients watch their objects with equal intensity. Actors in phobic dramas inevitably come to discover that they are fascinated and obsessed with their objects of horror; fetishists learn that their beloved scenes and objects, divested of their erotic power when they have served their purpose, fill them with disgust and horror.

Thus the *I*'s ambivalence in respect to its important objects becomes clearer as analysands gradually discover the reasons for their psychic creations. The ambivalence attached to them mirrors the love-hate feelings attached to the original parental objects. Their interpretation of the parents' exhortations, prohibitions, and incoherence had aroused mental pain and conflict that led to the creation of the symptoms of fetishism, phobia, and so on in order to ward off the return of these painful emotional states. In the case of neurotic symptoms the anxiety is displaced onto a new situation or object, and in the case of sexual deviation the anxiety-arousing situation is displaced onto a sexual act and anxiety transformed into erotic pleasure. When the inner characters involved in these highly condensed psychic theater pieces come to life again in the analytic situation, the power of the fetishistic or phobic objects diminishes. The analysands are then free to utilize differently the powerful libidinal and aggressive drives that were to a certain extent paralyzed by the symptomatology. Such psychic change permits a redistribution of instinctual investments, allowing not only a richer sexual life but also richer relational and creative activities.

AN OBSESSIONAL SCENARIO

Before discussing the final acts of these intriguing dramas I will introduce a third scenario, just as classical as the two that I have compared and contrasted. This psychic play is also constructed with displaced erotic elements, but in this case the object of fascination and mental pain is *thought* itself—in other words, the drama of obsessional neurosis.

Honorine, a woman of forty, had come to France because of her husband's work. She felt he was the right man for her in spite of the fact that he had always proclaimed he did not want any children. She was convinced that she deeply desired children but had renounced her wish in order to please her mate. She was totally unaware of another part of herself who, like her husband, did not want children. This character in Honorine's psychic theater who hated children was difficult to bring on stage and, like others in her internal world, would angrily demand the right to speak. But Honorine's *I* could only permit this in the form of obsessive doubts and compulsive acts.

In spite of six years of analysis, my patient still suffered from torturing symptoms, such as counting steps many times over and being unable to leave her home, or other people's homes, without complicated verifications. She did, however, allow herself a measure of professional success and sexual pleasure that she had not known before. Her ideal image of herself, in her mind's *I,* was that of a saintly woman who treated all humanity with bounty and love. At the same time another, deeply disavowed character would, to Honorine's utter astonishment, hurl out insults, obscenities, and hymns of hate. To combat this unwanted inhabitant of her secret theater, Honorine resorted to magical acts, gestures, ritual words, and symbolic numbers in the hope of casting a spell upon the unruly, hated Honorine.

Here is a typical session from Honorine's analysis:

H: In your waiting room I was looking at those lovely flowers.

This statement is followed by flattering and affectionate remarks about the analyst, then silence.

JM: Can you see what has stopped you?

H: I'm . . . embarrassed . . . an absurd thought, maybe a bit ridiculous. . . . Voilà! The thought burst into my mind that perhaps you were unable to have children, or maybe too old to have any. So you grow flowers instead. You see why I had to stop!

JM: Well, not altogether. Am I not allowed to see this person in you who has these thoughts?

H: What I said might hurt you—and maybe you would hold it against me.

JM: Perhaps you are lending me a thought of your own? Maybe you hold something against me?

H: I was just thinking of my mother with her three children.

Honorine then thinks, for the thousandth time, of all the special gestures and rituals she had to use in childhood to ward off danger or to heal people.

H: I always had to protect members of the family against death.

JM: Which ones?

In my mind is a floating hypothesis that comes up from time to time: Honorine was the last of three children, born much later than the other two; perhaps she holds herself responsible for the fact that there were no more after her. She has said she was always referred to as "the Little One." Was it a cherished position? Has she not, in a sense, got rid of all *my* children in the first part of the session? What about her own unfulfilled desire for children? All her rituals and conjurations —are they perhaps destined to protect children against her wish to eliminate them?

H: Oh, it's quite clear. I had to protect my parents and the big children.

JM: And "the Little One"? Why did *she* have to do this?

H: I always felt so alone . . . all through my adolescence I spent my spare time looking after other people's children. Everyone knew how much I loved children. Once, I knocked three babies over by accident; I was pulling them along in a little cart and suddenly it turned over and the babies all fell out. I picked them up and then they all fell out again. It's a horrible memory. (Long silence.)

I finally ask her to tell me more of her thoughts about my "flower-children." In attempting to do this she winds up recounting many occasions in which, in spite of her efforts, she could never accomplish anything properly. She was "without strength," "lacking determination," and so on. She tries again to think about my "flower-children" but brings up another old complaint against herself: if she let out all her aggressive and hostile thoughts, she would become a despicable person. In fact she is indicating that her feelings of hatred are dangerous not only because childhood megalomania invested them as all-powerful but also because there is the risk that she will kill everything within her that is loving and protective. (The latter were in fact genuine qualities of Honorine's.)

JM: In other words your magical aggressive powers don't really work? Nobody dies. Even the babies you spilled out twice onto the ground weren't really hurt.

H: So much anxiety for nothing—it's almost funny, isn't it? (She laughs.)

JM: The impotence of all those magical thoughts, the fact that they don't work—maybe that's an even more painful blow to your image of yourself?

H: Yes, that's true. After all, if all the bad thoughts that burst through me so often don't hurt anybody—well, what's the use of them!

Thus little Honorine, full of aggressive feelings, advanced timidly onto the analytic stage. Was this a new Honorine who, all by herself, had tipped out of the maternal womb all the children that might have "flowered" after her? In any case, this is the first time in six years that this particular Honorine has had a chance to speak her lines and to ask for understanding.

Behind the Oedipal Plots: The Drama of Death

If we think further about the ambiguous objects that have a central role in the *I*'s psychic theater—the fetishist object, the phobic situation, or the obsessive thoughts—the ambivalence of each creator toward these inventions is manifest. Above and beyond their power to protect the infantile *I* from the fantasy of castrative punishment (in which the interdiction of all sexual pleasure is felt to be deserved because of childlike incestuous wishes), they convey a succinct message in the final act of this play: the object in question always acts as a link between the subject and someone else. But who is this Other? And why must the *I* make the lengthy detour of a symptomatic act or thought in order to go about the business of living? It is not my intention to explore the many complexities contained in these individual psychic dramas but simply to show the last twist to each story.

The fetish that permits a certain form of sexual pleasure at the same time protects its inventor in two ways: against oedipal vengeance and also against the fascination of fusional sexual longings that spell psychological death (since their aim is to merge with the mother of infancy but at the price of losing one's own identity as an individual; the return to the womb is a desire for nothingness—nirvana). In this way the fetish fulfills the function of a *counterphobic object,* which magically preserves the individual not only from castration but also from giving in to a terror-and-wish to be devoured, to fuse with the primitive mother-universe.

The phobic object and the terror it inspires are the price to be paid for certain fulfillments. Its construction also acts as a barrier against identical archaic wishes. By its creation the *I* provides a safe area within which it may circulate, protected from the object or situation that represents the fascination of the mother's body: heights, cliffs, open and closed spaces all may serve this purpose, provided they symbolize at one and the same time the oedipal parent and the primitive "breast-mother."

The obsessional scenario too, in its first acts on the analytic stage, seeks to resolve oedipal difficulties. Its many disguises are different from those displayed in phobic symptoms (which demand flight), in that the primal scene fantasies are frequently marked by anal and sadistic themes that oblige the threatened child to attempt to use magic to get rid of thoughts, hands and their movements, body substances, habits, and so on, all of which may be experienced as dirty or dangerous. In this compromise with the oedipal drama, death is always in the wings. The actor must be continually on guard to keep a careful distance from any object of desire, for fear of destroying or being destroyed by it. This back and forth movement may last a lifetime; it attempts to avoid fantasized punishment for infantile longings as well as the disintegration that the actor fears would result from becoming identified with the unconscious image of an omnipotent, death-dealing mother.

These psychic scenes with their complicated staging have

been created against a common primitive fantasy—the leitmotive of castration have been secretly linked to those of death. To give in to the dream of melting into the womb of the universe awakens the fear of dying. But that is not all. An even more profound anguish is aroused by the fear that the mind's *I* might die, that is, the danger that one may no longer exist as a separate entity with one's own subjective identity.

The Theater of the Impossible

Thus we come to the threshold of the "Impossible," that is, the longing for "oneness," for narcissistic bliss in which separateness, sexuality, and death are disavowed as external realities. This repertory is part of everybody's psychic theater, and its basic theme is the obligation to create something, anything, to fill in the gap produced by the inconceivable existence of "otherness." The first response on the part of the infant is an attempt to annihilate the boundary that forever separates one human being from another, by means of what Freud (1911) called "hallucinatory wish fulfillment." How do we come to accept that it is impossible to cross this invisible barrier, that we can never enter another's mind or possess another's innermost secrets? How do we learn to give up this imperious infantile wish to invade another being, originally the mother, and by the force of our own desires control the desire of that other? Indeed, some people never do give up the attempt!

Then, again, how do we come to terms with the disturbing discovery of the difference between the sexes? Our sexual anatomy is as inevitable as our death. Here too there are certain individuals who play out, in their inner theaters, a drama in which they have the right to choose their sex. In a sense these creators are incurable optimists. Their scenarios belong to the domain of the inventions I have named *neosexualities* (chapters 11 and 12), going in some cases to the extreme solution of the transsexual. The defiance, stemming from earliest childhood choices, that leads to neosexualities is not difficult to understand. How do the rest of us manage to accept, without regret or rebellion, our ineluctable monosexuality? We must all find our own solutions to this narcissistic dilemma, but some are not aided in accomplishing the renunciations involved, when the parents' unconscious wishes and fantasies concerning their own sexuality and feelings of sexual identity are highly disturbed.

The final act of the human comedy, the somber reality of death, uses few words and most people handle with it with total denial, or perhaps a belief in an afterlife. In the unconscious mind death appears to be represented as a blank. There are neurotic exceptions, such as those underlined by Freud, in which preoccupation with death is a displacement of castration anxiety, giving rise to what might be called "castration hypochondria" and even leading to psychotic inventions in which certain parts of the body are believed to be dead. There are, however, two notable realms in which the individual may write his or her own death-script: the "appointment in Samara" may be advanced when, faced with libidinal or aggressive suffering, the *I* decides to be the master of destiny and commit suicide or when these same factors precipitate psychosomatic death.

The factors that contribute to psychosomatic death reveal a curious abdication on the part of the *I* when faced with psychic stress stemming from inner or outer tensions. The psychic stage is then apparently empty: no plot, no players, scarcely any recognition of impending danger in the face of libidinal loss, narcissistic wounds, unsuspected longings, or hatred. These are, to all appearances, cast out from the psyche without compensation. When the psychic theater closes down in this fashion, the drama runs the risk of being enacted in the biological functioning of the body itself. The individual, overwhelmed by affective storms of which he or she has no knowledge, may then suffer grave psychosomatic explosion and die for the wrong reasons.

The Psychosoma on the Psychoanalytic Stage

The characters in the psychosomatic theater are not primarily men, women, or children, nor even part object representations of penis or breast; they are more like functions that seem endowed with a life of their own. These characters can only be felt, smelled, breathed in, or pushed out of the body; anonymous, invisible, and mystical beings, they sometimes seem to function like a global "body-sex." How can we communicate with the monsters of the deep? Perhaps we must try to "listen" to the rhinencephalon, the oldest part of the human brain, using archaic sources of knowledge to lead us to what awaits us.

Psychosomatic manifestations have the power to force the *I* to recognize that its own body is another "person." The body speaks no known language, yet it serves, time and again, as a framework for communicating the psychic scenes of the internal theater. The way one experiences one's body, imaginatively and symbolically, determines the nature of the stage plays that will appear there. It may be a neurotic body-theater or a psychotic body-theater. Or it may be that representation without words that becomes the psychosomatic production. *I*'s insight into its neurotic and deviant sexual creations and even into its psychotic inventions is totally lacking in these mysterious somatic dramas. When there is a radical separation between psyche and soma, those afflicted do not understand what their physical manifestations have to do with their psychological way of being, since they are unaware that the mind is being deprived of its own body's messages. The *I* has, unbeknownst to itself, given up its creative functioning and allowed the soma to become the mime-theater of the mind, sending silent messages (albeit violent in their expression) as pseudo-solutions to mental stress. This means that the body has decoded the conflict, erroneously, as a *physiological* threat. Even if at these times the curtain falls upon the psychic theater of the mind, however, its ever-creative *I* still tries to make sense of its physiological catastrophes and to "explain" the inexplicable soma. The psychosomatic illness then becomes an object of interest to the psyche and as such becomes part of the analytic discourse, even being used at times to hide other problems of a recognizably psychological order. The following case is an example of this kind of drama (V.-G. Brahmy, personal communication, 1977).

Monsieur C. came to the psychosomatic department of an important medical center for a consultation. He had been sent by his general practitioner, because he complained of periods of mental confusion that occurred suddenly in the street as well as of a number of other problems that he attributed to a state of increasing physical deterioration. These confused states seemed to him the final calamity. He believed his diabetic state to be the fundamental cause of his present problems, but his referral to a psychosomatic center resulted from his doctor's conviction that his physical state was exacerbated, if not caused, by psychological problems of which he was totally unaware.

In his first consultation, Monsieur C. talked at considerable length of his professional life, his friends, and his family, always in terms of "before" and "after" some unnamed event or events. When he spoke of "before," it was particularly the admiration of women that seemed important. Since the onset of the physical deterioration that had culminated in the feelings of confusion, his whole life "had shrunk away." There was no sense to be made of it, and he could relate it to no psychological events. "It's like that, that's all! Because I am diabetic."

To clarify the way in which Monsieur C.'s *I* tried to give meaning to his experiences in external reality while at the same time refusing any exploration of his psychic reality, I present an excerpt from his first consultation.

> INTERVIEWER: And this bad temper and irritability you speak of, when did it start?
> c: Without any cause . . . no cause whatsoever!
> I: Yes?
> c: My family . . . well, if you want, there are variations for diabetes, you know . . . depends on the sugar level and you're more or less irritable and nervous, you see.
> I: Yes.
> c: When they're hypo . . . well, that's when it gets dangerous.

I: You are speaking in whose name there . . . when you say "they"?

C: Well, no, I'm speaking . . . diabetic . . . *diabetic* you understand . . . because I'm part of the group of diabetics.

I: Yes, I understood that.

C: Well, if it's not . . . in my own name if you like . . . let's say being diabetic, there's a certain variation in one's state of mind that's very . . . variable.

I: But is this what alerted you to the need for consulting your doctor? Or was it those difficulties in remembering, those times of confusion you spoke of? What exactly happened on those occasions?

C: Ah . . . listen! One day I found myself in the street and I didn't even know where I was going. I didn't remember what I was supposed to do. I didn't quite know where I was. Well, I was suddenly worried because . . . I was diabetic or something. I don't know. I went and ate something. I just don't know any more than that.

I: But you knew already that you were diabetic?

C: Well, yes. I've known that for twenty years!

In her paper on this patient, Monsieur C.'s analyst, Brahmy, discusses his slow acquisition of the capacity to remember her in her absence, accompanied by subtle changes in his way of thinking about himself and his troubles. She noted that on numerous occasions he seemed to use extremely logical thinking in order to block fantasies from arising, frequently attempting to use words as a discharge function. They appeared to serve as a protective screen against states of tension in his psychic world. Was Monsieur C. at last beginning to speak other languages than "diabetic," thanks to the painstaking work of his therapist? Nevertheless she talks in her paper of her extreme discouragement at her patient's lack of recognition of the value of their work together: she alone observes the changes that are occurring. It is an open question whether the psychoanalytic situation can provide a framework capable of awakening the paralyzed *I* of certain severe psychosomatic patients. Under what conditions might it help to build a bridge across the frightening gap that separates psyche and soma? And at what psychological cost to the individual?

The possible answers to these questions go beyond the scope of this chapter. It may nevertheless be said that when somatization is the *only* visible response to psychic conflict and mental pain, it constitutes a monumental challenge to analytical understanding. Psychosomatic incidents arise in every analysis (and in everyone's lifetime), particularly when depressing or anxiety-arousing events are pushed out of the mind instead of being elaborated mentally. Such phenomena cannot fail to awaken many questions in the psychoanalyst's mind. It is in dealing with severely somatizing patients (who have invariably come to analysis for quite other reasons) that the analyst encounters those walled-in structures that seem to hold the *I* prisoner, although the *I* itself is unaware of its predicament. Releasing such prisoners calls for a particular style of contact on the part of the therapist, perhaps what Winnicott (1971) has called "the creative capacity for play." Winnicott holds that psychoanalytic work in general can progress only through an experience that takes place between two psychic "play areas"—that of the analyst and that of the analysand. He remarks that a therapist who is not capable of play will not be able to engage in this kind of therapeutic work (Winnicott 1971, p. 54). The patient who has no psychic space for playing has to be helped to create one so that a psychotherapeutic process can be set in motion. This need seems to me to be particularly true of patients (like Monsieur C.) who demonstrate a so-called "psychosomatic personality." These people have indeed lost the "capacity for playing" in the Winnicottian sense. Uninterested in "being" and only in "doing," unable to recognize their own feelings or to invest with libidinal interest their own and other people's thoughts and psychic realities, unable therefore to reflect upon the meaning of relationships, they are unable to play out in fantasy different ideas about what is going wrong in their lives.

In an ongoing therapy, such psychic prisoners appear totally unable to daydream and frequently even to dream. In spite of this difficulty, however, it is sometimes possible to make contact with the subterranean stream of unconscious life in these patients. The empty psychic spaces then become filled with a multitude of people and memories and an outpouring of affect that sometimes terrifies the patient. If the psychotic patient flees into the world of delusion in order to render overwhelming mental pain tolerable, the psychosomatic patient takes flight into external reality. When this occurs the body itself begins to act in a delusional way. When a "psychic space for play" is created, the fantasies that arise usually differ from those of the "normal-neurotic" in that they have a specifically concrete content, showing the extent to which the world of corporeal reality continues to invade the realms of fantasy. The following case was discussed with me for some two years by a gifted young analyst who often used a play technique in which the patient makes clay models to try to discover imaginative capacities and to undertake an exploration of his or her own psychic reality (Cazas, personal communication, 1977).

Monsieur D., a thirty-year-old actor, had been referred to the analyst by a dermatologist. He was suffering from a variety of serious skin troubles, including a severe form of eczema; as a child he suffered for many years from asthma as well as recurrent rhinitis. The analyst, faced with a total blockage in the patient's capacity to associate any ideas to any thoughts or events that he recounted, invited him to imagine a story, sometimes asking him to bring a clay model to the session. Pieces of bodies predominated. The patient was at first unable to invent stories other than "This is a mouth" or "This is a nose."

As D. gained confidence in his right to make fantasies, he one day described "an enormous tongue, ten meters long, that moves forward like a snake." Encouraged to describe it further, he produced the details that it was "disgusting and full of filthy things." It had "a tiny little mouth that served no purpose and on its back were very small teeth which also served no purpose since its digestion occurred all over its surface . . . no one could do anything against this tongue." He then added that "no matter what you do to it you can never get rid of it; nor is there any way of breaking into it." The analyst in noting his impressions had written, "This opposition between an agitated surface and a body without organs no doubt reflects the way in which this psychosomatic patient sees himself as well as reflecting his symptoms" (A. Cazas, personal communication, 1977).

In the patient's accounts of his relationship with his mother, the latter seemed to correspond in every way to the "double-bind" parent (for example, the mother who says to her adolescent boy, "Please feel free to leave home; but if you do it will kill me"). Such parents sometimes produce total psychic paralysis in their children. It seemed to me that the patient was trying to make a concrete representation of an unattackable "mother-tongue" into which one could not penetrate, but at the same time from which one could not hope to detach oneself.

Some weeks later the patient brought another figure: "a pre-historic monster divided into three parts—head, body, and rear end." The head, balanced on several feet, had two globular eyes and a wide-open mouth from which projected a hand. On one side of the mouth were placed two nostrils, from one of which was hanging an eye and from the other a claw. The rear end "is armed with a sharp-bladed knife and a corkscrew . . . the body is only a tubular connection covered with scales between the head and the rear end." These elements, under the guise of play, provided a touching glimpse into the patient's experience of himself.

A further fragment, noted several months later, showed the patient's growing capacity to represent and give verbal expression to his inner psychic dramas. The fantasy gives insight into his painful effort to use words that would communicate not only the problem of his body-image but also its relation to oedipal conflicts:

> This is the story of a false nose, or rather a *false* false nose. I am in a play and my parents are in the audience. I must leave the stage for a second act in which I am obliged to put on a cardboard nose to play the role of an old man. The stagehand has lost the false nose. The audience gets agitated and they begin stamping their feet. My mother sends my father to find out what I'm doing behind the scenes. The stagehand, seeing my father arrive, cuts off his nose with a sharp-bladed knife and hands it to me. I put it on, not realizing that it is not the real "false" one. Once I'm back on stage everyone begins to scream because of the blood flowing down my face. I take off the false nose and recognize the

nose of my own father! I fly into the wings and grab the stage hand . . . [here Monsieur D. is embarrassed and finds difficulty in telling the end of his daydream, but he forces himself to continue] er, well, I take the sharp knife and I cut off his penis, then I bash his head against the wall until his brain splits. . . .

To be able to recount a fantasy was for D. an utterly unprecedented event and indicated that he was now able to get in contact with his childlike fears and wishes and to give them metaphoric form, even though of a less-than-subtle nature. (In French, there is also a play on words: "le faux-nez qui est le nez qu'il me faut" means "the false nose which is the nose I should have.") This false nose, metaphor for the paternal penis, must in the patient's mind be recovered in the flesh. There is no repression, and there are few other protective mental mechanisms in this scenario. In this way it resembles psychotic fantasies, which so often reveal a breakdown in the symbolic process. But here we are dealing with the same process *in reverse.* The crude fantasies are not a sign of breakdown, but of progress. There is a rudimentary displacement onto the stagehand, who must act out the role of the son bent on obtaining his father's phallic power by castrating him. In the next act, this same character must take the son's place in the punitive castration (of body and mind) that is to follow. It seems that this patient, up until now, has been able to "speak" only by means of his infantile asthma and eczema and only able to "think" or express affect in terms of rhinitis. Perhaps this is a form of archaic psychosomatic communication using the old visceral or rhinencephalon brain (which means literally the "nose-brain"). The archaic brain was associated with olfactory power and the primordial role of smell in relation to others, thus giving particular importance to the signifier *nose* and its primitive relation to the earliest memory-traces of the maternal body, first sought through the baby's sense of smell.

It is not impossible that D.'s oedipal problems and castration anxiety are built upon, and mobilize in him, reactions stemming from the prototypes of castration anxiety that occur in earliest infancy, during the first experiences of separation and, eventually, individuation. There are glimpses in this patient's material of an internalized image of his mother that suggest she may have replied with excessive violence to what she interpreted as her baby's needs. The infant D. would appear to have been unable to "take in"—that is, psychically introject—the "breast-mother" with those soothing qualities that allow the baby to breathe freely and with pleasure, as well as to invest the other autonomic functions of the body with libidinal feeling. Without this essential introjection there is the ever-present risk that no fantasy life will develop, since all libidinal activity is then automatically excluded from the chain of symbolic representations. All that remains for us to "hear" are the asthma and the rhinitis. The psychoanalytic adventure sometimes allows such patients to use the analytic stage as the first setting in which primitive psychic scenes of this kind may be played out, permitting instinctual drives to be verbalized and thus available for thought for the first time in the analysand's life. The actor was able to use the psychoanalytic stage, whereas Monsieur C. could not.

As long as the soma is the *only* theater in which mental conflict may be expressed, the defensive organization of the mind's *I* is fragile, and we are faced with dramas that are potentially more death-bearing than neurotic, perverse, or psychotic constructions. On the other hand, when the creative psyche fulfills its function by building a psychological fortress for the menaced self, it serves to protect not only the psychosexual and narcissistic life of the subject but the biological life as well. The soma's "delusions," due in part to the inadequate participation of the mind, lead to the production of an act without a scene, a story without words, force without meaning, resulting in a biologically senseless illness. Lacking precious information of an affective and sensory order, the *I* remains in ignorance of future dangers stemming from either inner or outer sources. (These themes will be more fully explored in chapters 4 to 8.) In a sense it may be said that the only recognizable pain is psychic pain, for in the absence of any *mental* representation of the affective reactions and corporeal sensations the body is conveying, these parts of human experience have no psychic existence for the individual. Thus serious somatic states resulting from total unawareness of psychological pain may lead readily to biological death, as opposed to the psychic death that is experienced in psychotic states.

THE THEATER OF DELUSION

Much less common than somatization as a response to unacknowledged psychic stress is what may be considered as a psychical equivalent, the solution of psychosis. (The relation between psychosomatic and psychotic states will be examined in chapter 7.)

To do justice to the Theater of the Impossible in its psychotic version would require an entire book (and an experience in the psychoanalysis of psychoses that I do not possess). I shall limit myself here to giving a glimpse into a psychic scene devised by a young patient suffering from paranoid psychosis. I was fortunate in being able to follow this patient's development far enough to make sense of his particularly dramatic stage creation, and also to see the growth, based on his psychoanalytic experience, of a slowly and painfully acquired sense of reality, in closer conformity with society's demands and better adapted to his intimate wishes and strivings.

Dominique E., a twenty-year-old man, was mandated by the French courts to have psychotherapeutic treatment. He had attempted to commit murder, and only fortuitous circumstances had prevented his project from being successful. He was also genuinely seeking to understand how to cope better with dramatic circumstances in which, according to him, "anyone might feel moved to murder." The eldest of three sons, Dominique had enjoyed for the first three years of his life what he described as a unique form of maternal adoration, although he did admit that at times his mother's devotion to him was "excessive" and "disturbing." His illusory paradise was brutally destroyed by the arrival of his first little brother, a banal event in many a child's life but experienced by this patient as the cause of intolerable pain and irreparable narcissistic damage. He was left with the impression that "he had grown up by the force of hatred" and he added, "this hatred is so strong that no power on earth will take it from me." According to others (his father, as well as some of the witnesses at his trial), he was a gentle, timid, secretive young man; he had always shown particular tenderness to the first of his younger brothers, and the two were the best of friends.

At eighteen Dominique left home to come to Paris and study in a field in which he was considered talented. There he was introduced to Louise, an older woman who had been his mother's schoolgirl friend. He fell "crazily in love" with this woman, and before long they became lovers. Dominique moved into her apartment and, according to both of them, they were extremely happy together. However, the young man persuaded his woman friend to accept as a lodger a younger fellow student with whom he had struck up a friendship. Gradually he began to suspect, and finally became convinced, that his friend and his lover were having a secret affair. In spite of her vigorous denial of his accusations, he became so insistent that she decided to ask the friend to leave the apartment, and he did. But the persecuted and jealous young lover was in no way mollified and secretly prepared his revenge. He decided he must kill his lover for her betrayal of him. Gravely wounded by numerous knife stabs, she screamed loudly enough to attract the attention of an itinerant tradesman, who walked in through the unlocked door and was able to take the young man by surprise and disarm him. The fact that Dominique had allowed himself to be overpowered was advanced as an attenuating circumstance in that there was no irrefutable evidence that he intended to go so far as to kill his victim.

People with neurotic character problems (discussed in the next chapter) look for others who are in complicity with their secret scenarios, whereas those with psychotic disorders do not necessarily choose partners who, in accordance with their own internal scenes, are eager to play a role in their psychic scenarios; frequently those chosen are unable to recognize themselves in the resulting plot. In the case of Dominique, it is probable that, as long as his psychic scene was dominated by love rather than hate, his lover, his mother-substitute, was in complicity with him to the extent that she too wanted a son-lover. Indeed she may have desired unconsciously to live out certain homosexual wishes or conflicts with regard to her schoolfriend through having a relationship with the son. But when the paranoid script took full possession of the young man's mind, it is rather unlikely that she sought to be killed by her lover's hand.

In contrast to productions on the transitional stage (chapter 3), which must take existing reality into consideration, the psychotic *I* creates a *neoreality* that overrides ordinary social reality. It dictates that what the psychotic wishes to believe is universal truth. With the invention of the new reality, intolerable conflicts magically find a more satisfactory explanation, which can help to repair the severe narcissistic damage from which the subject is suffering. From this standpoint a delusion is also an attempt at self-cure, since it enables its author to live with a narcissistic self-image in which subjective identity and self-esteem are not in constant risk of being shattered. What once seemed meaningless and intolerable with regard to one's place and value in the family constellation now makes "sense" in terms of the self-created reality. But this new psychic solution sends its creator out in search of certitudes. Any likely thread, as in Dominique's case, may be used to create from whole cloth the proof of the impossible—an attempt to reverse time and erase the past, accompanied by the wish to settle accounts with the past and rewrite history more in keeping with the infantile *I*'s megalomanic aims. In putting his show on the world's stage, our young patient could see no other reality than his own, the violence of an enraged child whose hatred found no solution other than the path to madness.

The Basic Dramas of Humanity

Fundamentally, the themes of the psychic theater vary little. According to the child's own inborn and acquired creative possibilities, the traumatic events that have molded each individual psyche lead to an infinity of psychic inventions, all intended to deal with the calamities of separation and otherness, of sexual and generational differences, and finally of aging and death. Each *I* must construct scenes capable of containing these dramatic situations in order to achieve psychic survival.

The psychic scenarios presented here are all linked to the discovery of the parents as a sexual couple, to the wish to be the only child, and to the desire to possess the mother entirely for oneself in narcissistic fusion. These banal wishes and their non-fulfillment are part of the experience of every child. What distinguishes the solutions to psychic pain and mental conflict found by Madame A., Monsieurs B., C., and D., Honorine, and Dominique? With regard to their fundamental exposure to universal traumas, nothing except the form of self-cure that each child-artist created. Why one solution rather than another? It is too simple to say that all is the "fault" of the parents. This question will never receive a satisfactory response, even though each new psychoanalytic adventure tends to reconstruct a coherent hypothesis to explain it, as the chapters that follow illustrate.

3

The Transitional Theater
and the Search for Players

Not all psychic dramas take place in the inner theater where neurosis and the delusional plots of psychosis are staged. There is another theater whose performances go on the world's stage. Here the producers attempt to externalize intolerable inner dramas that they do not wish to claim as their own. Sometimes the wish behind such complicated dramas, commonly called character neuroses, is to try to make sense of what the small child of the past, who is still writing the scripts, found too confusing to understand. Constructions that use others to play important parts of oneself or of one's inner world are neither psychotic nor neurotic creations, but they borrow techniques and ways of thought that belong to both. The social stage on which such psychic productions are presented and the nature of the tie to the characters who are maneuvered into playing roles in them characterize what I call the Transitional Theater.

This particular way of splitting off mental pain and conflict, ejecting them from consciousness so that they must seek a solution elsewhere, is not confined to what is known in the analytic literature as *externalization*. It contributes to character neuroses and constitutes a large part of what is included in the term "narcissistic personality disorders" (discussed more fully in chapters 9 and 10). Included in the Transitional Theater are all actions whose principal aim is to discharge painful tension through constant activity. In this theater the psychic economy is dominated by addictive compromises of various kinds. These addictions may be obviously symptomatic (as in substance abuse) or may be subtly disguised in taking as their objects sexuality, work, or other people. Work addicts, for example, are unaware that their endless activity is compulsive and represents flight from their internal psychic world and its underlying tensions.

In chapter 5, I describe these addictions as character patterns dominated by "action symptoms" and explore the hypothesis that such modes of mental functioning tend to increase psychosomatic vulnerability. When that point is reached, the externalization of inner drama is no longer on the social stage but is worked out instead upon the subject's own body, much as though the afflicted body has become what it was in infancy—a foreign object experienced by the psyche as part of the external world. When the soma is left to solve psychological problems without words or representations from the psyche to guide it, the result is an off-stage production from the vantage point of the psychic theater, as chapters 4 to 8 will describe.

The Addictive Play

Intimately linked to the scenarios of the transitional stage are all the substance dependencies. Here the actors are reduced to inanimate objects that take the place of once-valued part objects, in many cases the breast-mother of early infancy. The latter is still being sought in the external world because there is little or no identification with an internal caretaking mother. Etymologically, the term *addiction* refers to a state of enslavement; the slavery is in many ways similar to the extremely dependent relationship of the nursling to its mother. For the enslaved addict, the addictive object—whether it is food, tobacco, alcohol, pharmaceutical products, or opiates—is in the first instance invested as "good," in spite of its sometimes dire consequences. In many cases, its pursuit is experienced as vital to the subject's well-being or even as giving meaning to life. Yet once absorbed, the addictive substance is usually experienced as "bad."

Another associated aspect is destructive danger, frequently interpreted by analysts as an unconscious wish for self-punishment. While this dimension may form a part of the subject's internal drama, it is more apt to function as a secondary benefit than as the cause of the addiction, in that the *I* who is directing the action has at some time felt the need to be punished for having dared to possess, in this drug-like fashion, the desired breast-mother. That is to say, the individual has detached the object that unconsciously represents the breast (in imaginary fashion has "stolen" the breast from the mother) and can now use it with impunity for his or her exclusive needs. Included in this primitive oral fantasy, however, is a punitive father-figure (often sought in the outer world in the form of the law, the doctor, or the detoxification facility), who is unconsciously used to prevent the greedy child from endlessly consuming the mother-body. To the extent that objects of addiction fulfill the function of true transitional objects—that is, objects created by the infant as a halfway stage between the internal and the external mother— they might well be considered *pathological transitional objects.* Whereas genuine transitional objects represent the soothing magic and strength of the mother's presence in the process of being introjected, addictive objects create no lasting change in psychic structure and therefore must be sought ceaselessly in the outer world, as symbolic substitutes for the mother of infancy. (To this extent they might better be called *transitory* rather than *transitional* objects.)

Addictive stage plays need no description; their reiterative plots are well known to everyone. In the first act the addictive substance is sought as a good "mother" or "breast." After absorption, it becomes a bad, persecuting "mother" (or part object); this forms act two. What we might call the third act (described above as an interchange with a punitive representative of the father) consists of promising oneself—or some important external or imagined inner object—never to start again. All of us at times take flight from the psychic pain stirred up by life's disappointments and irritations by seeking momentary oblivion in excess eating, drinking, smoking, sleeping, and so on. For certain people, however, such simple creations are expected to deal with every conceivable life tension.

When *other people* are used as addictive substances, they sometimes function as tranquilizers and at other times as containers for all that seems too hard for the individual given to addictive relationships to assume as part of his or her own psychic theater. Staging such scenarios obviously requires the cooperation of other people's *I*. These others are often unaware that they are playing the roles of projectively expelled aspects of these analysands or of other inhabitants of their internal worlds. Addictive relators are equally unconscious of the fact that their words and actions have galvanized others into playing these rejected roles. It is often those closest and dearest who are designated to carry out these parts—usually, it must be admitted, because their own psychic conflicts suit them to the identifications in question. Addicts who succeed in this feat rarely realize that they are writing the script and frequently complain bitterly of the way the others are behaving. Blanche, whom we shall meet later in this chapter, firmly believed that her husband was the author of all their domestic tragedies. Yet such people are constantly on the lookout for suitable players to carry out the roles of the inhabitants of their inner worlds.

The other players have also been waiting to jump on such a stage and play out the relational tensions and unconscious roles for which they do not have the words, rather like Luigi Pirandello's celebrated *Six Characters in Search of an Author*. It sometimes happens that these malleable actors, once in analysis, discover their tendency to get mixed up in other people's scenarios and realize that the temptation to do so has a compulsive quality. A gesture or a word from another is frequently sufficient for them to recognize their cues. It requires the strength and courage of their more adult side to stop the eager, anxious, or angry child within from jumping into the opportune drama. Domestic scenes of this kind that are perpetuated by certain couples make one wonder if the partners have chosen each other in part because they invariably trigger off in each other the scenarios that are seeking to discharge unconscious tensions in quarreling, predestined "accidents," and so on. The patient I have called Blanche falls into this category.

Thus the players in the Transitional Theater do not seek to resolve conflicts through neurotic compromise and symptom formation or through the creation of a neoreality that society would term crazy. In a sense, such people throw themselves into a more perilous enterprise than that of psychotic and neurotic sufferers, in that they are always dependent upon the good offices of others to furnish the sought-after certitudes that will enable them to avoid mental conflict and its accompanying psychic pain.

The productions of the Transitional Theater resemble the perverse scenarios of neosexual creators (McDougall 1978, pp. 21–86), but the staging of the plots and the use of others as characters is more intricate. These psychic dramas are not consciously eroticized, and they require a more complex outcome than the orgasmic response of the sexual deviant as proof of the certitudes seeking to be proclaimed. It frequently happens, however, that the producers on the social stage are treated as perverse, not in the sense of perverse sexuality but of *perversity*—that is, a "character" perversion (Arlow 1971). They are accused of taking pleasure in attacking, embarrassing, or in other ways causing suffering to those around them. Since these scenarios require some manipulation of the external world and the people in it, the addict in fact unconsciously assumes that the others are mere parts of his or her own self and thus denies the basic postulate of otherness. When otherness is disavowed by the psyche, we are truly in the Theater of the Impossible, but since the play cannot go on stage without the complicity and credence of others who are not mere inventions of the subject's imagination (even if they are treated as such), the whole performance is also under the sway of external reality and thus subject to the limitations of the Possible.

The Case of Blanche

To illustrate what I mean by the Transitional Theater I offer an excerpt from a long analysis. Blanche had been married for twelve years when she first sought my help in dealing with depressive feelings she did not understand. In our initial interviews she referred to these states as "voids" or "empty spaces" in her days, in which she wanted to do nothing because she felt life was valueless. At such moments she would become the victim of a variety of skin allergies from which she suffered intermittently. According to her description, she would then proceed to attack her skin with needles and burn it with alcohol, in order to combat the allergic reaction. This treatment in turn required many hours of staring into her mirror as she applied creams and ointments to heal the damage. Once installed in the analytic relationship, however, she spoke little of these potential psychosomatic dramas and also gave no glimpse into the scenarios hidden behind her "voids." Instead she seemed to use her sessions to prove to me that she was always "right," not only with regard to her professional colleagues, her mother, and her sons, but also and above all in her perpetual disputes with her husband. She had chosen this husband with considerable care. As she frequently recalled, with unmistakable bitterness in her voice, he had "corresponded exactly to what [I] expected of a man." She had spent some time searching for this suitable mate, turning down desirable offers in his favor. What a fiasco! Having studied him microscopically for twelve years, she could now declare that he was a monument of selfishness, a ridiculously indulgent father, negligent both in his person and in his work, disorderly and distracted. He did stupid things on trips, he was clumsy in the house and even in bed, where he showed himself to be awkward and inattentive to her wishes. From time to time she neatly designated her husband's place in her internal theater with the words, "My husband is a turd!" (in French, *une vraie merde,* which means literally *a true turd*).

Throughout the first two years of analysis, Blanche's remarks were punctuated with equally emphatic statements such as, "You see—it's perfectly clear! Self-evident, isn't it?" I felt she was trying to open my eyes forcefully so that I would see the scenes that occurred between her and her husband exactly as she did. At other times it was as though she sought to lay before me legal evidence of her husband's misdeeds; I was given forty-five minutes to judge and convict the accused. During one of these tirades she became fed up with my silence and said in a firm little voice, "I want you to know this time I expect a reply." "Reply to what?" I asked. After a shocked moment she said in an incredulous tone, "But you *are* listening to me, aren't you?" To her surprise I replied at length. Yes, I had heard everything she had been saying. I enumerated her husband's misdemeanors of the past two days and added that it seemed to me she was waiting for a reply to a question that had never been formulated. Though irritated, Blanche nevertheless attempted to be more precise about her expectations of me. She felt that she had a right to some remark . . . something that would confirm her judgment of her husband . . . perhaps I could see some aspects of the question that escaped her . . . and after all, she was only in analysis because of her husband!

Sensing in this last remark that she was rapidly renouncing any attempt to put herself in question and was once more being drawn to put on stage the perpetual round of domestic tragedy, I interrupted her to say, "You are seeking some predetermined response from me. I have noticed that your husband always responds in a totally predictable fashion to what you are expecting." I myself had realized clearly for the first time that this husband-turd had always reacted exactly as she knew he would and had in fact *corresponded* to "everything she expected from a man," as she had told me in our first interview. She had then been referring to his suitable qualities, of course, but it seemed more than probable that she had chosen him also for his defects and clumsiness, of which she had been aware from the beginning. This uncomfortable knowledge, however, was split off from her consciousness or at least firmly denied. The scenes she recreated for me on the analytic stage were the bare truth. She invented nothing.

What do you do when your life-partner is "a *true* turd"?

Blanche knew the only answer her *I* had been able to find: she was entitled to a holier-than-thou anger, a theatrical drama that seemed to offer her endless satisfaction. But why? The violent and tormenting warfare into which she was compulsively drawn, day after day, cost her dearly. Of her husband's complicity in entering this bullring, perhaps provoking his wife to violent and saintly anger, I had little doubt, but he was not my patient. I could examine only Blanche's as yet unknown vested interest in this incessant conjugal drama. As with most character problems, Blanche's constant states of irritation and despair were more time-consuming and more wearing for her than many neurotic symptoms would have been, while at the same time they were less accessible to analysis. All that I was permitted to see was my role as judge and her insistence that her complaints were based on a true account of the facts. They were not fantasies; I was being provided with "evidence."*

When such a scenario is relentlessly staged, session after session, the "wickedness" of the accused is highlighted in the therapeutic situation, just as it is in everyday life, in order to show that all fault is in the other. This behavior has little to do with that chimera known in analytic literature as "reality test-ing." Blanche was using her husband to prove to me, as well as to herself, just how virtuous, worthwhile, and estimable a person she was, deserving no shame and exempt from guilt. These were essential aspects of her narcissistic self-image. And I was to confirm that she had attained the impossibly high ideal she felt she should meet. It requires no stretch of the imagination to guess that a profoundly painful task lay ahead of us in our analytic endeavor. Would Blanche ever be able to accept that, in spite of the reality of the facts she recounted, she herself was coauthor of this running serial? And that the guerrilla warfare that character-ized her domestic scene was the major interest of her life? Her professional work (which was reduced to a minimum and in which she used but a small part of her genuine abilities), her life as a mother, and her life as a woman were all sacrificed to this

---

*Since writing this chapter, I have encountered a most interesting paper by Ruth Lax dealing with "self-righteous" patients and describing identical phenomena (Lax 1975).

reiterative theater piece, which seemed made to measure—the only role in which she could find fulfillment and maintain her feeling of identity without falling to pieces.

I gradually came to realize that Blanche's husband, to whom she was constantly aggressive and who always responded as expected, was in spite of all appearances not only an essential but indeed a beneficial object in her life. In other words he held the place of an addictive object. Like a heroin addict, Blanche felt her addiction was destroying her, but she needed it and sought it out with unfailing determination. At least from the standpoint of her narcissistic economy, her true-turd husband played the role of a transitional object, one without which she would have felt empty, afraid, and valueless. How are we to understand the plot and the characters that made up most of my patient's psychic scenario, when she herself was unaware that she was putting this play on a transitional stage in the external world? By what means could she come to understand that the "true turd," who had the leading role and was felt to be so harmful, was a needed and indeed invaluable object? Here we are faced with a little Blanche of the age at which children play with dolls and give them important roles in the externalization of their inner fears, longings, and tensions. When we see a small girl giving her doll a severe thrashing because she has done badly at school, refused to eat her vegetables, or answered her mother back it would not occur to us to say, "Don't you like your dolly?" She loves it as though it were a part of herself, and indeed the doll is not only required to submit to painful *experiences* that the child herself has had to endure but is also invested with all the undesirable *traits* that she herself does not wish to recognize as her own, for fear of losing her parents' love. The game serves to reassure her that she is a child beyond reproach, an ideal child perhaps, trying to meet what may have been interpreted as parental demands for perfection.

As a child Blanche had in fact been asked to meet standards of behavior and to accept painful emotional situations (she had to make an absolute choice between her parents when they divorced) that are not within the capabilities of any child. I do not wish to dwell here on Blanche's historical reality; I am mainly concerned with illustrating an aspect of the mental processes by which she was able to create and maintain an illusory identity, one that appeared to her as to be the only means of meeting senseless demands. In order to feel loved, she had to forgo most of her instinctual wishes and had become something of a psychic cripple. Thus she had achieved a remarkable feat in discovering a husband able to express and carry into action all the aspects of her own needs and wishes that she had had to disown. In order to preserve a tolerable narcissistic image in the face of her internal persecutors, Blanche lived out, through her husband, all that was for her—in all senses of the word—unthinkable. *He* could be sexual, clumsy, dirty, careless, and casual (as well as overindulgent with his children in ways that she had never known in childhood), and *she* was there to see that he was suitably punished for it. He embodied all that she had been accused of in childhood, enabling her to guard intact the belief in her own ideal self. In order to be, she had to be perfect.

This primitive method for dealing with intolerable psychic pain is of course only one of the many possible manifestations of such a predicament. Most of Blanche's psychic energy was directed toward seeking proof that she actually possessed the valued qualities she believed were necessary in order to be esteemed and loved, or indeed to be allowed to exist. In many ways she used her husband as a mirror, as though seeking her own image in reverse. "He is the epitome of evil, not me!" But in order to maintain this constant psychic production, she had been obliged to cut herself off from almost all instinctual satisfactions; she found pleasure in few activities, and her relationships with others were either conflictual or meaningless. Unable to observe either herself or others, she was deprived of the means of reflecting on her difficulties and of understanding the periods of emptiness in her life. In a sense she had thoughts for no one but her husband. The worse he became, the more she was convinced of her goodness. Unknown to her, her husband was the imaginary recipient of her own instinctual life. All that was forbidden to her she enjoyed vicariously, rather like a preacher engaged in the passionate pursuit of sinners whom he hopes to redeem for the many sins he is unable to commit. But her husband did not always fulfill this designated role. Sometimes he would turn upon her in anger, and once she reported that he had broken down and cried, saying he would never understand what she wanted from him. At these times, or during his absence, her living nightmare ceased, to be replaced by the feelings of emptiness and inner deadness.

Blanche's inner theater evolved slowly, allowing her to reflect on her frustrations and discontent instead of plunging into quarrelsome action in an attempt to flee all knowledge of her painful feelings about herself. In particular, the empty spaces began to fill up. She became psychically richer as she came to accept the many precious and so-called "bad" impulses that she needed to possess in order to feel truly alive. The awkward, mean, little "turd-girl" became an important character on the analytic stage and was able at last to be recognized as having the right to exist and something important to say. The small turd could now talk to the parental objects that she had so brutally introjected into her psychic structure in childhood. She was able to discover how much her conscious *I* had identified with their apparently cruel and impossible demands. As she began to let the wicked little girl within her speak in the first person, her hitherto hidebound identity-representation enlarged its confines, allowing the dramatic scenes that had always been played out in the external world to find an interior elaboration.

Addictive Relationships and Transitional Phenomena

This tortuous way of placing internal dramas on the world's stage is more complicated to maintain than the creation of a delusion or the construction of a neurotic symptom, if only because of its inherent fragility. The scenarios of which the individual is the unacknowledged author also require a certain manipulation of other people and must relentlessly seek the needs and weaknesses of others in order to discover those who will play the predetermined roles. Anything that does not fit within the framework of the predestined scene receives no libidinal investment

and quite frequently is not even perceived. The author is endlessly driven by the need to obtain with certainty, through unconscious exploitation of the external world, the confirmation of
self-illusions.

To clarify the processes at work in the externalized theater
and its particular use of the psychic and social space between the
subject and the others, I shall take the model of object relating
implied in Winnicott's (1971) concept of transitional objects and
activities (Modell 1969). As with any such concept, this one can
represent only one aspect of the phenomenon to which it is
addressed, in this case the beginning of the *I*-World relationship.
This extremely important phase in the development of the infantile *I* includes what Winnicott called the recognition of "not-me"
objects. At this stage children become capable not only of differentiating themselves from others but of maintaining an image of
an object in its absence. This concept took as its starting point
Freud's illuminating discovery of the underlying significance of
the infant's game of peekaboo and play with the wooden spool
(Freud 1920). The transitional object, like the spool, is neither a
purely psychic activity (which would not require a concrete object in order to exist) nor purely a part of the external world. It
differs from the rest of the "not-me" world of people since children have already learned that they have no influence over people
and therefore recognize them as beyond their magic control. Such
is not the case with the spool. What Winnicott has underlined is
the precarious nature of the equilibrium that children at this stage
have established between personal psychic reality and the experience of controlling a real object in the external world. This maturational phase precedes the capacity to be alone without fear of
losing identity and without the danger of being overwhelmed by
anxiety. This period of development also foreshadows the ability
to effect genuine exchange with others without fearing dangerous
invasion of either oneself or the other. People like Blanche are
stuck at this stage of development, as far as their significant
relationships are concerned.

The inanimate thing or the activity that has succeeded in
becoming a genuine transitional object then embodies the earliest
external expression of self-engenderment (in contrast to hallucina-

tory wish fulfillment), in that it is the child who creates the meaning of the object in accordance with its internal reality organization. The proof of the success of this creation lies in the fact that the object stands for or contains the mother's image and indeed the whole maternal environment. It is an object in the process of becoming internalized, although it is still far from being the foundation of what will one day be an internal symbolic structure. A small child is not yet capable of identifying with (and is therefore still unable to use) such an internal object, in that the possibility of being a good mother to oneself and assuming a maternal function for oneself still lies in the future. The transitional object or activity represents a union with the mother that helps the child to support her absence, just as later on the ability to use the word *Mommy* will allow the child to think about her in her absence and image her there.

According to Winnicott's conception, if this process is hindered by environmental factors or by the conscious or unconscious problems of the parents, the young child has only one course open to it, namely, to split the self-image in two; one part encapsulates the child's secret, subjective world, while the other complies with the demands of the external world. This second self is a false (albeit vital) self that is an adaptation to the outer world but detached from the child's intimate psychic reality. Such children run the risk later in life of living as though they were "not entirely real." They may then feel that they do not understand the world around them; they come away from others with nothing—in other words, "empty."

This kind of split in psychic reality may well predispose people to addictive ways of dealing with the feelings of unreality and emptiness. In place of the transitional object of infancy, with its capacity for soothing the self, the child within the adult may continue to seek transitory objects—drugs, sexual rituals, other people, or endless compulsive pursuits that bring only temporary relief.

When other people are chosen for an addictive and drug-like role, they are subsequently expected to fulfill one of the normal functions of the self-soothing transitional object of childhood— that is, to supply the subject with the feeling of being real and having individual value. In other words, they are required not only to soothe and to maintain the subject's narcissistic homeostasis but also to fill holes in the *I*'s feeling of identity, holes created by a parental discourse that seemed to give the child no place in the family constellation or that set up an impossible ideal as the measure of personal value. In the fantasy of the subject, the chosen other is held entirely responsible for everything that happens; happiness is expected not as a desire but as a duty to be discharged by the transitional person or drug-substitute. Inevitably, this special other sooner or later proves inadequate to fulfill these expectations and may then be accused of indifference or lack of perception of the subject's urgent needs. Like small children under the sway of infantile megalomania, people who use others in this way tend to feel that the failure of the drug-other to take full responsibility for their happiness is proof that the other does not care about their personal desires and wishes or even about their continued existence. These persecutory projections reveal the pathetic attempts of the child to make sense of the thoughts and feelings that were incomprehensible during childhood.

The Role of Primitive Defense Mechanisms in Addictive Relationships

Although this psychic solution to mental pain does not qualify as a delusional formation, primitive mechanisms requiring splitting and projective identification, as described by Klein (1957), Segal (1964), and Grotstein (1981), are at work, and the secondary processes from which verbal thought is constructed are infiltrated with elements of primary-process thinking, that is, dreamlike ways of reasoning (Freud 1900). From the point of view of the psychic economy, the fragility of such relationships, when they play a crucial role in the maintenance of psychic equilibrium, is evident. They can be understood as addictive in the full sense of the word, in that the dependence on the other is extreme, yet the other is treated as a substance rather than as a person. The creator is totally unaware of writing the script for all that happens in the relationship.

In unconscious fantasy such ways of utilizing external objects as though they were inanimate form part of the infantile belief that one has created by oneself everything that exists. But the unhappy creators of these scenarios must also suffer the uncomprehending pain of the small infant whose hallucinatory wish fulfillment fails and who then experiences all that happens as the effect of the other's omnipotent capacity (interpreted as a wish) to make the infant suffer. At this stage of infant psychic development, omnipotence has changed sides, a sign that primary-process thinking is beginning to coexist with secondary-process ways of thought. In Bion's terminology (1962b) "alpha" functioning, which includes the capacity for thinking without psychotic distortion, is intact, but a fusional view of the relationship with others still persists.

Thus we come back to that transitional area that in so many ways falls into two worlds and two ways of experiencing the world. For this reason I regard the malleable others as stand-ins for what should have been, in infancy, a genuine transitional object—that is, an object that represented the mother but was also regarded by the infant as its own creation. Since the addictive object in adult life is recognized as having an independent existence and therefore as being able to hurt or frustrate the subject, it escapes magic control and thus fails as a transitional object. And since there is little identification to an internal caretaking mother for self-soothing and narcissistic well-being, the transitional other must be manipulated, although such manipulation is demanding and exhausting work. This system of maintaining a feeling of identity is complicated, but the very fragility of these psychic structures and the profound, unconscious pressures that render them necessary endow them with such resistant strength that the possibility of modification through analysis is sometimes uncertain. As in drug addiction, there is profound ambivalence toward the need-object, as well as a feeling of incapacity to tolerate, elaborate, and eventually resolve emotional tensions.

The fundamental ambivalence attached to the person or persons chosen in adulthood to fulfill transitional functions is destined to display its strength in the analytic relationship as well. The analyst, like the privileged external object, is also experienced as a primitive mother who is alternately excessively good and excessively bad. In the analytic relationship the intensity of the unconscious demand (to merge with the object and recover all the idealized dimensions of oneself that are projected into its representation) is clearly impossible to satisfy. At the same time the limitless rage that such a situation is bound to create seeks continually to be externalized in the transference. Analysands are torn between a belief in the analyst's beneficial powers and the illusion of being in the clutches of a magician capable of making them suffer simply for pleasure. Analysis of the transference relationship then becomes more than usually difficult, since the *I*'s identifying landmarks are as confused as they are in external relationships. The patient frequently feels that the analyst is responsible for the ensuing confusion. In this tormenting transference situation, impregnated with hostility and extreme dependence, such patients do not readily put forth on the analytic stage the scenes of love and hate that need to be put into words and rendered meaningful, perhaps for the first time. If, however, a feeling of trust in the analyst and in the analyst's capacity to accept and understand feelings of love and hate is established in the relationship (and it does not always happen), then the analyst, the substitute transitional object, can be experienced as both a real and an imaginary object in the space between their two subjectivities, so that between the *I* of the analysand and that of the analyst a genuine encounter may take place.

4

The Staging of the Irrepresentable: "A Child Is Being Eaten"

When he first came to see me, Isaac claimed that he had never suffered from any psychological problems until the age of forty —when he was stung by a wasp. Ever since then he had suffered excruciating attacks of anxiety, an anxiety neurosis of such violence that no amount of psychiatric drugs could alleviate his symptoms for more than a short period of time. After four years he now recognized that he had become frighteningly dependent on drugs and that as a result his work was suffering. On the advice of a friend he consulted an analyst, but he hadn't the slightest hope that psychoanalysis could do anything for him.

The chief interest in a clinical presentation lies in the theoretical issues or unresolved questions to which it gives rise. Since these factors often motivate our choosing one patient over another, they require consideration. Why did I accept Isaac in treatment, even though I had too many patients at that time? And why did I take so many notes during his analysis? The latter requires quite powerful motivations, over and above interest in one's clinical work and one's patient. In this case, Isaac's story promised to give me insight into theoretical questions that had nagged me for several years, such as the relationship between hysterical and psychosomatic states and what distinguished them, a question I had already tried to resolve in an earlier publication (McDougall 1978, pp. 337–96).

Despite the intriguing question of why a man would wait forty years—and for a wasp sting—in order to develop an anxiety neurosis, I might not have accepted Isaac for analysis had he not revealed to me in our first two interviews that during his forty supposedly trouble-free years he had suffered from a variety of psychosomatic ills: gastric ulcers, attacks of tetany and asthma, and ill-defined cardiac symptoms. For some time I had nourished the idea that the missing link between psychosomatic and hysterical formations might be partially revealed in those intermediate formations that I call acting-out disorders and that sometimes take the form of Freud's (1898) little-used category of actual neurosis. And here was Isaac, with a full-blown anxiety neurosis, a psychosomatic history behind him, and an apparent absence of hysteria or any other marked neurotic symptoms! In addition I found him engaging—intelligent and a little crazy in a way that appealed to me (although before his analysis began Isaac considered himself one of the sanest people he had ever met). In all fairness to myself, I should point out that I did offer to find him another analyst since I could not take him for some time and his symptoms and suffering were considerable. But Isaac firmly refused my offer. He was prepared to wait a year, provided he could see me from time to time. I agreed. It seemed we had chosen one another, for better or for worse.

Isaac and the Wasp

Here briefly is Isaac's background as he presented it in our first encounter. Forty-four years old, married to a woman ten years older than himself to whom he feels deeply and affectionately attached, with teenaged children. He has come for help because of frequent uncontrollable outbursts of unmotivated anxiety. These happen in the street, at work, when he is alone, when he is far away from home. He suddenly begins to sweat and tremble and he has difficulty in breathing, accompanied by frightening tachycardia and a pulse rate of 120. At these times he feels that death is imminent. The anxiety attacks began four years ago, after he was stung by the wasp. Since then he has seen several doctors and psychiatrists; the attacks are controlled for a while by heavy medication, but eventually the calming effects diminish and the medication has to be changed. Isaac is frightened by his dependence on psychiatric drugs (he never took such things before) and equally perturbed to note that his symptoms seem to be getting worse. He has always enjoyed his own company, but he is now afraid to be alone and therefore cannot concentrate properly on his work. As a writer and a filmmaker, he must be away from home for days at a time during shooting sequences. Tension has grown up between him and his wife; he finds he is losing sexual interest in her, and they have been constantly at loggerheads for the past year or so.

Up to the age of forty, he was a thoroughly "normal" human being, with no psychological problems whatsoever, and now he is a total wreck. And in spite of what "they" say (that is, the doctors who are always reassuring him that there is nothing seriously wrong with his heart or his lungs), he is convinced that he is going to die of a coronary or some other cardiac disaster. When I ask why he has decided to die of heart failure rather than something else, he recounts his father's history of two myocardial infarcts. These happened well before Isaac's fortieth year, but until recently he had given little thought to them. Now he is constantly preoccupied not only with his own imminent death but also with his father's. He tells me he is "so fond of [his] father that the thought of his dying is intolerable" to him. His mother, on the other hand, gets on his nerves—but she is in excellent health. (He seems to suggest that nothing could kill her; she's immortal.) So I get a first inkling of a hysterical identification—to his father's heart attacks—although there is nothing in his history to indicate that his symptoms are genuine hysterical symptoms or that they are a metaphorical expression of his sex life. On the contrary he asserts that he has "never had any sexual problems" (but I shall return to this important question later in this chapter).

The circumstances of the first anxiety attack are as follows. Isaac and his wife were spending the weekend in the country with close friends. While dining outside, Isaac was stung on the neck, from behind, by the wasp. The moment he felt the sting, everything began to spin around him, his heart raced madly, he had a sudden intuition that he was dying of a myocardial infarct, and he fainted. He was given urgent medical attention and assured that he had suffered a severe allergic reaction. This diagnosis surprised him, because he had often been stung by wasps and bees and had never had any violent reaction in the past. Of course he might have built up an allergic reaction to wasp stings, but the interesting factor was the unconscious breakthrough, a psychological accompaniment to the somatic event in the form of a terrifying and anxiety-arousing fantasy. There was very little content to it—simply, "I am going to die." During the ten to fifteen years in which he had suffered from similar symptoms (asthma and cardiac dysfunction) in addition to his gastric ulcers, Isaac had never suffered the frightening idea that death was close. On the contrary, he seemed rather insouciant about his health and life expectancy.

The Psychosoma and the Mother

I find this insouciance to be a common feature in people with proliferating psychosomatic symptoms, as though they are being looked after by some divine providence—that ever-loving mother of early childhood. Once their illness has been diagnosed, however, many become excessively attentive mothers to themselves. They care for the sick part of the body as though it were a child. This observation raises the question of whether psychosomatic explosion may bring about a reorganization of ego functioning in a positive direction. It has sometimes been suggested in analytic writings that such a reorganization may be the secret aim of the illness, but I believe it to be in the nature of a secondary benefit, not a causal factor in psychosomatic illness. However that may be, insouciance is frequently transformed into hypochondriacal concern. This development at least indicates that life forces have been mobilized to combat unsuspected death-seeking factors in the unconscious. They give rise to the fear of psychic death in the form of ego fragmentation, as well as archaic castration fears expressed in fantasies of bodily disintegration and biological death. These are psychotic rather than neurotic anxieties, but in patients like Isaac no defenses have been created against them. It is interesting to recall that to the components of the actual neuroses Freud (1914) later added hypochondria, which he felt to be a narcissistic investment of libido in the somatic self. The undoubted stimulus to hypochondriacal concerns, in which the illness is treated like a sick baby, may be necessary and valuable in instituting care and concern for the body and its functioning, sometimes for the first time in the patient's life history.

To return to Isaac and our initial interview, Isaac insists that he does not believe in analysis, at least not for himself. (His wife has had an analysis that was beneficial to her, but then "she had had problems and [he] didn't.") Secondly, he is very afraid of what analysis will do to him. I ask him what it might do, and he replies that it could destroy his creativity. Isaac has a personal theory that psychological illness makes people creative, "provided they do not probe into it" (an interesting form of castration anxiety that is common to many creative people). In view of his suffering, however, he is prepared to take the risk—provided I promise not to do a "full analysis" on him (just a partial castration?). His next objection is that he is not a "typical analytical case." I ask him what this is, and he replies that he has never suffered from any sexual problems. He is thoroughly "normal." Not wishing to appear Socratic and persecutory I refrain from asking him what "normal" means. His final reservation about analysis concerns what he has heard about transference and his observation of his wife's profound attachment to her male therapist. He does not wish to get emotionally involved with anybody in this way; he is an independent man and would bitterly resent any feeling of dependence on another person.

In fact, without realizing it, Isaac was desperately afraid of becoming the instrument of another's will, just as he had in childhood been the instrument of his overfeeding and overcontrolling mother. Such mothers sometimes use their children as parts of their own bodies or selves. They may project upon the child some of their own conflicts and then attempt to control these conflicts through the child's somatic functioning. A mother might, for example, give her child frequent enemas in order to get rid of an anxious feeling or an unconscious fantasy that she herself is dirty. Such children grow into adults who are terrified of being colonized by people like their mothers. They protect their limits and boundaries with ardor. At the same time, within this secure area they may grow up not fully convinced that they possess and are therefore responsible for their own bodily parts or functions. These may later be nodal points for the formation of psychosomatic symptoms; alternative consequences may be the creation of psychotic beliefs or sexual perversions.

Patients like Isaac reveal to us in the course of analysis that they have had an addictive relationship to their mothers—and here was Isaac, already terrified of becoming addicted to his analyst! Instead of an identification to a "good-enough" internal mother (Winnicott 1960), there is in these patients an "adhesive identification" (Meltzer et al. 1975) to an external figure (or inanimate object, in the case of substance addictions). In psychosomatic patients the tendency to addictive relationships often becomes polarized upon the treating doctor in a kind of oedipal triangle composed of the doctor, the patient, and the "child" in the form of the imploding, somatically dysfunctioning organ. Just as in early infancy, the body is unconsciously experienced as an external object for the psyche.

In spite of his fear of becoming addicted to analysis and therefore hopelessly dependent on it, Isaac was able to come and see me because he knew from our first telephone conversation that I had no place for him. The compromise that I would see him occasionally until such time as I could offer four sessions a week on the couch suited him perfectly. The waiting time turned out to be eighteen months, with Isaac calling up more and more frequently for extra sessions. When these were not available, he would record his own free associations on a cassette and bring it to me.

In the interval I learned important facts concerning the onset of Isaac's ulcer troubles that gave me valuable insight into the "irrepresentables" that had contributed to his psychosomatic afflictions as well as his anxiety neurosis. His ulcer history began after two important events that occurred when he was nineteen: despite his success as a student, his failure to pass a very important examination (the "Baccalaureate"), and his first sexual experiences. The latter, unlike the examination, he felt he had passed with success. But this apparently felicitous entry into his adult sex life had mobilized profound and primitive forms of anxiety of which Isaac was totally unaware.

During the initial eighteen months of sporadic contact, Isaac also reconstructed the emotional climate in which he had received the famous wasp sting. He discovered to his surprise that he had been feeling very jealous of his friend Pierre: not only had Pierre and Isaac's wife been talking together about *their* psychoanalyses, making Isaac feel excluded, but he also felt that Pierre allowed himself to be influenced too much by his own wife, to Isaac's intense irritation. (This was my first "free-floating hypothesis"— that the wasp sting may unconsciously have represented a feared-and-wished-for homosexual penetration, in which Isaac's unconscious desire would be to take the place of the two wives in relation to Pierre. It seemed to tie up with the hysterical identification, in his fantasy, to his father's infarct, as well as his irritation with his mother.)

Terrors and Smother-Love

I shall resume at this point Isaac's first year of intensive analytical work. In spite of his determination to have "nothing to do with transference," Isaac became rapidly attached to his analysis, and we went through the usual honeymoon of oedipal projection: he kept a jealous eye on signs of other patients, speculated lengthily about the other rooms in my apartment, decided —in spite of evidence to the contrary—that "there was no man in this place," and so on. Among his associations Isaac made out a case for incest and could not see why it should be forbidden. All this led eventually to his rediscovery of the important role he had always played in his mother's life. An only child, he had been "her little man," and for many years she called him *mon petit soleil* ("my little sunshine"). When his parents quarreled, his mother would come and sleep with Isaac. He maintained that his parents had no sexual relations, but these memories led him to accept that they did nevertheless share the same bed most of the time. In any case, the contact between Isaac and his mother seems to have been unusually intimate, and his father appears to have taken no steps in the early years to separate them, rather as though he gave Isaac over to be his mother's phallic completion. At least Isaac had interpreted it this way. Isaac seemed in implicit agreement with Freud's hypothesis to the effect that woman's major desire was to be possessed of a male child. But as the analysis proceeded, Isaac began to wonder, for the first time, whether his father were jealous and angry with him. He really felt he had taken his father's place with his mother.

Certain ineradicable childhood memories and historic details also formed an important background. Isaac's was a nonpracticing Jewish family that fled Paris at the time of the German occupation. A recurring memory was that of a bombing attack in which Isaac's mother threw her body over the little boy's back to protect him. The different contexts in which this memory surged forth, in spite of the poignant and tender feelings it evoked in Isaac, made me ask myself whether a "wasp sting" fantasy could have crept into Isaac's unconscious memory, like the wasp that took him by surprise from behind.

During this same period Isaac was sent to a Catholic school, for security reasons. He had a memory of feeling different from the others. Apart from the reality of the situation and the knowledge that the danger was genuine, we came to understand that the "difference" included the feeling that he had a different and more dangerous relationship with his mother than did the others. The historical reality, which undoubtedly heightened the mother's intense protectiveness of her little boy, is not a sufficient explanation.

Since childhood Isaac has had a recurring nightmare in which a cat wound itself around his neck and threatened to smother him. In associations to this repetitive dream, the "smother-love" of Isaac's over-loving mother came through very clearly and could be connected to his frequently recurring fear that I and the analysis would "smother" his creativity.

Pussy has the same slang meaning in French as in English, and associations to this word-image led Isaac to another memory in which he would get under the skirts of the babysitter, there to be "smothered" with delight and giggles. Isaac had a number of asthmatic attacks during this phase of the analysis, but he denied that his respiratory suffering could have any relationship to the "stifling," "smothering" memories impregnated with a mixture of excitement and terror. That these frightening affects were unconsciously linked to fantasies of the female sexual organs and the feminine body left no doubt in my mind, but they were inaccessible to Isaac, who could accept no connections of this kind. He reiterated, as though he anticipated such interpretations, that fortunately he had "absolutely no sexual anxieties." Around this time he reported on several occasions that he behaved cruelly to his own cat and was surprised by his unkindness toward this animal, which he loved dearly. A clue to his underlying quarrel with the cat came about in an association in which he recounted that he often jumped with fright when his wife came up behind him. The chain of signifiers that included his back covered by his mother's body, the wasp sting from behind, the many terrors coming from the cat of his dreams, the exciting sexual smother-game with the babysitter, and finally the fear of his wife's approach clearly indicated global anxiety of an overwhelming kind attached to his mother's body and sex,* but one that Isaac was not yet able to comprehend.

The constant "terror of something coming up from behind," which he felt acutely as a nameless dread when walking alone in the street, was first approachable through the transference. On many occasions I was that danger; Isaac feared my words and even more my silence. I asked him whether my interpretations or my anxiously awaited silent thoughts about him could be put

---

*Isaac could equally well have developed an allergic reaction to cats and cat fur, a common manifestation in patients with similar fantasies attached to the mother's body.

into images and was rewarded with associations that allowed us to see that I might "penetrate" him disastrously with my "wasp sting" interpretations or my treacherous silence. All these images were invariably attached to a male figure. I was the castrating father and only much later came to be feared as an invasive mother. The early memory of his mother flinging her body over him was still felt as reassurance. She alone could protect him from the bombs of the enemy and the other "attacks from behind" that filled his fantasies.

As Isaac reiterated that the danger of attack was exclusively attached to the mental representation of a man, it became clear to him that this was a justifiable scenario, a castrating attack in which he would be punished in his back, where he and his mother had been in such tender and intimate contact. But it was only toward the end of our first year of work that Isaac could admit that the danger concerned his relationship to his parents as a sexual couple and in particular the notion that his mother might have sexual wishes of her own.

The First Glimpse of Neurotic Symptoms

This material led Isaac to become conscious first of all of a number of neurotic symptoms and hitherto unrecognized inhibitions concerning women. Formerly, the feelings that might have become conscious regarding woman's sexuality had either been avoided by counterphobic means or discharged through immediate action of some kind. For example, Isaac stumbled upon the association that he had never been able to watch a woman undress, and should he happen to see female underwear anywhere, he rapidly averted his eyes. He came to realize that he was filled with feelings of panic and disgust at the sight of women's underwear, particularly his wife's or his mother's clothing. Eventually the elaboration of these feelings led him to the frightening fantasy of the woman's sex as a hungry cat that could smother you with its desire; the prettier and the more exciting the underwear, the more it revealed evidence of woman's devouring sexuality. (It is interesting to compare Isaac's inhibition with its perverse counterpart, as seen in fetishist formations in which the same dangerous elements have been eroticized and thus serve to triumph over castration anxiety as well as the underlying archaic fears of the mother's body as an object with cannibalistic intentions.)

Around this time I had made the following notes: Isaac also has many "looking" inhibitions: he is afraid of mirrors, especially of catching a glimpse of someone's eyes in the glass, and is afraid in general of looking and being looked at. He fears certain sights. For example, he cannot watch couples embracing or even walking hand in hand without strong feelings of anxiety; he always turns his head away. Even in the cinema he closes his eyes during love scenes. (His own films are more concerned with violence than with love.) He is unable to watch funeral processions and lowers his eyes "in case this sight may precipitate his father's death."

Toward the end of our first year, Isaac managed to recognize that up to the age of eighteen he had had many inhibitions against sexual knowledge. He had, for example, no mental image whatsoever of the female body and felt that its sexual conformation was totally unknown to him. He had denied all sexual relationship between his parents and was astonished at the psychic splits that had been required to maintain this illusion.

Behind this reassuring oedipal material, which brought some significant changes into Isaac's psychic life, the more primitive underlying fantasy content was already visible, though as yet difficult to interpret in a way that would be other than intellectual for Isaac. It was abundantly clear that in his imagination he feared penetration from a man—feared, that is, that he might find such a wish within himself. Protection was therefore sought from the woman (mother and analyst). But behind this first layer of unconscious fantasy, a second terror was already becoming evident —that of a dangerous phallically invested woman who might invade and take possession of him (like a smothering cat), all the while denying him access to a protective and needed phallic father (who figured in his dreams and associations as a magical and elusive penis). In the first year this material appeared only in the form of shapeless fears of being stifled or drowned or of having his respiratory system squeezed to pieces from within. In the absence of such fears, he would suffer once more from asthma. I came to consider these attacks as a mute way of communicating the same anxieties.

Because of his strong unconscious wish to receive a magical penis from his father, Isaac had created the belief that he was in imminent danger of being penetrated by a man. His as yet undiscovered longing for this fantasy was required not only to reinforce his phallic representation of himself (among other neurotic fears, he had worried all his life about his penis being "too small") but above all to limit the dangerous representation of the woman's sex and body. To Isaac it was an empty chasmlike void, and he ran the risk of being sucked into it, squeezed and swallowed up by it. With no image of his father's penis as playing any sexual role in his mother's life, the mental representation of her sex became limitless, an abyss waiting to take him to his death.

The different layers of fantasy delineated here are relatively commonplace in psychoanalytical work and are the basis for a number of neurotic symptoms and neurotic character patterns, as well as the nucleus of many psychotic fantasies (such as the "influencing-machine" delusion [Tausk 1919]). But the important point is that Isaac had not developed any such symptoms to combat or deal with these primitive terrors. They were not subsumed under phallic castration anxiety, nor were they held within a sufficiently integrated oedipal structure. Isaac went blithely on with his sex life, with no restraining or buffering psychic symptoms to protect him against global anxiety in which his whole body and being were felt to be threatened. Instead he developed gastric ulcers, cardiac dysfunctions, tetany, and asthma. For some forty years, the ejected representations and the stifled affects had left him without the slightest psychic compensation for their loss.

I consider the capacity to eject from consciousness both the ideas and their associated emotions to be a major contributory factor to psychosomatic vulnerability. Under the appearance of "normality"—if such a state can be defined in other than phenomenological terms—the psychosoma is in a state of constant readiness to affront lethal danger, but there is no psychic awareness of danger and therefore no compensation in the form of psychological symptoms. The "buffering effect" that neurotic symptoms may produce in the psychic structure in these cases has been admirably stated by Engel (1962).

By the end of our first year of analysis, Isaac's heart pains and anxiety attacks had notably diminished. The only psychiatric drug he still took in any great quantity was Valium, and this mainly during breaks in our analytic work, when his somatic symptoms tended to flood back.

Isaac discovered that behind his irritable feelings and aggressive behavior toward his mother he felt deep affection for her and indeed, as a little boy, had loved her ardently. The tender memory of her throwing her body over his back led him to construct the idea that it was only to be expected that a paternal figure would creep up and punish him from behind. Thus the wasp sting acquired its first symbolic meaning: a castrative attack from the oedipal father, because of his interest in his mother's sex and his wish to take his father's place.

By now Isaac was less concerned with his real father's health and had ceased being disagreeable to his real mother. Instead he became interested in exploring his fantasies concerning the parents as "inner" objects of a complex kind. He no longer jumped nor had an anxiety attack when his wife came up behind him ("After all, she's not my father") and also once more began to find her sexually attractive ("After all, she's not my mother"). But these symptomatic changes were not connected with the underlying levels of unconscious terror—that is to say, the archaic smothering-mother image and the search for homosexual support from the father. Nor was there any change in Isaac's pattern of psychic functioning, namely, somatization and anxiety attacks when these pregenital and homosexual layers were unconsciously revealed.

The Birth of a Phobia

I come now to the first session I noted fully in Isaac's analysis. We were in the middle of the second year of our work together. The session is an interesting example of the way in which pregenital phobias are constructed and also of the different projective and introjective mechanisms involved in such constructions.

Isaac has had a dramatic experience touched off by being hungry. Although Isaac had never known this, hunger was for him a constant "actual" trauma whenever it occurred. He always had to eat immediately—no question of dealing psychically with the frustration. In this session we see that being hungry calls up unconscious sexual impulses of a primitive kind and of an oral-sadistic nature. But Isaac projects this infantile amorous and oral-sadistic impulsion onto a crowded supermarket, into whose bowels he must "penetrate" in order to get food.

Isaac looks pale and shaky and is reluctant to lie down on the couch.

I: Yesterday . . . I had a terrifying experience . . . never been so close to death in my life. Even now my heart's racing; can't breathe properly. I was hungry . . . went to buy some biscuits in the basement of the supermarket. So anxious I even had to smoke a cigarette going down in the elevator. I got into the line and suddenly couldn't go forward—you know, you go through a sort of iron turnstile—click, clack! (Isaac mimes this with his fingers, as though they were teeth or jaws closing.) And after that you can't get out. I tried to back out but the crowd pushed me on. I was afraid I would scream.

JM: So it wasn't just a "grocery store" you were getting into?

I: Ah, no! As it clicked behind me, I said "This is my tomb!" (He is silent and I ask him to tell me what he is thinking or feeling.)

I: Funny. I had an erotic thought in telling you that—the idea of being sucked into the grocery store to die. Why should I link up death and sex?

JM: This "tomb"—is it associated to a woman's body, then?

I: Last time Anne and I made love I got suddenly anxious; that's never happened to me before.

Isaac says this in an accusing tone of voice that he often uses. In other words, the analysis is interfering with Isaac's hitherto smooth-functioning operational sex life.

JM: Anxious about being "closed in"?

I: (Isaac meets this question with a swift denial.) Oh, no. Everything about sex, different positions and all, that enchants me. Not afraid of getting stuck . . . but . . . huh . . . well, sometimes right in the middle a strange idea gets grafted on. As though I ought to get out quick.

JM: Like in the grocery store?

I: Sort of . . .

It might be noted that in a neurotic organization, such a fantasy about getting swallowed up or stuck could, in childhood, have been imagined, formulated verbally, experienced affectively, and subsequently repressed. The result might well be symptoms of premature ejaculation, loss of erection, or loss of pleasure. But such was not Isaac's lot. It may be postulated that Isaac has been able to remain unaware of his massive anxiety arousal. Instead of forming a mental representation of the woman's body as dangerous (thus forming the nucleus of an eventual neurotic compromise), his hidden anxiety, instead of producing a signal, would seem to have been regressively resomatized in the form of somatic discharge (increased gastric secretion, asthma, and so on).

Now, thanks to his recent capacity to capture anxious affect, Isaac is beginning to create fantasies to accompany or "explain" these emotions. In fact, he is beginning to create—or recreate—infantile sexual theories without which there can be no neurotic formations and perhaps no psychotic ones, either. In any case I propose this theoretical notion.

So Isaac is finding outer support for his until-now-inarticulate inner theater: the grocery store mother; the crowded and stifling inside of the woman's body; the click-clack teeth that she has at her "entrance"; the death that awaits him if he is hungry (desires her) and then wishes to penetrate within to satisfy this desire. These mental representations, which could have produced a neurosis or a delusion, begin for the first time to produce neurotic defense of a hysterophobic kind. This process gives some insight into the way in which phobias come to be created. To Isaac's dismay, he began to develop more and more phobias. We were at the crossroads of somatic explosion, anxiety neurosis, and true neurotic symptom-formation. With the latter came the possibility for the first time of Isaac's being able to delay the somatic discharge and to think about what was going on in his own psychic reality and his relationship to the outer perceptual world.

In "On Narcissism: An Introduction," Freud says, "Our mental apparatus . . . [is] first and foremost a device designed for mastering excitations which would otherwise be felt as distressing or would have pathogenic effects" (1914, p. 85). Isaac's infantile libidinal wish to devour his mother had remained defused from its sadistic component, and his mental apparatus had done nothing with this dilemma (that is, loving equals destroying). We might say that up till now Isaac had never had any "signal anxiety" (Freud 1926) nor devised any means for mastering excitation. In consequence he was totally overwhelmed.

> I CONTINUES: Yes, the grocery store and the woman. Got to get out quick. I'm beginning to wonder whether I have a problem with my sexual wishes. But I've always been completely free of sexual problems. Is there something in me that is hostile to my desire? What's going wrong here? I no longer think of my father watching over me; and I no longer think of Anne as my mother. We make love better than ever before. And she really likes it. What's wrong with sexual longing, anyway?
>
> JM: (Thinking of that devouring grocery store.) Something wrong with woman's sexual longing?

I: Aha! That's a thought. But I've always wanted women to desire me. It's the man I've always been afraid of. Uh . . . I think. You know . . . the ogre that's going to eat Tom Thumb.

So Isaac has become little Tom Thumb and has projected his ogre-like oral wish onto the man—no doubt to protect his passionate infantile tie to his mother. I decide rather precipitately to unmask this defensive maneuver.

JM: But going into the grocery store you were the one who was hungry—a sort of reluctant ogre?

In between the introjective and projective mechanisms I now have Isaac thoroughly muddled.

I: Merde! It's all upside down. I was the one who was in danger. The grocery store was going to devour *me.* It was going to suck me into its entrails, and that was going to be my death. Voilà!

These frequent interjections of Isaac's are intended to put an end to the problem of having to think any further; they are a way of using words as an act, a discharge mechanism. I drop Isaac's desires and go back to his projections.

JM: As though the grocery store desired you?
I: Huh—there's nothing to stop you getting absorbed in there!

If, because of the disturbed early oedipal organization transmitted by the parents' unconscious, the representation of the woman's sex is of a limitless chasm, then there's no knowing where you might end up. In fact there is a psychic risk of continuing projection on the child's part, leading to persecutory ideas concerning the relation to the mother and her body. A thought-provoking paper by Noël Montgrain (1983) on the representation —or the failure to create a representation—of the female sex and sexual functioning (based on the analyses and fantasies of several woman patients) corroborates many of my own observations. My similar findings are, interestingly enough, mostly based on male patients. No doubt these two research paths imply, above and beyond possible countertransference aspects, that this is a unisex fantasy. We have all had to come to terms with the chasmic mother and her "limitless" female body. In his paper Montgrain states, "[The representation of the vagina] may remain that of an insatiable 'hole' that takes in, swallows and consumes, and thus functions according to a model of purely instinctual economy" (p. 171). (He might have added "greed," the greed that the infant projects upon the mother's body and into her desiring eyes.) He adds, "This fantasy may well be one of the principal reasons for man's immanent fear, when first confronted with women's genitals . . . [which are] felt to be the site and origin of an engulfing pleasure that is difficult to contain" (p. 172).

The point I wish to emphasize is that Isaac had never been able to attach any such anxiety to the genital organs. Among the many consequences of this inability was the fact that the difference between the sexes (and their complementary role) had received no true symbolic significance.

Isaac is only just beginning to verbalize his fantasy of the chasmic mother and to attach it to a mental representation of her sex. At the end of the session he says:

I: When I came in today, I thought you looked attractive in that pink suit, but I was terrified to look at you.

JM: Maybe it's the same drama. Who's devouring who?

As he goes out he looks me straight in the eye and says, "Well, I have no difficulty in looking at you as I go out! It's only terrifying when I enter!"

I do not resist saying, "It's a relief to get out of the grocery store?" And we both laugh.

I might add that I frequently have to be on guard not to make seductive remarks with patients who have had seductive mothers. While it is tempting to place the blame on the analysand's discourse that encourages such repartee, it is my task to elaborate it afterward. For example, that night Isaac dreamed that he had to protect himself from an ogress who had eyes made of mirror! It was a dream-image of the Narcissus myth. Narcissus could not find his own reflection in the eyes of his adoring and possessive mother, Liriope, only her desire for exclusive possession of her son. Nymph of the waters, she became the tomb from which he would never again detach his gaze.

The Chasmic Mother and the Cork Child

As the weeks went by, Isaac brought more associations to the fantasy of the internal mother-image as an "abyss," a "chasm," a "void," coupled with the idea that his role as a child was "to keep her filled," or at times to act like a cork that would keep her enclosed. The following fragment of a session took place just before the summer vacation break. Coming separations often brought about a violent recrudescence of the asthmatic and cardiac symptoms, sometimes during the sessions. With the threat of the separation Isaac always began to lose the transference image of his analyst as a protective father-mother; I would become once more the chasmic mother, but one that now hid a detached sadistic and persecutory paternal phallus in its depths, as in the associations to the following dream.

I: I dreamed last night I had to plunge from a great height to catch hold of a woman's body lying on the ground—as though I had to hook her up with my penis and then fly into the air again. As I get close I see that she's a witch. I'm terrified and excited at the same time.

The image of the penis as a sadistic hooking instrument is subsequently projected onto the woman's body, now felt to contain the dangerous part object. Isaac's associations lead him to thinking of his terror when swimming; when he is

99

able to see through clear water to the seabed, if there is no obstruction, he is "afraid of something surging up from the depths." He adds, however, that he is quite unafraid of *diving* into deep water. I ask him what makes the difference, and he replies, "Well, when I dive, I always close my eyes. Otherwise I'd be terrified." The parallel with Isaac's sexual pattern is striking.

JM: As though otherwise you might lose control, get swallowed up in the "void"?

I: Exactly! . . . (After a pause) That reminds me of masturbation. My father said I'd lose my memory and not be able to think. I was terribly frightened, but I did it anyway.

JM: You had to make a "void" in your thoughts? Shut your eyes?

I: Yes . . . just had to plunge on without thinking too much.

It seems to me that Isaac had been doing just this most of his life. There is a counterphobic dimension to the so-called operational way of being. It is possible that certain people who give the impression of being "super-normal" or "super-stable" have marshaled defenses of this order against primitive anxieties that have never been elaborated verbally. The fantasies that developed later indicated that Isaac had, so to speak, emptied his mother's body of all its contents, in order to avoid meeting not a protective but a dangerous and persecutory penis within the feminine body. To "close one's eyes," as Isaac did whenever he saw couples in the street or on the screen, in order to shut out the source of danger is, in a sense, a distinctly psychosomatic defense against threatening fantasies and feelings: we might call it a roller-coaster response. Although shutting one's eyes appears to remove temporarily the need to deal with anxiety-arousing situations, it certainly cannot be considered equivalent to repression. It is more akin to foreclosure or repudiation by the psyche—more akin, that is, to a psychotic defense allied with a disavowal of perceptual and external reality. The same counterphobic mechanisms may be found in addictive symptomatology and other acting-out disorders. In character problems based on the externalization of inner conflict, one closes one's eyes to other people's psychic reality. The story of Blanche in chapter 3 illustrates this way of fighting mental pain.

Isaac had talked at length about his masturbation fantasies in our first year of work, and slowly he came around to telling me that he still masturbated very frequently without quite knowing why and that it in no way replaced his sexual relationship with his wife. I am always interested in masturbation fantasies, since they contain in condensed fashion so much of our analysands' infantile sexuality and indicate where the greatest anxiety is concentrated (McDougall 1978, pp. 141–68). Isaac's erotic scenario is as follows: "I am picked up by a young prostitute and taken back to where she lives. Her mother is waiting for her, and it is she who orders me to make love to the girl. When I am sufficiently expert I shall then be obliged to make love to the mother. That is the acme of my excitement."

At the banal oedipal level, the fantasy is transparent, and we see that the guilt for sexual desire is attributed (as always, from Adam and Eve onward!) to the woman and, as so often, to the mother herself. Thus Isaac is "forced" into his love act. But it now becomes evident, as with many masturbation fantasies and sexual rituals, that these are also destined to contain and cope with the strongest anxiety-arousing features, by eroticizing those very elements. Here, Isaac's unconscious terror of the mother's sexual desire is made into the most exciting part of the fantasy.

> I: I still wonder why I choose prostitutes for my sex dreams. I've never had anything to do with prostitutes. Why is it such an erotic idea?

Although the prostitute fantasy frequently carries homosexual excitement with it, in that the man is having sexual relations with a woman who has had numerous other male partners, it seems to me that Isaac is much closer to realizing his need for assurance that the woman is not an unfathomable chasm whose vagina has never been represented as limited or defined by a penis

(Montgrain 1983). The oedipal rival becomes instead, at this more primitive narcissistic level, a much-needed protective figure. This assurance alone can give meaning to genital differences and provide the child with a recognized place in the family structure and a sexual identity. Without it there is the continual risk of that "plunge into the void," the limitless, irrepresentable maternal sex. I take this up with Isaac:

JM: The prostitute may be reassuring? No plunge into the void, since many men have been there before you?

I: Aha, yes! The most frightening women to me are young virgins.

JM: Uninhabited? The way you describe your mother? (In French *bite* is a slang term for *penis;* "inha*bité"* in primary-process thinking, therefore, has a double meaning.)

I: My mother? She's still a virgin! The idea that she ever had a penis inside her is unthinkable. *That's the void.* I— I can't breathe properly. (And indeed Isaac begins wheezing.)

JM: You plunge into this limitless chasm?

I: Yes—with my eyes shut!

Somatic Symptoms Give Way to Psychological Symptoms

This material was developed over several months. Here is a later fragment, halfway through the third year of analysis, in which Isaac describes the exfoliating phobic symptoms that appear to be taking the place of somatic phenomena, in particular of his asthma and cardiopathology.

I: It's a terrible discovery to realize that my mother desired me sexually. The look in her eyes—my head spins when I think of it. I've always wanted to find that look in a woman's eyes, but can't tolerate the idea that I wanted to see it in my mother's eyes also. Whichever way it goes—whether I find it or whether I don't—it means my death. (After a silence): Did you see that film of Woody Allen's—*Interiors?* What did you think of it? (He doesn't expect an answer; direct questions are always a sign of anxiety with Isaac, as with most patients.)

JM: You want to know how I see things? With what eyes I look into people?

I: I feel suddenly terrified . . . I want you to like me, to like what is inside me . . . but it's as though I'm afraid of being engulfed by this idea.

JM: I might be like your mother. You said she "devoured" you with love.

I: She often said "I'm going to eat you up." She would run after me and make a gobbling noise and I loved it. It was one of our favorite games. Am I afraid of being eaten? I feel such panic right now—but why? I *loved* that game.

JM: Maybe you wondered whether you were all she had to eat? What if she were really hungry?

I: *Mon Dieu!* She always called me her little sunshine. *Little* —you understand; and I really was small, and there were no others for her to gobble up . . . I can now stand the idea of her desiring my father. But *me*—no, thank you. I'd get eaten alive! My mother kills everyone with kindness and devours them all.

JM: So the kinder and more loving she was, the more you felt frightened?

I: Yes. And yet I had such a terrible need of her presence. Couldn't deal with anything by myself. I would rush into her arms—and at the same time I was rushing to my own death. She was just waiting to eat me. How'd I get on to all of this?

It may be noted that Isaac as a child was unable to use an inner image of his mother; he needed her real body and presence, which I have referred to elsewhere as the "drug-mother" (McDougall 1978). I had once suggested that it was as though he felt she wanted to "breathe for two." Isaac was very struck by this intervention of mine and developed the idea of their "respiratory relationship" for some months. He refers briefly to this intervention, then repeats the question:

I: How'd we get on to all this?
JM: Woody Allen and *Interiors.*

Interiors is about a woman who stifles her husband and children with her own desires and wishes. Isaac is very interested in Woody Allen, not only because he is also a filmmaker but because he has recently learned that Woody Allen has had twenty years of analysis—and it hasn't destroyed his creativity! Isaac finds this fact reassuring since I, as the devouring mother-analyst, was going to eat out all his creativity and leave him nothing with which to create stories and films.

I: Ah, yes! Interiors and insides! You know, lately I'm scared of getting stuck in small spaces where there's no air. I never go near the Metro any more, and I keep away from narrow corridors and streets. Afraid of feeling shut in—stifled. I never had any of these problems before coming to analysis! I'm sure the analysis is responsible.
JM: It probably is. You imagine things you never let yourself imagine before, like the kind of places you could blame because they make you feel "stifled." But what is this feeling—is it similar to those asthmatic attacks? (To my astonishment he replies:)
IA: Well, no. I breathe fine now. Didn't I tell you? Haven't had any asthma for months. But these phobias are really something.

Analysands often "forget" to tell us about changes like the disappearance of longstanding psychological or somatic symptoms. They are less concerned with reassuring the analyst than with maintaining the transference projection of the anxious mother with the sick child.

My hypothesis in the present session is that Isaac is learning to find, in the form of phobic objects, psychic representations for the archaic terrors attached to his love-hate relation with his mother—that is, the primitive terror-fantasies of getting stuck, stifled, eaten, or drowned. Formerly, in situations that called forth the desire-and-fear of the devouring mother, Isaac was totally unaware of his panic and would have an asthma attack instead. His lifelong somatic responses are becoming verbal and metaphoric and thus give him the raw primary-process material with which, subsequently, to create neurotic symptoms to protect him. It is certainly easier to avoid small spaces and subways than to face archaic castration at every turn. The economic gain that neurotic symptoms achieve is evident; they may have biological, life-preserving functions as well.

> Isaac looks around my very small consulting room and notices on my desk a large pot of winter branches that are sprouting tender spring leaves in the indoor warmth.

I: Heavens above—look at those little leaves! Did they open out here? Inside?

JM: In my "inside" you might expect them to stifle? (In French, women refer to their homes as *mon intérieur*.)

I: Aha—what opens up here are my phobias. Well, I guess it's better than not being able to breathe. *Tiens!* I think there's a little more space for me inside you than there used to be. A safe space!

During the following session Isaac comes up with the idea that his indulgent mother would have allowed him to do just about anything. In fact she was the original "prostitute." In his terror, he was obliged to make his own laws to protect himself from her overpowering love. He had to take care not to be penetrated by her invading ways. His hatred of her underclothing now appears to him to be closely connected to a fearful fantasy that he would "be eaten by the grasp of her strong thighs," a theme that developed over several sessions.

I: But until the wasp sting I was immortal. Now I know I've been afraid all my life of being eaten by my mother. Always waiting for me like a hungry spider. I'm continually expecting my death.

This is not phallic castration anxiety but a more primitive fear of being possessed or devoured (which we might call narcissistic castration or fear of annihilation). At the same time Isaac is projecting onto his mental representation of his mother his own primitive sexual wishes, for it is *he,* the devouring infant, who wants to eat his mother (the grocery store projection).

So the wasp sting has acquired one further symbolic meaning: it now represents the devouring and intrusive mother-image of early infancy—that is, the mother who gazes upon her baby with desire in her eyes. This thought leads Isaac to recall once more the memory of his mother throwing her body over him to protect him.

I: Mon Dieu—the weight of a mother is a heavy load to bear!

5

Psychosomatic States,
Anxiety Neurosis,
and Hysteria

Some Hypotheses on Psychosomatic States

The fragments of Isaac's analysis described in the preceding chapter will serve to illustrate an exploration of some hypotheses about psychosomatic regression, which may contribute to an understanding of the kind of mental functioning and dynamic personality organization most likely to increase psychosomatic vulnerability. My first proposition concerns the possible links between psychosomatic symptoms and hysterical symptoms as they may be observed in the course of psychoanalytic treatment. In earlier research (McDougall 1978), in which the difference between the two types of symptomatology was examined in detail, I proposed that psychosomatic phenomena, in contrast to hysterical manifestations, were devoid of repressed fantasy content capable of being verbalized and thus had no direct symbolic meaning such as we find in the unconscious structure of neurotic symptoms. I have come to question this total lack of symbolic significance, in the course of discovering the massive defense measures that certain patients employ to render psychic pain inoperative, including the radical elimination of any representation of intensely affect-laden ideas. (This question is explored more fully in chapter 7.) To begin with, I was unable to appreciate the underlying archaic significance of psychosomatic reactions to psychic conflict, that is, the extent to which they depended on extremely primitive body fantasy. I began to see somatic functioning as a form of communication and became interested in the economic role of somatization on the psychic structure. Perhaps a brief might be held for the notion of "preverbal symbolism," detached from any verbal links in *preconscious* functioning (Freud 1915b), which might subsequently give rise to an archaic form of hysteria. This is my first proposition.

The Oedipal Constellation

A second proposition is that of a specific personality structure in which oedipal representations and conflicts are infiltrated by an underlying fantasy of a primitive, preverbal kind and in which the infant's body is little differentiated from the mother-body. Any close erotic contact, therefore, is unconsciously experienced as engulfment and death. At a later stage the normalizing role of the father-image serves to obliterate the fact that the oedipal organization is built upon the archaic relationship fantasy that I referred to in the previous chapter as the "chasmic mother and the cork child." (This process is exemplified not only in Isaac's analysis but also in the analysis of Paul, whose story forms the basis of chapter 8. These two men both suffered from gastric ulcers and other psychosomatic maladies, and although in many respects their psychic functioning was widely different, their histories show striking similarities in the elements that contribute to their oedipal organization.) It is my contention that this kind of oedipal structure leaves the subject prone to future psychosomatic regression, particularly in situations of external or unrecognized internal stresses of a continuing kind. In addition to the unconscious body fantasies, the psychic economy is frequently characterized by a form of mental functioning in which disturbing ideas and painful affects run the risk of being ejected and foreclosed from the psyche rather than repressed or countercathected by the use of neurotic defense mechanisms.

The Psychic Economy

A third consideration is that of a specific way of discharging tension in which action and reaction tend to take precedence over mental elaboration. The psychic activity that might otherwise lead to constructive thought or sublimatory expression—or to the construction of neurotic and psychotic symptoms—is instead short-circuited and discharged through immediate or repetitive action. Such acts, which I refer to as action symptoms, are in no way a solution to the conflict-ridden instinctual reality or the stressful external reality with which the subject is faced. They are merely a flight or withdrawal from painful and anxiety-arousing situations (Engel 1962) accompanied by psychic destruction (rather than denial) of the unwelcome ideas leading to swift evacuation of the affects attached to them. Thus throughout his life Isaac had merely closed his eyes, smoked a cigarette, or given way to a compelling need to masturbate whenever an anxious, guilty, or angry feeling was aroused in him (for example, when he saw affectionate couples, funeral processions, or feminine underwear displayed in stores).

It must nevertheless be admitted that symptomatic actions of this kind form part of everyone's psychic armor on occasion. Drinking to drown a passing sorrow; smoking or overeating to weather life's daily frustrations; taking a pill to calm anxiety or ensure sleep; stealing insignificant objects compulsively or destroying valuable ones "by accident" under the sway of certain erotic or aggressive tensions; temporarily using people addictively in stressful circumstances—all are relatively commonplace occurrences among people who in most respects are not considered psychologically ill. Everyone tends at times to get rid of tension and psychic pain through inappropriate action or dependence on external agents, in situations where thought and emotional containment would be better indicated and even required for a more durable solution. From the point of view of the psychic economy, the important factor with regard to action symptoms is that they involve minimal psychic elaboration and indeed often take the place of it altogether.

In certain analysands we may observe that this kind of mental functioning is the predominant method of maintaining psychic homeostasis whenever the libidinal economy, whether invested in other people or in the self, is felt to be threatened. We see it clearly in a number of clinical categories such as organized perversions, addictive behavior, certain forms of character pathology, and in all situations in which psychic stress precipitates somatic dysfunction or facilitates infection or other forms of physiological disease. Psychosomatic symptoms of this kind come at the very end of the action symptom series I am proposing here, in that psychic elaboration in this sector is at a minimum if not totally absent. The roots of such patterns of mental functioning are to be found in the dawning of psychic life (McDougall 1982a), and evidence of their disturbing effect may be clearly observed in small infants. Since the baby cannot psychically work through situations of a stressful, mentally painful, or overstimulating kind, the pathological manifestations are invariably of a psychosomatic nature such as infant insomnia, the continual regurgitation and reswallowing of the stomach contents known as merycism, cyclic vomiting, and spasmic reactions of various types. Such observations present psychoanalysis with challenging research problems in both the theoretical and the clinical fields.

Acting Out and Psychosomatic Phenomena

In psychoanalytic work with adults, these action-reaction phenomena tend to escape the analytic process and therefore furnish serious stumbling blocks to progress. The Freudian concept of *acting out* merits reflection in this context. Originally this concept was applied to the psychoanalytic situation to describe phases in which conflicts mobilized by the transference relationship were dispersed through some form of action, usually outside the analytic setting, instead of being verbalized and worked through in the sessions. Despite this narrow clinical connotation, however, acting out is theoretically an economic concept in that it involves the immediate translation into action of instinctual impulses, fantasies, and wishes in order to avoid certain ideas and emotions of a painful, overly exciting, or conflictual kind. It also comes under the category of psychic repudiation or foreclosure.*

The use of the word *out* in translating *Agieren* as acting out conveys a twofold notion pertaining to the psychic *economy:* first, something that should have been kept inside and dealt with psychologically is put outside (of oneself or of the analytic situation); second, tension is being drained out or away so that no trace of the internal conflict remains. This is a fundamental notion in Freud's writings (Freud 1938b). Thus anxious or depressive affects with which the subject might not be able to cope do not achieve mental representation. The psychological mechanism of foreclosure goes hand in hand with the economic tendency toward acting out and the discharge of tension.

Applying the concept of foreclosure rather than that of repression to psychosomatic phenomena leads to the supposition that mental conflict is disavowed and thrown out of the psyche, to be discharged instead through the body and its somatic functioning. At the beginning of psychic life the body is experienced as an object belonging to the external world. This state of perception continues to exist in dream life and in certain psychotic and mystic states; that is, the body itself or certain of its zones and functions are treated as independent entities and sometimes as belonging to and under the domination of an Other. (For example, in psychotic states in which severe self-mutilations are inflicted the subject may be totally unaware of any immediate sensations of pain.) The important question here concerns the possibility that in what we might call psychosomatic mental states certain body parts and functions may still be regarded unconsciously in this fashion—that is, they may be considered as

---

*Freud frequently employed the term *Verwerfung*—repudiation or ejection from the psyche, for example in *The Wolf-Man* paper (1918)—to designate a specifically psychotic mechanism to be distinguished from repression *(Verdrängung)*.

not being the subject's own property but belonging to someone else, the mother of early infancy.*

This structure would then be in marked contrast to the psychic structure underlying hysterical *conversion,* in which primary-process thinking gives to certain zones and functions a symbolic significance of an instinctual kind. As already emphasized in chapter 2, neurotic and psychotic symptoms are primarily endeavors to achieve self-cure through some form of psychic activity that leads to the creation of the symptom as an attempted solution to mental conflict. Psychosomatic symptoms, on the other hand, although they may acquire secondary symbolic significance (and sometimes bring *secondary benefits* in the form of concern from the environment), are primarily the result of avoidance mechanisms uncompensated by the creation of psychological symptoms. These avoidance mechanisms of course might also be envisaged as rudimentary attempts to cure oneself by ejecting from psychic awareness any form of mental pain.

Individuals who use such escape devices to an exaggerated degree tend to give an appearance of normality in that they are symptom-free and often, because of the stifling of affect, appear able to cope with adversity in all circumstances. It is precisely this latter aspect of acting-out phenomena—especially when these phenomena take a psychosomatic turn—that renders such manifestations so tantalizing in psychoanalytic practice. The analyst hears an associative discourse that, while eminently coherent, seems to lead nowhere. At such moments we sense that something is lacking—a missing dimension, often of an affective order; it is rather like hearing the words of a song without the music. This discourse is very different from that in which repressed thoughts, fantasies, and denied feelings, although unconscious to the analysand, seek by numerous means to give clues to their existence, not only through the symptoms themselves but through dreams, sudden associations, slips of the tongue, and so on. When the communication is not of this order but is instead reduced to actions and reactions, as it is in all of us from time to time, then we know that the inner theater is not being elaborated

---

*A similar hypothesis with regard to the predisposition to drug addiction has been advanced by Krystal (1977).

internally, even in the form of neurotic or psychotic symptomatology, but rather is being externalized on the world's stage, or discharged somatically.

External Factors that Precipitate Psychosomatic Phenomena

The shift from mental elaboration to discharge in action is particularly likely to occur when we are subjected to sudden narcissistic wounds or to unexpected object-loss. Such events frequently produce unusual behavior or precipitate mild or severe psychosomatic manifestations. I am using the term *psychosomatic* here in a broad sense, from a uniquely psychoanalytic viewpoint. That is, I am concerned with the body and the somatic self as it is revealed in the course of analytical experience. Thus I am referring not only to well-recognized psychosomatic maladies such as gastric ulcers, bronchial asthma, and ulcerative colitis, but also to ill-defined anxiety and depressive states that are invariably accompanied by physical symptoms such as fatigue, sweating, trembling, and listlessness. To this array of psychosomatic phenomena must then be added accident proneness and increased susceptibility to infection in times of stress. The psychoanalyst has many opportunities to observe such phenomena and is in a position to formulate hypotheses different from those made by psychosomaticists, who, while seeing many more patients, are less likely to be able to follow them through the intense experience of a psychoanalysis or ongoing psychotherapy.

Although we all have a threshold for psychic stress beyond which our capacities for coping mentally may fail us, my clinical observations have led me to postulate that psychosomatic vulnerability is noticeably increased following any perturbation in our narcissistic economy (McDougall 1978). The more fragile our narcissistic balance, the more likely we are to deal with internal or external tension with some form of acting-out behavior or the action-symptom of somatization. In the case of somatization, subjects usually remain unaware of their mental conflicts and psychological pain. In any case it is perhaps the rare person who thinks of his or her physiological ills as also being psychological ills. Recall that for forty years Isaac was unaware of psychological problems in any domain. Although he suffered gastric ulcers, asthma, cardiac pathology, and tetany, he did not regard this array of somatic maladies as having a psychological dimension. His defensive structure was such that he was as unaware of the extent of his narcissistic fragility as he was of his underlying terror of all libidinally invested relational situations. People like Isaac, and they are legion, are able to plunge ahead with their lives, in both professional and love relationships, with no knowledge whatever of the continual—that is to say, *actual*—psychic stress to which they are subjected, day after day. The lack of awareness that follows when the mind rapidly evacuates any emotional arousal precipitates in its place grave somatic dysfunction.

It appears to me that in such situations the body is defending itself as though threatened by biological illness and therefore marshals survival techniques in a mistaken situation. (This notion is more fully developed in McDougall 1978, pp. 421–52.) It is perhaps this very unawareness of excessively painful or exciting affect, with its mental conflict, that contributes to the by-now-classical description of a supposedly "psychosomatic" or "operational" personality structure, in which catastrophic events that would cause most people considerable psychic pain are met with apparent calm and the unusual affectless state known as *alexithymia.* * My observations, during many years of work with analytic patients, lead me to emphasize that this condition is not necessarily due to a lack in either the psychic or the biological neuronic structures. The traumatic events that so frequently precede the outbreak of severe psychosomatic affections—loss of security, abandonment by one's love objects, sudden loss of self-esteem—might instead be considered as having caused pain and perturbation that lie too deep for the subject to bear or that stir up anxiety of psychotic dimensions. In other words, operational ways of relating and the ejection of affect may be extremely

---

*Alexithymia (Sifneos 1973; Nemiah 1978) means having no words for emotions, or a state of being incapable of distinguishing one emotion from another. Chapter 7 deals extensively with this concept.

primitive mental defenses. The concomitant but unrecognized fears of being overwhelmed by uncontainable affect and pushed to mad action, of "falling to pieces," or of losing one's sense of identity and capacity to function, sometimes come to the fore in analysis. The unwelcome ideas and painful affects have up to that point been eliminated so rapidly that the subject retains no knowledge of their ever having existed. (An example of such a case is described in chapter 8.) It might be added that when tension of any kind is reacted to as a narcissistic threat at the level of one's infant narcissism (in which the body is as yet little differentiated from the mother's body), then the psychosomatic response to instinctual tension and environmental stress is an accusation against that part of one's bodily self that is felt to belong to the mother or to *be* her. In other words, the illness becomes another unconscious link with the mother; her body too is under attack.

On the basis of many years of experience as psychiatrist and psychoanalyst attached to a psychosomatic unit, Lefebvre (1980) observed that "psychosomatic vulnerability is notably increased in patients who in childhood were exposed to traumatic events at the separation-individuation phase depicted by Mahler." He proposes that "the somatizing patient appears to show at the time of somatizing a relational mode which, when chronic, is characteristic of the so-called narcissistic personality. . . . *Confrontation with such self-other differences provokes a relational and economic impasse* which itself leads to 'giving-up' affects—and a somatically expressed regressive disorganization" (p. 6, my italics).

It seems to me that many people have created a psychic armor-plating with the result that they neither think nor feel too deeply in certain circumstances. These circumstances may consist of catastrophic external events, as suggested above, but they might also be daily occurrences (such as sexual or work situations, or simply meeting people) that contain a hidden traumatic potential. For example, the events leading to Isaac's severe gastric pathology were his failure to pass an important examination and the beginning of his adult sexual life. Isaac was aware of feeling defeated and narcissistically wounded by the failure, but he remained unaware of the underlying traumatic elements that were constantly reactivated by his sexual experiences. Consciously, he regarded these as satisfactory.

Reconsideration of Actual Neuroses

Isaac was destined to become afflicted with a new area of psychological perturbation, also of a psychosomatic order, that is, his severe anxiety neurosis. The actual neuroses are those in which strong affect is consciously experienced, though it is diffuse and unattached to clearly defined mental representations, in contrast to neurotic symptomatology. The early Freudian texts (1898, 1914, 1916–17) that deal with this concept are, in a sense, the first psychoanalytic papers on psychosomatic phenomena. The old-fashioned term *actual neurosis* included two categories, *neurasthenia* and *anxiety neurosis* (to which Freud later added the category of *hypochondria*). The signs of neurasthenia included physical fatigue of "nervous" origin: headaches, digestive troubles, constipation, diminished sexual activity, and so on. Anxiety neurosis, such as Isaac presented, was characterized by sweating, trembling, palpitations, and breathing difficulties. Many of today's analysands describe these identical symptoms as vividly as did those of Freud's time. Indeed, with today's much longer analyses we frequently find that, following the disappearance of the neurotic symptoms that bring patients to analysis, these and other discharge patterns risk becoming another rock upon which many an analysis may founder. The symptoms are gone and there are many inner psychic changes, but the analysand still feels empty, anxious, unhappy, or unfulfilled. And so does the analyst! (McDougall 1984)

Freud of course attributed the origin of the actual neuroses to the blocking of libidinal affect due to a lack of sexual satisfaction or to masturbation. Such explanations seem inadequate today, and perhaps this dubious etiology did much to discredit the concept. I should like to extend Freud's causal hypotheses in several directions. I consider, as Freud did, that depressive, listless states and anxiety neuroses are indeed mobilized and set off by "actual"—that is, everyday—tensions, but I attribute this activation to a specific form of mental functioning, the discharge-in-action that has just been described. This way of functioning is closely linked to the nature of the primitive fantasies that lie behind the urgent need to act rather than to reflect and the need to stifle emotion rather than to contain it. The origins of such psychic patterns, however, may be traced to the early physical and emotional transactions between mother and infant. In severe psychosomatic and anxiety states, we tend to find a primitive oedipal organization in which the mother, while not repudiating the father, nevertheless is felt to have related to her child as a sexual complement or as a narcissistic extension of her own self, thereby establishing a specific form of relationship to her child's bodily self. This organization is frequently linked with an image of the oedipal couple as taking second place to the important mother-child unit. The situation would also appear to require a somewhat complaisant father who, in accordance with his own unconscious problems, permits the incestuous relationship to continue and maintains his exclusion from this magic and overly gratifying circle. The child then runs the risk of feeling seduced, in danger of invasion, and a prey to archaic libidinal longings and terrors. At times these children may become convinced that they have no true existence for their mothers. Because of their incapacity to deal with overstimulation at this early age, their image of the primal scene also tends to be condensed and sadistic.

I therefore suggest that while the psychosomatic manifestations of the actual neuroses may frequently be traced to unrecognized libidinal tensions, as Freud suggested, these are set in motion by present-day libidinal blockage only when the blockage derives from very early sensual and emotional tensions and traumata. If Freud's theory of the pathogenic effects of sexual frustration and masturbation receives any credence today, it is only in that perturbing elements may be built into the child's psychosexual structure by the parents' unconscious sexual conflicts and dissatisfactions. The child's body and self may in that case become an object of undue and terrifying investment, and the conflict one in which primitive wishes and fears—desire for fusion, fear of disintegration, and loss of identity—take precedence over phallic-oedipal strivings and anxieties. The outcome is of course not necessarily a psychosomatic one; it may be the creation of sexual perversions as a means of short-circuiting the anxieties and wishes at both the oedipal and the more primitive sexual levels. These matters are considered at length in chapters 11 and 12.

In addition to libidinal conflict, we also emphasize today the importance of aggressive tensions as contributory factors to psychosomatic phenomena, in particular the role of primitive sadism that has failed to be integrated within the idealized mother-infant relationship (see chapter 8). While oral sadism might well be the aftereffect of the child's projected greed and envy, it may also include the mother's unacknowledged ambivalence and the envy of her child. In this respect it might be noted that Freud did not leave much room for the idea that things could go badly between mother and infant, convinced as he was that the period of infancy formed the nostalgic basis for the belief in Paradise. In fact, however, an exclusive mother-infant relationship of this order, in which the child, male or female, is required to replace the father as the object of desire and libidinal longing, is potentially pathological even at the nursling stage. In such a case the child represents for the mother an object of vital need rather than one of desire. The object of desire is a child born of mutual adult love and embodies the wish that it too will become a loving and desiring adult and parent. The child who is an object of need (rather than desire) reflects the parents' unresolved sadistic and sexual conflicts as well as their unsatisfactory narcissistic and sexual experiences. With such patients one frequently has the impression that there was no project in the parents' minds with regard to this child's future independence and adult sexual life. On the contrary, such an eventuality appears to have been denied or feared.

Such mothers are often excessively "maternal," not "good enough" in Winnicott's sense but "over-good"; they overlove, overfeed, over–care for, and over–worry about their children. The children are likely to experience this treatment as psychic abandonment, in that they are cared for by mothers who appear totally indifferent to their psychological needs and affective states. Many such mothers are remembered later as having been uninterested in their children's mental pain but quickly aroused by and involved with any bodily pain or physical symptoms. Apart from the obvious risk of creating in such children's minds the conviction that they exist as separate human beings and interesting people only when they are ill, the apparently gratifying aspects of the relationship run the risk of creating the impression that the children are indeed the mother's sexual and narcissistic extension and that nothing they can ever do will repair her or satisfy her. She is the chasm waiting to be filled. Their needs and desires do not count. At the same time such children cannot leave her without psychic stress. This is the dilemma of the cork-child, needed to keep mother together. One might wonder why such children have not become psychotic or sexually deviant. I have only a tentative explanation to offer, drawn from my clinical experience with patients whose major reaction to psychic stress was somatization and who, in other respects, were neither notably neurotic nor perverse, nor ostensibly psychotic.

Psychosomatic versus Perverse Organizations

Although a thorough exploration of the similarities and differences between psychotic and psychosomatic states requires further research and goes beyond the aims of this chapter (see chapters 7 and 8), I shall discuss briefly the perverse structure and its relationship to psychosomatic psychic structure. In my experience a major differentiating factor involves the parents' problems and their ensuing discussions with the growing child concerning sexuality and sexual identity. In adults whose lives are largely conditioned by compulsive or deviant sexual pursuits, we almost invariably find in their childhood history that the mother's attitude toward their sexuality tended toward total disavowal of its importance accompanied by frequent sexual seductions of a pregenital kind, such as the ritual giving of enemas, exploration of the child's genitals, and so on. Another strikingly common element is the parents' derogatory or frightening communications with regard to the opposite sex. These features are discussed more fully in chapters 11 and 12. In the majority of somatizing analysands I do not find this kind of communication. The mother, although often remembered as seductive or overly concerned with her child's body and health, is not felt to have denigrated sexuality nor to have created phobic reactions to the opposite sex. Isaac's mother, for example, who called him her "sunshine" and said that he would always be her "little fiancé," nevertheless did not communicate to her son the idea that girls or sexuality were disgusting or disagreeable.

With regard to the father's part in the child's psychosexual structure, it is a notable clinical fact that with children who become sexual deviants, the mother frequently presents the father as an object of little esteem whom the child may ignore or dislike with impunity. This denigration of the father often persists in the child's mind through adolescence and into adulthood. To the denial of the father's place is added a distorted image of the primal scene and the oedipal structure, with an inescapable weakening of the father's symbolic role as upholder of law and order. There is also an inkling of the father's complicity in keeping a distance from his offspring with regard to sexual matters and sexual identity in general.

In patients with severe somatizing tendencies, on the other hand, I have more often found that the father, although apparently playing a distant role in early childhood, is remembered as having been considerably more active during latency and adolescence and indeed as having discussed sexuality in a normal parental fashion, perhaps even with a nuance of overemphasis on the young adolescent's future sexual role. For example, Isaac's father, while ostensibly playing little part in his early upbringing, insisted emphatically when his son was still in puberty on the importance of "virile" behavior and sexual experiences. (An identical paternal portrait was presented by Paul, whose analysis illustrates chapter 8.) Isaac's father also allowed his son to have knowledge of his extramarital sexual relations. Although such a paternal discourse may play a "normalizing" role with regard to sexual activity as such and may imply that the child has a right to a future adult sexual life, problems arise if this kind of encouragement is grafted onto a terrifying infantile sexual fantasy of being devoured by the mother, in which the father's structuring phallic role—that is, his function as a figure who will protect the child from such danger—is minimal. Behind the facade of a normal oedipal organization may lurk overwhelming anguish, with regard to both the mother's limitless sexual void and the representation of a detached, avenging, and persecutory paternal phallus. This combination can lead to an adult sexuality that appears normal but is of a pragmatic kind in which the partner is regarded as a function or a thing rather than an emotionally alive person. Such primitive defense against feeling has the potential for pathological consequences of a psychosomatic kind, rather than of a neurotic hysterical nature, such as may result when there is regression from the oedipal situation. The progressive movement from the psychosomatic to the psychoneurotic register, under the impact of the psychoanalytic process, was illustrated in the last chapter and is also in evidence in chapter 8.

To this attempt to contrast a pseudo-oedipal organization in somatizing patients with a lopsided oedipal structure in sexual deviants, I would add that many analysands with deviant sexuality also suffer from psychosomatic manifestations such as allergies of all kinds. The converse is not true, however; the majority of psychosomatic patients do not reveal organized neosexual inventions. Instead, their outwardly normal sexuality is pragmatic and delibidinized rather frequently, while manifestations of primitive libidinal body relationships are expressed under cover of the psychosomatic symptoms. These reveal an implicit disavowal of the oedipal triangle and in its place a hidden somatic fantasy tie to the mother-body as well as unacknowledged sadistic hatred turned back upon the subject's own body. Attention given to the symptom often hides a deeply buried fantasy of repairing the mother (the "cork-child"), while neglect of the symptom, or the suffering caused by it, becomes a secret weapon intended to destroy the hated or destructive aspects of the maternal imago through destroying a part of one's own bodily self.

Henry Krystal's penetrating observations on the "basic dilemma" in drug-dependent individuals apply equally well to many patients with psychosomatic dysfunction. Krystal (1978b) writes that the alcoholic or drug-dependent patient "experiences some vital parts and functions of his own as being part of the object representation and not self representation. Without being consciously aware of it he experiences himself unable to carry out those functions because he feels that this is prohibited for him, and reserved for the parental objects" (p. 215). Krystal goes on to cite examples of patients with psychosomatic pathology who have been able to obtain help through biofeedback devices, increasing their control over certain areas of the autonomic nervous system. The patients frequently demonstrated "guilt and anxiety over gaining control over vital functions and over parts of themselves which they assumed to be beyond their control. . . . Early mothering is experienced as a permission to live. . . . Some [patients] experienced fear that taking over such maternal prerogatives would cause them to destroy themselves" (p. 217).

To Krystal's conception I would add the important role of archaic primal-scene fantasies in which children of both sexes may experience their bodies as the mother's sexual complement; for such patients, taking psychic possession of one's vital functions and body parts is tantamount to destroying the mother, whereas maintaining the pathological functioning unconsciously represents being at one with her while at the same time wreaking sadistic havoc upon her body through one's own dysfunction. The primal-scene imagery has thus regressed from a three-body relationship through a two-body relationship to a one-body erotic death struggle in which there is no inner identification to a caretaking maternal object. (In some of the sessions quoted in chapters 4 and 6, Isaac expressed similar ideas in poignant fashion.) If the psychological dependence upon the mother is recognized, patients are often able to discover their profoundly addictive relationship to all significant present-day objects. They come to find that these function as outside "substances" to which access is needed in order to survive. In the context of such a narcissistic relationship we can readily understand the perturbation in the psychic economy caused by the loss of this very object that so often precedes the outbreak of severe psychosomatic pathology. The object cannot be mourned since it cannot be relinquished; a part of the subject dies psychically instead, and this psychic death may threaten biological survival.

The Split Between Psyche and Soma

It is evident that, on the psychoanalytic stage, such analysands are going to fight furiously against the transference relationship if they have the slightest inkling that the experience may awaken feelings of narcissistic or libidinal dependence. This observation brings me back once more to the question of psychic representability and the awareness of affective arousal. If psychotic anxieties have not given rise to the creation of psychotic symptoms—if instead the frightened child has dealt with painful fantasy, overwhelming excitement, or terror by creating a sterile space between the self and the engulfing void that others represent —a space will at the same time be created between the child's affective experience and its mental representation. In other words, there will be a radical split between psyche and soma.

We would not be astonished, therefore, to discover that all that is visible to the outside world of the lifelong struggle to survive psychically is the impenetrable armor-plating against any representation of emotional arousal or psychic pain. All that is offered in the consulting room is a pragmatic, operational kind of discourse and a nonreflecting alexithymic image (see chapter 7). This discourse may even contain emotional words and phrases, expressions of joy, hatred, love, and anger and yet be empty of all feeling. There is no such thing as an idea that is painful, frightening, or exciting in itself—unless the idea is accompanied by a conscious awareness of emotion. Such *disaffected* people (McDougall 1984) have created a primitive defense against all danger of violent intrusion and are thus sheltered from the risk of being made the vassals of another's will.

With a defensive structure of this profundity, the subject who lives within these fortified walls no longer needs to cut the ties to important objects or to break contact with external reality. But the maintenance of such decathected or *false-self* links is acquired at the cost of a profound break with part of the individual's internal reality and a consequent distortion in what Freud (1915b) termed *preconscious functioning.*

We can imagine that this is the way Isaac protected himself from psychic dread for forty-odd years. I do not know if, before the onset of his psychological illness, Isaac presented to the world a smooth and smiling surface that revealed nothing of the emotional turmoil within, while all the time these unrecognized storms were flooding and breaking down the barriers of his corporeal kingdom. He himself suggests that this was the case; he was "the most normal man he had ever known." No psychological problem had cast the smallest shadow on his mind, and thus he was left without warning of the gathering tempest.

Isaac's analysis, therefore, did not begin at the point at which his psychosomatic pathology commenced but at the moment when his own carefully constructed armor-plating against affective invasions and awesome fantasy cracked wide apart, leaving him in a state of anxiety beyond his control or understanding. The operational and affectless tranquillity of his past life was brutally revealed as a fortress against an anguish of chasmic proportions. This anguish might have remained forever irrepresentable to his psyche, had not a wasp fortuitously offered itself as the psychic representation of literally unspeakable terror and nameless dread.

But for the sudden mobilization of his crippling anxiety neurosis, Isaac would probably never have dreamed of engaging in the experience of a personal analysis. It is highly probable, nevertheless, that this outbreak of an actual neurosis enabled him to avoid further, and perhaps more serious, psychosomatic disorganization. In addition, his analytic adventure brought a deepening of his love relations and a widening of his creative potentialities through the lifting of many strong inhibitions of which he might otherwise have remained totally unaware.

As we shall see in the following chapter, in spite of the resurgence, in other areas of his life, of the same somber psychic drama that invaded his psychic theater, Isaac continued his struggle for self-knowledge, to the point where he no longer recalled his old self-image of the "super-normal" man, nor could he remember the reasons that originally brought him to my door!

6

Elaboration and Transformation of the Psychic Repertory

The Compulsion to Repeat and the Antilife Force

To illustrate further the work of the mind that I referred to in chapter 1 as *psychic elaboration* (on the part of both analyst and analysand), I shall again use excerpts from the analysis of Isaac. Clinical fragments of analytic work frequently give little insight into the slow struggle on the part of the psychoanalytic couple to bring new elements to light and the constant need to work through material already gathered and interpreted as it repeats itself in other areas of the patient's life. The loss of symptoms, which may be considered as a secondary benefit on the path to self-knowledge, frequently gives the impression that a piece of constructive work leading to profound understanding of under-lying conflicts has been achieved once and for all. As every ana-lyst knows and every analysand comes to discover, however, the intricate maze that has contributed to the maintenance of uncon-scious structures and the dynamic force that emanates from them are of infinite dimensions.

Thus it is that the same dramas, the same disavowed desires, the same conflicts that gave rise to inadequate solutions may readily surge forth in a new context. The inexorable drive to maintain one's basic identity (Lichtenstein 1977, pp. 23–122) that is revealed in this tendency might lead us to ask whether this thrust to psychic continuity might not be equal in strength to the force of the life drive itself in its biological aspects. To this question may be added another consideration: the vital drive to survive in many ways reveals a counterpart that is a parallel striving toward the *extinction* of the life force with its endless quest to satisfy desires—in other words, a desire to be free of all desire. Every member of the human race must deal with both the pull of the wish to live and the pull of the wish for nirvana. The latter does not necessarily imply a wish to die, but in fact, when its strength exceeds that of the life force, this wish leads certain individuals to give up the struggle for survival, in which case death may be hastened.

Freud discovered this counterpart to the drive to survive in the course of his clinical experience and sought to conceptualize what he had observed in his paradoxical work titled *Beyond the Pleasure Principle* (1920). It is not my intention to discuss here Freud's third and most controversial theory of instinctual drives, known as the turning point of the twenties. I simply wish to give some glimpse of the way this instinctual duality may leave its trace on the continuing work of the psychoanalytic process.

The back-and-forth movements on the winding paths of the analytic adventure, the discovery of the renewed upsurge of old anxieties, and the return of psychic pain astonish and sometimes disappoint our analysands—just as these issues disappointed Freud and have disappointed all analysts since his time. Over and above therapeutic considerations, there is a desire to understand this human phenomenon. How can we accept that we ourselves are responsible for replaying our old scenarios, for producing, on our life stage as well as in our internal theaters, old anguishes in a new disguise, old failures in a new field? Or that we are instrumental in resuscitating the drab drama of depression, when we have already learned that it is up to us to give meaning to our own lives, that we alone are responsible for severing the bonds that prevent life from being a creative adventure? The fact that the stage—its lighting and its backdrops as well as its characters—

may change when old productions once more go into rehearsal allows us to regard these apparently new psychic creations as the result of circumstances. Human beings do not want to recognize that there is within them a driving force toward *antilife,* equal and sometimes stronger than its counterpart, the conscious desire for a happy existence and the wish to triumph over adversity.

No one knows better than the analyst that everybody is likely to suffer from catastrophic events in the external world and at the same time to be the victim of an internal psychic theater that never closes down. Although analysts are usually alert to these factors in their own external and internal realities, patients are more likely to blame the analyst when they too find themselves returning to old psychic productions that they believed were finished forever. To take a banal example, the right to the enjoyment of sexual pleasure frequently reveals itself to be a delicately balanced acquisition. Sexual impotence may leave the field of love relations to reappear as failure in professional achievement; in the face of unexpected libidinal or narcissistic setbacks, it may just as readily recur in one's erotic life, the mind's *I* having decided to pull an old script out of its psychic archives as a solution to present conflict.

The Maintenance of a Feeling of Identity

Thus all analysands must come to recognize the quasi-permanent possibility of reliving the forgotten stage plays of the mind and the fact that this tendency underscores the human need to cling to identity patterns and ways of maintaining libidinal and narcissistic homeostasis. The fundamental value of the psychoanalytic experience is that the analysand becomes conscious of the compulsion to repeat and also of possessing the means to analyze just what is happening and why it is happening at that precise moment. The psychoanalytic process itself never comes to an end, and those who have engaged in this venture into their inner worlds possess knowledge that combats the drive to repeat old and uncreative solutions. They can refuse the role of mere player on the world's stage, manipulated by an uncontrollable destiny. If the *I* freely admits that it cannot control the desires and decisions of those who inhabit the external world, any more than it can control and rewrite the events of the past, at least it can now accept total responsibility for its inner world and the way in which it keeps alive painful as well as pleasurable relationships with all the characters of the psychic theater.

The *I* is also better equipped to detect those moments at which it identifies with cruel, traumatized, or disturbed people in the inner psychic world, thus treating its own child-self, still anxious to grow, with the same severity or incoherence as the adults of the past were felt to have done. It no longer suffices to hold the inconsequential, overconscientious, or crazy mother, or the absent, weak, severe, or dead father, or the envious siblings, or the family's race, religion, or life events responsible for one's difficulties in living. Each of us must choose what we will make of all that has happened in our lives and whether to use it creatively or destructively. Such is the harvest of the psychoanalytic field. It does not suit everyone. Many people *prefer* to throw the responsibility for their unhappiness or failures on the figures from the past or on those who surround them in the present and thus preserve the lifelong identity patterns in the service of psychic survival.

To come back to Isaac, let us follow a little further his own fascinating psychic theater and some of the repeat performances that his mind's *I* found occasion to stage. We left Isaac's story at the phase in his analysis in which he had become convinced that his psychosomatic states and anxiety outbursts were closely linked to his infantile incestuous tie to his mother and the image of his father as a fantasied castrator. He furthermore accepted that these inner convictions were fantasies of his own making. As we shall see, he still sometimes holds his mother responsible (not as an inner object, but as a person in the external world) for many difficulties that are in fact linked to his strong infantile attachment to her. And he continues to struggle against the emergence of his father as anything other than a "castrating wasp"; the fact that he might also harbor tender homosexual child-wishes toward his father is, to him, a reprehensible idea.

The fragments of sessions that follow came a month after the last session reported in chapter 4. At that time I noted "in regard to his symptoms Isaac is making considerable progress: he is no longer afraid of being alone; no drugs; working well; psychosomatic symptoms greatly diminished." But the asthmatic and tachycardiac attacks were destined to return with the upsurge of homosexual material. With the primitive mother-image reduced to life size, it was as though an archaic fantasy of the father (a sort of idealized, detached, cruel phallus, which could be lodged anywhere in the body in fantasy constructions) now became analyzable in the same way. There was finally room for the fantasy representation of a penis that could be desired as well as feared.

Following the pattern of his heterosexual anxiety, Isaac's homosexual fears likewise had found no protective symptomatic structures of a neurotic kind (see chapter 4). They too appear to have been a source of continuing—that is, "actual"—stress, and therefore they carried the risk of stimulating the soma to cope with the situation as though it were a biological threat. Since the soma cannot think, it can only work along the lines of its own biological laws. In psychosomatic maladies the body mobilizes its forces in what seems like incoherent activity, serving no known physiological purpose. But somewhere it must make sense, and with this conviction I felt encouraged to pursue to their analyzable limits Isaac's unconscious bodily dramas (and those of others with similarly mysterious body-mind symptoms).

It will be noticed in the fragments that follow that Isaac now becomes conscious of his emotional states and imaginative ideas more readily than before, because he is on the lookout for them. These feeling states and fantasies are often first aroused by somatic sensations. In turn, they are slowly being transformed into affective experiences and the psychic representations of ideas.

The Homosexual "Wasp"

The following session, which I noted rather fully, gives us further insight into the process by which neurotic symptoms are created. In this case neurotic defenses were marshaled to contain anxiety connected with hitherto unconscious homosexual conflicts and their associated libidinal strivings. The session followed a weekend break. On the previous Friday Isaac had brought up associations that linked the celebrated wasp sting to ideas of homosexual danger, envisaged by Isaac as anal penetration. I had interpreted the fantasy as fearing a "sting from behind" and later on had said that everything about the session in question seemed to point to his mingled desire-and-terror regarding a "sting" from his father's sex. (I should add that in French the word for an insect's sting, *le dard*, is also a slang word for the penis.)

Isaac comes in, in a terrible state:

I: Mon Dieu, haven't been able to breathe since Friday! Not really asthma but could be so at any moment. It's as though my esophagus was twisted. As though it might close up altogether. My lungs feel as if they're going to turn inside out—like a glove. I sound completely crazy; it's only here that I feel calm enough to ask why all this happened this weekend.

Now Isaac unfolds the propitious circumstances.

I: My wife's been away for three days—no panic. I was delighted because I needed the time to work. Saturday evening I went alone to see a play . . . the theme was more or less homosexual. And I suddenly became aware that the audience was nearly all men. I began trembling —everything inside me was shaking. I rushed home and fell upon the Valium.

Valium has once again become the "good breast" that is required to calm and protect Isaac from every conceivable danger.

JM: So you tried to calm the fear—or the wish—to be stung?

I: My God, you don't know how true that is—I only allowed myself one thought: "Where's the homosexuality in all this?" Now why can't I even think about sex between men? After all, what can it do to me?

JM: Twist your esophagus?

I: God, it's so obvious, isn't it? In my mouth! The thought didn't even get through. I just close up and shut down everything against such ideas.

This is once again the "roller-coaster response," a psychosomatic attempt to control affect. The whole body, instead of the mind, is tensed against painful ideas, as though to evacuate them or keep them out in this way—a somatic and not a psychic way of dealing with frightening affect. But Isaac elaborates his experience in this session.

I: I do everything to prevent that penetration. (He goes on to recall a story of men in prison in which one man is sodomized by a number of others, and he starts to wheeze and tremble.)

I: My heart's racing; I can't breathe properly. I've got to think about this, damn it! I close up everything against such ideas—my throat, my lungs, and my arteries.

We have here a condensed fantasy of a sodomizing paternal phallus and a stifling "breast-penis." They are only just beginning to be separated into two distinct fantasy representations, while still retaining a measure of self-object confusion.

I: The idea of homosexual rape is humiliation and horror at the same time, for me. . . . Funny, I don't feel the same way about women being raped. Somehow that's rather exciting . . . as though the girl would sort of enjoy it too.

JM: You have to be a girl to enjoy being raped?

I: Huh, I seem to get more and more obvious. Do I want to be a girl? Mummy likes getting "stung" by Daddy— and a little girl can look forward to it. But what's a little

boy to do? Makes me think of what you said last week:
"How can a little boy feel strong if his dad's not around
to help?" I've got to get hold of that strong penis somehow—and mine always seemed too small.

JM: Too small for what?

I: Smaller than my father's, of course—but I couldn't have
known that. I know this sounds stupid—but I really
didn't know he had one. Funny—no wonder I always
felt so small with my mother's devouring love. Her big
chasm—it would just eat me up!

JM: Now it seems you'd like to eat up your father's strength,
his penis, so you could get to be a strong man like him.

It may be noted that the "twisted esophagus" comes close to
being a hysterical conversion symptom.

I: Remember that mad idea I had a few weeks ago? Whenever I saw dog excrement in the street I felt I might
suddenly eat it?

Isaac had been very distressed by this, as well as by
the idea, entertained by many who are afraid of fantasies, that psychoanalysis will turn one crazy. In fact,
Isaac's development of neurotic obsessional ideas of this
sort is a sign of psychic progress in that hitherto unconscious fantasies and impulses are now becoming accessible to consciousness and oblige Isaac to think further
about their meaning and their relation to his problems.

I: Now you said I wanted to absorb something, but we
didn't know yet what it was and that it had to take this
unacceptable form.

JM: Maybe the excrement has something to do with an idea
of your father's powerful feces?

It's reassuring to me to be back to the elements of infantile
sexual theory and the raw material of neurotic fantasy.

I: Ha—that could make my esophagus close up, couldn't
it! Makes me think of those times when I just couldn't

stop eating. And I've got another crazy idea I've never mentioned—a terror when I watch certain men, that I might suddenly jump at them and kiss them on the mouth. It's nothing to do with the wish to kiss a woman —that's exciting and wonderful, but this is horrible. As though I want to attack the man. Just like the bulimia. Look, these ideas are making me feel sick!

The zonal confusions and the role of everyday addictive behavior—excess smoking, drinking, and so on—are ways of discharging and thus avoiding unwelcome ideas and painful affect. Isaac's "bulimic" fantasy of devouring the man, or his penis, makes him "feel sick."

I: I'm not a homosexual, am I?

JM: You don't want to allow for the little boy in you who admired his father and wondered just how you could get his strength and virility into you. Eating his feces? Biting him on the mouth? Swallowing him? Something like primitive people eating the heart of the lion, maybe?

I: I've just had a crazy idea—maybe I want to eat a man's sex organ? Remember last year when I got excited thinking about my mother's sex and climbing inside? When you asked me what I would be looking for [I had expected he was going to say "babies"!], I said, well, it was the idea of finding excrement in there. But I don't see how these two ideas go together.

The basic fantasy here seems to be the problem of getting the father's and the mother's excrement (as a regressive substitute for the genitals) together. In fact, Isaac still has trouble getting his two parents together on any level, but especially on this level of childlike pregenital fantasy. The important advance, however, is that the formerly archaic and irrepresentable confusion of the relationship between two bodies is now attached to and contained in these part object representations. Isaac is now capable of distinguishing the fear of being stifled in his mother's body from that of being penetrated by his father's sex. What Bion

(1962b) would describe as "beta elements" have now become "alpha elements," the elements of verbal thought processes, and these permit Isaac to pursue what every child, from babyhood onward, seeks to discover: the sources of pleasure and how to control them. Thus Isaac is beginning to piece together his forgotten childhood sexual theories.

> JM: As though strengthened by your father's penis-and-feces you could now safely approach your mother's inside and fecal matter?
>
> I: That suddenly seems like an erotic idea. Oh là là—again I'm getting the feeling of not being able to breathe. Just like I'm stifled, all engulfed inside my mother. What a ghastly session! What's it all about?
>
> JM: The small child in you that wanted to make love to his mother—wanted to climb right inside her, as you put it —and in that way wanted to be like a man seems to have gotten terrified because he thought there was no man around. No good penis inside her—the limitless chasm. You might get drowned in her feces.

It should be noted that the feces are thought of as both good and dangerous inside his mother's body, at this point in time, whereas formerly the two fantasies coalesced.

> I: (who is wheezing and breathing heavily): Loving her was like going to my death.
>
> JM: Well, wanting your father's sting-penis, even if you were afraid of it, might have helped you face the dangerous things in your mother and not get drowned.
>
> I: What a ghastly session!

Even though Isaac found this phase of analysis painful, during the following sessions he came to wish for an image of his parents as a complementary and sexual couple. He no longer saw his father as a castrate, nor his mother as an empty chasm to whom he must play the role of the cork-child. The anal-erotic signifiers began to acquire both reassuring and phallic qualities, and at the same time they were also envisaged as dangerous and life-threatening fecal matter that might be encountered in the mother's body, there to behave like an avenging phallus. We can, however, leave aside the working through of these primitive fantasies and their early oedipal significance, to focus attention on the important question of Isaac's psychic functioning. A further fragment of analysis will illustrate this aspect. This excerpt is taken from a couple of consecutive sessions noted three to four months later. They demonstrate rather clearly the continuing swing between acting-out phenomena and psychic elaboration.

The Return of the Anxiety Neurosis

Isaac has missed several weeks of sessions because he was away on locations, and he comes back to analysis in a disturbed psychological state. As in the earliest days of his treatment, he is pale, sweating, "heart racing day and night," and he adds, "Naturally when your heart races you think of death at every turn." The anxiety neurosis is back in full swing.

I ask him what he feels might have caused this return of his symptoms, and I imagine he is going to invoke circumstances such as his absence from analysis, the fact that he has been plunged into many phobic situations by his traveling and the fact that he was working on the new film with a team of men. The latter factor may well have reactivated the homosexual material with which we had been dealing just before he went away. But what does he reply? That "it's all due to coffee"! He does not like coffee, but for hours on end there was nothing else to drink. So he has imbibed unusual amounts during this work period.

In a sense this is a cultural symptom—in France it is considered sheer madness to drink coffee after a certain hour. I am not denying that everyone has specific physiological patterns, but people (like me) who drink two cups of coffee before going to sleep are held to be crazy rather than endowed with a different metabolism. This might be an interesting example of "operational thinking" on a broad social scale. It is the social discourse that finally determines, irrespective of individual differences, what is sane and what is insane in any country. So here Isaac is using secondhand ideas instead of thinking.

By dint of encouragement on my part to elaborate on this inadequate theory of coffee as the source of anxiety neurosis, Isaac finally comes to exploring the anxiety-arousing conditions with which his psyche has been coping—or not coping—during the last few weeks. Toward the end of the session I question him also about his interpretation of the racing-heart symptom as an inevitable forerunner of death. Isaac has of course been back to see his cardiologist, but fantasy is stronger than reality.

> I: But when your heart races like crazy, what else could it be?
>
> JM: Could there be more pleasurable circumstances to make your heart race and your breathing rapid?

This is an alexithymic problem; Isaac doesn't distinguish between pleasurable excitation and dying. In a way it is a problem of metaphor and reflects the historical impact of the mother's words on the child's sense of reality. (What did mother say it was called?) Perhaps the problems of the parents, which dictate their admonitions and explanations, furnish us with another missing link between psychosomatic and hysterical formations.

> I: Of course! Sexual excitement—and even when my work is going well I feel excited, and my heart beats faster. Funny, I didn't think of it before. Why should good things like sex and work be connected with death?

The Sacred Heart

In the Roman Catholic church calendar, the date of the following session was the Feast of the Sacred Heart. Although Isaac showed no sign of remembering this fact, his psyche, as is so often the case, kept a secret calendar. Even if the adult Isaac did not recall it, the thoughts and metaphors in this session suggest that the child who went to the Catholic school knew it. And now we learned for the first time how he interpreted the religious teachings in terms of his fantasy world and his sexual conflicts concerning his mother.

Isaac begins by saying that his symptoms have already diminished considerably since yesterday. He is still scared, but he is relieved to have realized that there could be some psychological significance to his revived cardiac symptoms. He then recalls a vague memory of the time he spent as a child in the Catholic school. Before proceeding further, however, he suddenly cries out as though in pain and says he felt a "stabbing pain," a brutal "knife thrust" *(coup de couteau)* in his heart *(coup* is also a slang expression in French for rapid intercourse). These metaphors are precious signs of preconscious fantasy formations and therefore of the possibility of bringing to light through verbal links symptomatic expressions of a psychoneurotic rather than a psychosomatic order.

I: There, you see—I shouldn't think about these things. I should forget about my heart: it's making me ill. As if my heart were cut in two.

JM: Well, what were you thinking about when that "cut" came?

I: We were all in the church for Mass—and something got held up in the air—I think it was Christ's heart that was being offered up. And that way you would get salvation or resurrection or something. That's what I was thinking about when the cut stabbed my heart. [Pause] Why do I kill my heart? Now what was it you said yesterday about the heart? I've forgotten.[!]

JM: We explored the idea that "heart" troubles weren't only connected with death—they could also be attached to pleasure, excitement, and love.

I: Aha, yes! Interesting that I should have forgotten. I wasn't supposed to know about such things when I was a kid. Now who was getting into Christ's heart?

JM: Who do you think?

I: Well, God, of course!

From here Isaac goes on to explore his homosexual fears and wonders for the first time if the stabbing cut might be concerned with the terror of "something creeping up from behind." "Your heart could get stabbed from behind," he says. (Isaac is always apologizing for his fantasies, as though using his imagination were a guilt-ridden activity or a sign of craziness.) I think to myself that this is in fact another version of the wasp sting and all it has come to signify. Isaac then recalls our discussing his continual search for an ideal penis as the representative of an ideal father.

I: But why do I need his knife in me to make my heart beat fast? [After a long silence] I'm thinking of a song my mother used to sing to me when I was a child. [I encourage him to try to find the words, and they come back to him suddenly.] She used to sing "I give you my heart" —it's a well-known folk song! [This is said a little defensively.]

JM: And did you give her your heart, too?

I: I'll say I did! Absolutely. I promised her I would be her "little fiancé" forever. Even today that song brings tears to my eyes. But why does this cut my heart in two?

JM: Maybe you felt two ways about it: seems as if you needed to get your heart free at the same time.

I: Of course. And my father never gave me that vitally needed cut to help me get out of her clutches! To detach me from *her* body and mind.

This is another version of the homosexual material we were analyzing just before Isaac's recent absence. The "Sacred Heart" is his mother's heart, as well as his own, offered up to her. She was for him the image of the Virgin Mother and he, the Christ Child. But now he comes to realize his need for God the Father to play a more active role in his inner theater. After a long pause Isaac concludes:

I: You know, I might even get to like drinking coffee!

End of session

Rage and the Psychosoma

My aim in this chapter is to show the elaboration and continual transformation of conflictual elements in the psyche that
touch both psychic and external reality. I shall give some indication of the way in which Isaac eventually came to link certain
manifestations of his cardiopathology and sudden asthmatic
crises to the mobilization within him of hitherto unsuspected
experiences of *rage* with which he felt unable to cope or for which
he could find no satisfactory expression.

On his return from a vacation spent with his wife and children at his parents' home, Isaac remarked that in spite of his
now-tender and affectionate feelings for his mother, he found her
excessive concern with his physical well-being extremely irritat-
ing. ("She told me at least twenty times during the week to put
on a sweater before going outside, even when I protested that I
was not in the least cold and didn't need a sweater!") It was only
after some working through of his feelings about this type of
incident that he suddenly came up with the insight, "I know
what's so horrible about this kind of struggle with my mother—
it's as though I don't really exist! She flies into me with her wishes
and tries to take possession of my body as well as my mind. I
suppose she was always like that and I just took it for granted."
In order to pursue further Isaac's own part in maintaining this
form of relationship with his mother (that is, with the mother-
image *inside him* who wanted to control his mind and movements),
we came to "listen" closely to the cries of his soma, particularly
when asthma attacks and the like would arise during the sessions.
(I have learned over the years, with all my patients, to treat such
incidents as part of "free association.")

Isaac first produced fantasies of sudden explosive action
(rather than explosive asthma or excessive gastric secretion)—for

example, "I suddenly want to smash a window!" He stretched a leg out in the direction of my consulting room windows; "I'd like to smash everything by kicking my foot into it—a truly strong desire. . . ." We were able to link this impulse to my inability to change one of his session hours. Later on in the session Isaac recounted, for the first time, various serious and unexpected acts of physical violence that he had actually committed in the past and that had astonished everybody, since he was usually a rather calm youngster. For example, he nearly killed a classmate by deliberately throwing a large metal object at him, narrowly missing the boy's face. The youngster had unexpectedly come into a room where Isaac was studying, and this intrusion had filled Isaac with a sudden uncontrollable rage. Following such incidents Isaac often realized how close he had come to committing unforgivable and incomprehensible acts. As he grew older he became wary of such sudden destructive violence, until he no longer felt moved to compulsive behavior of this kind and finally was not even aware of ever being angry. There is good reason to suspect, however, that the uncontrolled violence continued unabated in the form of violent psychosomatic "acts."

We were able to reconstruct, in the light of Isaac's recent return to the parental home and his subsequent reactions in the session, that many times in his boyhood, circumstances that may have reminded him unconsciously of his invasive and controlling mother led to acts of physical violence toward other people. Since in Isaac's inner theater there was also a quite different maternal character who, unlike the one that induced hatred and rage, was felt to be tender, loving, and totally reassuring against all danger, Isaac had split his image of his mother into two distinct personalities. The hated mother was pushed out of consciousness and came on stage only in the form of someone else in the external world, such as the boy at whom he had thrown the metal object. This split allowed Isaac to protect the image of the loving and essentially needed mother. During this and the following session, Isaac explored many similar sensations and impulsive wishes to take brutal action. He expressed these in terms like "I have a desperate need to make some space around me" and "I need more air between myself and X" or "between myself and my mother" and was able to link these ideas to their base in his inner world. They no longer needed to involve other people and in particular his *real* mother, since he was now capable of realizing that she too suffered from psychological problems stemming from the many quarrelsome and difficult people that existed in *her* inner universe. Instead he could now come to grips with some of the "internal mothers" whom he permitted from time to time to dominate his psychic life. "The very fact of being able to say all that and to talk with my mother inside me, not quarrel with the outside one, makes me feel strong and relaxed. The tachycardia I felt at the beginning of the session has completely disappeared."

The following hypothesis comes to my mind when I am trying to uncover in patients like Isaac the infantile roots of the kind of psychic functioning that is likely to increase psychosomatic vulnerability. The tendency that Engel (1962) observed some years ago for severe psychosomatic manifestations in adults to be preceded by an attitude of "dropping out" and "giving up" may represent in the *infant's* psychic history an attitude of "giving in" to the invading, controlling, and colonizing mother. Perhaps this giving up, in place of struggling and fighting back as most small children instinctively do, is chosen because of the need to protect one's love for the mother. Or perhaps infants give up the struggle out of sheer exhaustion. They learn to stifle hostile affects and eventually, no longer aware of their rage and violence, they conform to what they realize is expected of them. In other words, they *become* the mother, their minds controlled by hers, and it is perhaps here that the door to psychosomatic explosion stays ajar.

While it may be said that psychic elaboration is first and foremost a question of mental representations and the working over of the ideas to which these give rise in a repetitive way, it must also be added that the body too is subjected to the repetition-compulsion. These repetitions form part and parcel of psychoanalytic communication. The aim of analysis is, of course, to render such mute messages audible: they must find verbal expression as they disclose the affects that accompany them. Only then can they be truly elaborated in the course of the analysis—frequently with the consequence that a whole new area of psychic experience comes into being, while the repetitive somatic manifestations tend to disappear. It must once again be emphasized that psychic change of this sort depends upon the joining of words and affects. A delibidinized or alexithymic discourse may be studded with affectively toned words, but as chapter 5 indicated, there is no such thing as a "sad idea" or an "exciting prospect" if the affects named are not felt. An idea in itself cannot be happy, tragic, hurtful, or in any way emotionally toned if the emotion is not perceived and experienced by the subject who pronounces the words or presents the idea. Isaac's violence in the lines quoted above was no mere "violent idea" but a truly felt experience that, since he was unused to feeling his rage, seemed to him difficult to control. The fact that verbalizing such emotion brought a feeling of relief was to him an important discovery.

The Struggle Against Nirvana

Two years later, Isaac was coming for sessions only twice a week. The reduced schedule had the effect of heightening his awareness of and reaction to separation anxieties and enabled us to explore further not only the fantasy that separation is the equivalent of death but also its contrary—that the wish to fuse with and become part of the other is similarly a form of psychic death. Certain symptoms also returned during his absence from analysis. The session excerpts that follow brought forth the fantasy of being able to reach a state of nirvana, the desire for a state of nondesire, which attracted Isaac as much as it frightened him. But the elaboration of his psychic theater continued, and a new theme emerged.

After three weeks' absence during which he was shooting sequences for a new film, Isaac begins by saying that he feels "nostalgic" for his analytic sessions when he is obliged to miss them because of his work. He complains that he is "full of problems and suffering" and that his analysis is far from finished. The fear that perhaps his analytic adventure is drawing to a close adds to his feeling of insecurity and his need to insist on unresolved symptoms.

I: These breaks in our work are painful for me. Yet I must admit that life is so much easier than it used to be. But the sicknesses of the mind are something like a cancer —it grows again just when you least expect it, and where you didn't imagine it would break out. The central illness has gone, but there are metastases. You see, I still think of death! This analysis is by no means finished! The other night after my return I made love with my wife. It was just marvelous, but a few minutes later I was sure I was going to suffocate. Isn't that incredible? For about ten minutes I was filled with panic —just like in the old days. A feeling that something horrible was about to happen, as if I had my head under water. You see, I still have sexual problems!

Isaac no longer recalls that before beginning analysis he never at any time associated his anxiety attacks with his sexual life. To the asthmatic and cardiac pathology that long preceded these, he did not attribute any psychological significance. His capacity to connect thoughts and feelings, accompanied by expressive metaphors, has greatly increased.

I: I suddenly said to myself that I was writing a whole script and this was ridiculous. It was over and I fell off to sleep. Then another time after making love I woke up every three hours, obsessed by something I'd read about men who have spontaneous orgasms, without wanting them, and they can't do anything about it. I was convinced this would happen to me and that I'd die of an infarct after all.

Isaac thus reveals briefly a new bodily fantasy concerning the loss of his body substances—one more neurotic punishment for sexual desire?

I: You know, the fear of seeing couples has come back again. In my new film there are several little love scenes. That's progress! But during the shooting I get terribly anxious. One problem at least has gone—the homosexual thing. No more anxiety on that score. Get on well with my whole team. But this fear of being killed by an orgasm is crazy. I must find out how one can get disgusted with sexuality.

I point out to Isaac the ambiguity of this last statement, in that his expression may be understood either as a need to understand his disgust or a need to become disgusted.

I: Of course, there I go again, as though I'm never sure of my sexual wishes because love and death are so mixed up in my mind. You see—analysis doesn't help you much. After all, I came to analysis because of my sexual problems.[!] I've hardly talked of anything else, have I?

I cannot resist pointing out to Isaac that this was not the way I remembered it, that it seemed to me he was convinced he had no sexual difficulties of any kind, and that he had even questioned whether on that account he could be regarded as a genuine analytic patient.

I: Zut! You know, I'd completely forgotten that! Of course I had all sorts of ailments, but everything else worked like a charm. Now I'm totally well physically. But my sexual life seems sort of—what'd you call it— sort of neurotic, isn't it? Anyway I've got over that problem in my work. In the new film I've put the lovers in the limelight and you can see their mouths united.

This latter phrase struck me as odd, something like a mutual devouring. Was he projecting an unconscious fantasy of his own onto the film characters? I ask him if he has any other thoughts about this part of the film.

I: Well, I had the feeling that I shouldn't watch things like that—as though it could do harm or like it was forbidden. I've never watched scenes like that anywhere . . . er . . . my parents . . . I just don't know . . .

JM: What don't you know?

I: Well, they were always kissing each other, but I never saw, because I always closed my eyes. Why does that give me a sudden stab in my heart?

JM: This is an old scenario, isn't it? "Either I recognize that my father and mother complete each other sexually and that I can have my own sexual life, or else I shall close my eyes to this because otherwise I might want to kill my father with an infarct and give my heart to my mother. Then my heart will get stabbed instead." Perhaps you close your eyes to all that? And meanwhile you get panic attacks when you make love.

I: Yes, I made the bad choice of not keeping my eyes open! But my mother didn't help me all that much either. She didn't respect the contract—let me believe instead that I was the only one she loved. Yet I've always known my parents loved each other; they just had problems. So she would look at me with that love light in her eyes and say "If I didn't restrain myself I'd eat you." But I'm beginning to think that's what I wanted. Wow! It must feel good to be eaten; what I really resent is the fact that she didn't do it!

JM: Once inside you'd be sheltered?

I: Right! Nothing would ever bother me again—no sexual problems, no sleeping problems. [Long pause] Mon Dieu! Is it possible that I said that? That *that's* what I desire? What's wrong with me? Is this survival, or am I really wanting to die? Please say something, I feel paralyzed.

JM: Effectively it sounds rather like a desire for death.

I: But that's not what I want. Me—I want to live!!

After a long silence Isaac continues by saying that the compulsive thought of eating excrement has recently come back. I ask him to tell me more about it, and he explains that his horror of the idea is worse than before because it no longer pertains to dog droppings but to human excrement. He is anxious when going into public toilets, as this stimulates the obsessive thought.

I: Am I going sheer crazy to have such ideas?

JM: Maybe a small child in you might find it quite normal to be fascinated with human excrement. Perhaps that was less forbidden than being fascinated with what adults did together genitally.

I: Well, when I was a kid, that's funny, but I always believed that sex had to do with their feces and anuses . . . yes, a kid's fantasy . . . but right now, I don't quite know why, I'm thinking about my work. It gets stuck. I'm always behind. And sometimes when it's going particularly well I have to stop, as though I absolutely have to make love—or to shit.

JM: Shitting . . . working . . . making love. Is there a link between them?

I: Of course. In a way they're different versions of the same feeling. Good God, why didn't I ever think of it? *Shitting* is allowed. But I see now why I often can't make myself work—it's forbidden, it gives too much pleasure. If only sexuality didn't exist, life would be simple, wouldn't it?

JM: Once castrated, no further problems?

I: Merde! I'm again reaching out to death. What a solution! I'm fed up with living all areas of my life like a castrate. The other day one of my female colleagues told me I was like sunshine around the place. Mother's little sunshine. I just melted with the wish to be right inside her—and felt panicked by this thought at the same time. It was not a wish for her sexually, but really to be totally inside her. Mon Dieu! It's true—that's my deepest desire. Mommy, Mommy, eat me, *please eat me!*

7

Reflections on Affect:
A Psychoanalytic View
of Alexithymia

The Role of Affect in the Psychic Economy

Going beyond the stage presentations of the scenarios of psychic life—their unconscious plots and internal players—this chapter will provide a glimpse of what is happening backstage and of the work of the stagehands and electricians without whose constant labor no play would ever be produced. It may afford an opportunity to observe the *construction* of psychic stage sets, with their capacity to create illusion and to highlight certain scenes, actors, and actions while keeping others in total darkness. The *I* who is responsible for this spotlighting and the kaleidoscopic effects it produces on the psychoanalytic stage acts, of course, as though it were quite unaware of the backstage world. At best it proclaims that the unseen hands who manipulate the machinery and shift the scenes are incomprehensible in their maneuvers and that the electricians are more or less crazy. In other words, dynamic fantasies are unconscious, as are the modes of mental functioning that create and maintain symptom formation.

Our analysands' communications about their psychic theaters deal only with finished productions and pay little heed to the fundamental elements that make up psychic structure, namely, *words* and *affects*. The psychic economy must bring these elements together in order to channel instinctual drives and give them symbolic significance, in turn structuring the individual's system of relationships and way of mental functioning. The finished productions are of course an amalgam of the subject's personal past and the creative efforts made by the child to come to terms with reality restrictions, parental attitudes, and social prohibitions.

It is not my intention to recapitulate Freud's fundamental concepts concerning words; the laws of unconscious mental functioning that combine word and thing presentations and confer specificity upon preconscious and conscious psychic functions need no further elaboration here. In this chapter I am principally concerned with pathological aspects of affect economy and the study of words and ideas that are potentially affect-laden but that have in effect become denuded of their emotional connotation. The *I* who uses these words with apparent freedom may remain "un-affected" by them. Since language is the principal means of symbolic communication among adults, we would expect affective psychic elements to be in constant circulation in all forms of verbal expression, and indeed we might well suppose that if language were not strongly impregnated with rather powerful libidinal and narcissistic investments, no child would ever learn to talk! The fact that as human beings we are obliged to *speak* our needs and desires if we hope to have them satisfied is one of our most severe narcissistic wounds. Why are we not magically understood, without words, as in infancy? Clearly a powerful libidinal cathexis has been required to transform the painful and narcissistically wounding aspects of language acquisition into a pleasure as well as a necessity.

It is well known that in certain psychotic states subjects lose the desire to communicate verbally. What is less obvious is that many people constantly use language without any wish to communicate something to somebody. They may talk (and insist that others listen) for secret reasons such as the need to prove that they exist. In this case, the others, by listening and responding verbally, act as reflecting mirrors. Still others converse without pleasure simply because they have long understood that humans talk to one another and they are striving to behave as the world expects. This mode of communication corresponds to Winnicott's (1960) "false-self" concept. It invariably indicates a desperate attempt to survive psychically in the world of others, but without sufficient understanding of the emotional links, signs, and symbols that render human relationships meaningful. We might well wonder where the "true" self is hidden in people who function in this manner and what factors may have forced them to imprison themselves in this way while maintaining a superficial appearance of normal relationships.

Affects and the Psychoanalytic Stage

In analysis, patients who unconsciously use language as a screen between themselves and others, rather than as the privileged means of exchanging ideas and communicating emotional experience, present a particular challenge to the analyst. The analytic relationship and process depend mainly upon the creation of vital verbal links, that is, thoughts that are charged with affects of varying kinds. Since no other action in reality takes place on the psychoanalytic stage, an analytic discourse that functions like an affectless screen between analyst and analysand gives to the psychic themes that are brought to the sessions a flat, colorless, and frequently fatiguing tonality (McDougall 1978, pp. 213–46; McDougall 1984). The analyst may well begin to wonder what the story is all about, what thoughts and feelings it is supposed to arouse, and why the patient is taking the trouble to put on stage a show that appears to have no more interest to the analysand than to the analyst.

Psychoanalysis is a science centered upon meaning, and its underlying logic is the logic of language, as Modell (1971, 1973) has succinctly expressed in his research into the nature of affects. An associative discourse in an analytic session is meaningful only to the extent that it is dynamically infused with affect, and the analyst's interpretative function depends to a large extent on the ability to capture the affectively charged elements in the analysand's communications. By identifying introjectively with these, the analyst becomes more attuned to what is being withheld from the manifest content of the session. The latent significance of the patient communications depends to a considerable degree, above and beyond its meaning, on the tone, mood, and emotion conveyed by the analysand's voice, manner of speaking, gestures, and body posture. The psychoanalyst also needs to be keenly aware of his or her own emotional and bodily messages, while introjecting those of the patient. This interchange then provides the analyst with floating hypotheses about the analysand's inner world, although it usually requires considerable time before these ideational and emotional insights result in interpretations that further the understanding of the analysand's private theater and personal psychic themes.

Even when the analyst feels ready to communicate this understanding, it must first be determined whether or not the patient is ready to receive the interpretation in question. Just *who* is in the consulting room at this particular session? Mr. X is there, of course, visibly stretched out on the couch, but of the numerous people who express themselves from within him when he says "I" ("I believe, feel, fear . . . this or that"), it is important to sort out which *I* is speaking. An angry child? An incestuous one? An excited or frightened lover? A condemning father, or a seductive mother? This way of listening, in an attempt to identify the varied cast of characters that inhabits each individual, explains why analysts, after a number of sessions of being relatively silent, are suddenly motivated to inject a word or phrase or to give a complex interpretation. Such interpretations appear to surge forth from unknown recesses of the mind, sometimes surprising the analyst as much as the analysand. These contribute to what Strachey (1934) aptly named "mutative" interpretations.

The patients I wish to discuss in this chapter, however, rarely provide us with the occasion for, and the analytic pleasure of giving, such interpretations. To the unspoken question, "Who among the characters in my patient's psychic theater is speaking at this moment?" we sometimes have the disquieting impression that there is no one there at all. If someone *is* present, that person may be carefully concealed behind the words that fill the silence of the session. This way of being—or of not being—in contact with another undoubtedly represents a specific form of transference in that such patients are relating to the analyst just as they relate to people outside the analytic situation and, indeed, just as they learned in infancy to relate to those closest to them. Transference affect, whether positive or negative, is notably absent. It should perhaps be mentioned that even a totally silent patient, unlike the fluent but affectless verbalizer, may be authentically present, the silence rich in emotional content and thereby contributing to the psychoanalytic experience. In sum, the constant intermingling of affect and psychic representation is essential to the continuation of the analytic process.

Freud's Conceptualization of the Vicissitudes of Affect

If certain of Freud's writings give the impression that the fundamental element in producing psychic change is the recovery of mental representations through the liberating effect of words, it should nevertheless be emphasized that Freud sought constantly to discover the links between verbal expression and emotional experience. He claimed not only that the analytical technique was therapeutically efficient to the extent that forgotten events were rejoined to their accompanying affective states, but that verbalization in itself provided a form of discharge of emotional tension.

Advances in the conceptualization of the metapsychology of affect usually involve entering mined territory, an exploration that has been recognized as hazardous since the birth of psychoanalysis. We have only to recall Freud's dilemma when trying to make a clear-cut distinction between the psychic presentation of ideas (things and words) and the psychic presentation of affects. In his paper on *Repression* (Freud 1915a), using his economic model, Freud refers to the "quota of affect," which "corresponds to the instinct insofar as the latter has become detached from the idea and finds expression, proportionate to its quantity, in processes which are sensed as affects" (p. 152).

From the time of his earliest research into hysteria, however, Freud was preoccupied with the vicissitudes of affect when it is separated from its mental representation. This brings us to the thorny question that preoccupied Freud as to whether an affect could be unconscious. The term *unconscious affect* would appear to be a contradiction in terms. Anyone with common sense would refute the suggestion that one is actually feeling an emotion that one is *not* feeling. Nevertheless affects, like ideas, are clearly capable of being kept out of consciousness. ("At the same time I was not aware of how terribly frightened, angry, excited . . . I really was.") The question of which *I* was experiencing the emotion and which was unaware of it is a difficult one to answer and raises a number of other questions. How is affect kept out of conscious awareness? In what way does its state of un-consciousness differ from that which is designated as an unconscious idea? In his attempt to untangle this complicated knot, Freud came to refer to the *repression* of ideas and the *suppression* of affects. These metaphors suggest two quite different mental processes: ideas are said to be *pushed back* from consciousness and affects to be *squashed out* of the psyche.

Where does affect go when it is rejected from the consciousness of the person in whom it has, if only momentarily, been mobilized? Freud provided a partial clue to the fate of unavailable affects. In *Studies on Hysteria* (Breuer and Freud 1895) as well as the papers on *Repression* (Freud 1915a) and *The Unconscious* (1915b), he speaks of the autonomous quality of affects and of their subsequent "transformations." The latter falls into three categories: the conversion of affects into hysterical symptoms; the displacement of an affect from its original representation onto another representation or set of representations, as in obsessional neurosis; and the transformation expressed in the actual neuroses, that is, anxiety neurosis, neurasthenia, and hypochondria. With regard to this last category, as we saw in previous chapters, these states are strongly impregnated with emotion, but the affects involved are massive, anonymous, and detached from any specific ideational representation. They manifest themselves somatically rather than psychically.

According to Freud's economic theory, affect that is suppressed from consciousness is then invested (or discharged) in neurotic symptoms or in the depressed and anxious states of the actual neuroses. It appears to me that we might also posit other transformations in the vicissitudes of affective experience. Certain people are capable of disavowing their affective experience, or segments of it, in such a way that it is radically repudiated or foreclosed from consciousness, creating a gap in psychic experience that still achieves some recovery of what has been lost, in the neurotic organizations discussed above. The recovery of ejected emotionally charged ideas may occur, for example, in many delusional states in which a neoreality must contain and try to make sense of the affects aroused. A similar mechanism is at work in what is referred to as *externalization,* in which the subject attributes rejected emotions to other people and attempts to deal with them through unconscious manipulations and interactions with others. This idea of course finds a theoretical framework in the concept of projective identification. The "scenes from psychic life" described in chapters 2 and 3 give glimpses into each of the above-mentioned eventualities.

There remains one further possibility, in which affect is not only strangled but split within its own specific structure, its psychic element severed from its somatic aspect. Following such a split there is no compensation for what is lost, either through the neurotic symptom formations described by Freud or through delusions or externalization. Affect that receives no psychic elaboration or compensation for its suppression, leaving in its wake nothing but a mental blank, runs the risk of continuing as a purely somatic event, thus paving the way for psychosomatic disorganization.

Another form of mental blank requires mention. It is pertinent here to reiterate that affective experience may be radically severed from the emotional words being used to express it, thus giving rise to paradoxical communications in which the psychic presentation of an affect, with its specific "quota," is neither experienced nor expressed in neurotic symptoms but exists purely as a disaffected idea. As I have already emphasized, an idea can be painful or pleasurable only when it is joined to a corresponding affect. The situation is complicated by the fact that the concept of affect, like that of instinct, is a borderline one, partaking of both somatic and psychological expression. We might postulate, therefore, that owing to their peculiar structure, affects may, phenomenologically, express themselves in three different ways.

First, one may be capable of giving a precise and differentiated account of what one is feeling, describing not only the overall affective state but also the mixture of emotions and sensations that are included in the particular experience.

Second, one may have an affective experience dominated by a massive emotional outbreak such as anguish but be unable to attach this arousal to any clearly defined situation. One may even be incapable of knowing whether what one is experiencing should be described as anxiety, depression, anger, or pleasurable excitement.

Third, one may be strongly "affected," both psychologically and in the general sense, by an outer or inner event and yet give no more than a second's attention to what one is feeling. Instead, all trace of this affective presentation is rapidly ejected from psychic awareness so that *neither the idea nor the affect remains.* When this occurs, affects may be split within their own peculiar structure in such a way that the psychic pole is divorced from the somatic pole and the affect is reduced to a pure physiological expression, while the subject remains unaware of the changes in bodily functioning that are occurring. In this case the emotion cannot be used as a signal to the mind, and therefore its message can be dealt with neither by thought nor by action, leaving the subject open to the danger that the soma may "think" its own solution to the event.

Affect Pathology

My interest in the pathology of affect, other than in the classical transformations described by Freud, first arose during the analyses of patients in whom the psychoanalytic process would from time to time come to a paralyzing halt; in some cases it would appear permanently stalled. These analysands had varied clinical problems, but they had this in common: all showed marked perturbation in their psychic economy when it came to dealing with strong affect. Instead of mentally elaborating their emotional states, they tended to discharge their feelings outside the analytic situation, often in inappropriate ways: through disputes, ill-considered decisions, or a series of accidents. The result was therapeutic failure or, worse, the disquieting experience of "interminable" analysis.

I came to realize that such patients, because of their *internal* fragilities, were unable to contain and work through the powerful affective states that had been stirred up by *external* events. They preferred to plunge into some form of action, or rather felt they had no choice but to do so. Some would try to drown their feelings in addictive substances (as described in chapter 5) or frenetic sexual exploits of a perverse or compulsive kind (chapters 11 and 12). Others would create havoc by unconsciously manipulating those closest to them to live out or play into their own unacknowledged crises. (Blanche, described in chapter 3, is a case in point.) Finally, I observed that many of these patients showed a strong inclination to somatize when under increased pressure from instinctual or external stress. As I mentioned in chapter 5, events such as the death of a parent, the birth of a baby, the loss of a love object or of an important job, and similar libidinal and narcissistic wounds were frequent mobilizing causes. In the case of Isaac (chapter 4), both libidinal and narcissistic conflicts appear to have prepared a terrain favorable to psychosomatic disorganization. If, from the point of view of the psychic economy, we regard sexual and character perversions and all forms of addictive behavior as compulsive ways of avoiding affective flooding, it is conceivable that sudden perturbation in the narcissistic economy may lead to the breakdown of the defensive structure and thus increase psychosomatic vulnerability.

A second group of patients who aroused my interest in affect pathology were those I have referred to as "anti-analysands in analysis" (McDougall 1972). I proclaimed myself stumped by them, with regard to both their underlying structure and their insistence on clinging to their analytic sessions. In view of their apparent lack of either neurotic or psychotic manifestations, they might more aptly be named *normopaths*. Unlike the acting-out patients I have described, these patients appeared to have no psychological problems. The neurotic and character symptoms that in fact they frequently displayed held no interest for them. Instead they seemed to have achieved in early childhood a robot-like adaptation to the demands of external reality. As might be expected, these analysands also had difficulty in identifying with other people's inner realities and often found themselves at odds with those close to them. Since they were not in touch with their personal psychic theaters, they tended to recount, in a tedious and compulsive way, endless chains of external events that appeared to have little emotional significance for them. The sessions went by like the months, one after the other, with little change to show for our analytic efforts.

These patients paralyzed my analytic functioning, and I would become frustrated, bored, and finally guilty, since I could neither help them become more alive nor get them to leave analysis. To my dismay, in spite of their conspicuous lack of transference affect and their inability to explore their psychic reality, I found they tended to become addicted to their analytical experience, despite their continual disappointment and dissatisfaction with the whole adventure. Their expressed lack of pleasure in the analytical work was scarcely surprising in view of the fact that their analyst, confronted with a sound barrier, could not hear anything that might further the analytic exploration. The striking lack of neurotic or psychotic symptoms led me to refer to these analysands as suffering from a form of "pseudonormality." I feel today that I understand better their mysterious psychic functioning, although this understanding frequently has not noticeably alleviated what might be described as their state of tranquil despair in the face of analytic failure. Today I would say that among their numerous psychological problems they also suffer from severe affect pathology. Their tendency to cling to the analysis as though to an outer source of vitality is perhaps reinforced by an unacknowledged hope that the analytical adventure will bring their inner affectivity to life.

In several personal histories among both the acting-out and the normopathic patients, one parent, usually the father, had died or left the family in the patient's early infancy. The mothers were frequently presented as overpossessive and overattentive while at the same time heedless of the child's affective states. In other instances the mother seemed to have been psychologically absent because of depression or psychotic episodes. These mothers appeared therefore to have been either too close or too distant in their relationship to their babies. It seemed to me that, for whatever reasons, a truly caretaking mother-image had never been introjected into the child's inner psychic structure, there to remain as an object of identification, allowing the child to become a good parent to itself. Thus in adult life the original maternal image, essential for dealing with emotional as well as physical pain and states of overstimulation, continued to be sought unremittingly in the external world in the form of addictive substances, addictive sexuality, or the addictive use of others, as though to repair a gap in the inner world and create an illusory, if temporary, experience of self-care. I have already referred to these activities in chapter 3 as pathological transitional or transitory objects.

Krystal's Research into the Nature of Affects

Henry Krystal (1977, 1978a, 1978b), who has spent many years in research into the affect pathology of holocaust victims, drug addicts, and psychosomatic patients, has remarked on the limited capacity of such patients to play a protective parental role toward themselves, as though they expected someone else to deal with their emotional and even their physical needs. Krystal has extended his concept of "impairment in the capacity for self-care" to include autonomous neurobiological functioning as well. He writes:

> The usual state of man in regard to the autonomously controlled part of his body is analogous to a hysterical paralysis. . . . [This

inhibition] of the exercise of volition over the autonomous or affective aspect of ourselves is, like any conversion paralysis, the symbolic representation of a fantasy . . . [but one that pertains] to the vital functions. (1978b, p. 221)

Krystal goes on to say that for certain subjects it may be an act of transgression to take in the maternal object "for the purpose of acquiring the walled-off, self-soothing and comforting functions . . . [because these are now experienced as] forbidden and punishable" (p. 222). This important insight illuminates for me the phenomenon that I had formerly described as the vestiges, in adult behavior, of the "drug-mother" in early childhood.

In his development of a genetic theory of affects, Krystal (1978a) posits a regression in the expression of affects due to traumatic events in adulthood. With regard to infants, he infers that continuing failure on the part of the mothering parent "to prevent the infant's affect from reaching an unbearable intensity and overwhelming him may result in a state of psychic trauma . . . [and] may cause an arrest in the organization of affective experience and its representational links" (p. 96), resulting in a lack of affective development. While I recognize the validity of this hypothesis, I suggest that what appears to be a lack of or an arrested development may, in many cases, cloak a massive but extremely early preneurotic defense against affective vitality. A brief might be made, therefore, for a concept of "developmental inhibition." This point can be pursued from another research approach.

Psychosomatic Research and Affect Pathology

Many researchers in the psychosomatic field have advanced the theory that the inability to recognize or express affective states is not a form of defense in the psychic structure but rather is due to a vital lack. In my first attempt to conceptualize the kind of failure in the psychoanalytic process displayed by my acting-out and normopathic patients, I had already noted a striking similarity to the "psychosomatic personality pattern" described by those of my psychoanalytic colleagues in Paris who were engaged in psychosomatic research. This personality organization is marked by operational thinking (Marty and de M'Uzan 1963) and by pragmatic ways of relating to life events and to other people (Marty 1976). Although it is evident that this kind of mental functioning is not limited solely to psychosomatic sufferers, the research of the psychosomaticists demonstrates that such structures tend to increase psychosomatic vulnerability, particularly when the operational mode of existence—basically a delibidinized way of relating both to oneself and to others—is the only mode at the subject's disposal for dealing with life events.

Pursuing my interest in blocked affect, I later became acquainted with the work of psychoanalytic colleagues in Boston who were engaged in similar research. Their concept of *alexithymia* immediately caught my interest (Sifneos 1973, 1974, 1975; Nemiah and Sifneos 1970). This clinical concept was directly inspired by the publications of the Paris School of analyst-psychosomaticists, but the continuing research of the Boston analysts led them into other fields, notably that of neurobiology. The more recent papers of these research workers, for example, posit defective functioning of the dopaminergic tracts.

The psychoanalytic conception of alexithymia may prove to be complementary to the neurobiological one. *Alexithymia* (from Greek *a:* "without," *lexis:* "word," *thumos:* "heart" or "affectivity") means, according to Sifneos, having no words for emotions.* The concept refers to a series of phenomena that have been studied extensively by the Boston psychosomaticists. It includes not only the difficulties that patients may have in attempting to describe their affective states but also the incapacity to distinguish one affect from another. It should be noted that the apparent disavowal of affectivity is not limited to painful affects. In these afflicted people, there is an equally pro-

*Greek scholars have suggested to me that the word might be more adequately related to the prefix *alexi,* that is to say, "against" or "vanquisher of" affect, if my thesis of defensive operations were to be accepted.

found inability to experience satisfaction and pleasure. Krystal (1981, 1982), referring to these as the "welfare affects," has named this phenomenon *anhedonia.*

The authors of the alexithymia concept do not discuss its extension beyond the patient's own psyche, except indirectly in speaking of common countertransference reactions to these patients. It is evident, however, that an inability to capture and become aware of one's own emotional experience must be accompanied by an equally great difficulty in understanding other people's emotional states and wishes. Trapped in this psychic impasse, subjects experience an overwhelming difficulty in knowing just what people mean to them and they to others. All relationships and exchanges with others thus tend to be pragmatic, that is, operational. For this reason, in the analytic relationship countertransference affects usually provide the first warning that certain analysands are dominated by operational thinking or suffer from alexithymic defects.

Nevertheless it must be reiterated that everyone is likely to function in operational or alexithymic ways from time to time. Faced with overwhelming events, we may all find ourselves temporarily out of touch with certain areas of our psychic reality. At such times we may fail to contain and reflect upon the experiences that besiege us. We are likely instead to drain away in action the affects that have been mobilized—and equally likely to fall ill.

Psychoanalytical and Neurobiological Theories of Affect Pathology

If my investigation of the varied phenomena of alexithymia seems somewhat opposed to the conclusions of the psychosomaticists, it should nevertheless be stressed that scientific options, while they have a basis in unconscious factors, are also determined by professional circumstances that lead us to concentrate on the problems that confront us daily. These may concern a patient on the couch, consultations in a psychosomatic service, or work on a psychiatric ward. In each case we are confronted with alexithymic patients, but they tend to reveal different aspects of their personalities to each specialist, and what each of us seeks to discover about them also varies.

Neurobiological research, for example, is always more concerned with intracerebral phenomena, whereas psychoanalytic research, in observing the same phenomena, always seeks for evidence of early psychic trauma and attempts to retrace the forgotten infantile past (Dayan 1981). I myself read articles dealing with the mysteries of the limbic system and the probabilities of hemispheric dominance with the fascination of an earth-dweller wandering about Mars. Such excursions into the field of affect pathology, however, have led me to reflect further upon the theoretical concepts of *psychical* causes as compared with those of *neurobiological* causes. A blind man uses a stick to tell him what he cannot see. What stick does the neurobiologist use? And what is the analyst's stick? For we are like the blind men describing the elephant. We are both trying to sound out and understand the multidimensional nature of psychosomatic man, and we are each limited by our specific disciplines and scientific beliefs.

What are the differences? And where is the interface? What links may be found between the specific hyperactivity or underactivity of certain chemical mediators in the synaptic transmission of a given patient's *neuroanatomical* system and the specific *psychological* system developed by that same patient for dealing with thoughts, affects, fantasies, and desires? A scientific synapsis may be required to link our different findings!

To return to our disaffected alexithymic patients, we might do well to recall that infants, unable to speak or to organize their emotional experiences, are by definition as well as by reason of their immaturity inevitably alexithymic. Infants (from the Latin *infans:* "not speaking") depend on someone else to deal with their emotional states and eventually to name these states for them. Might it not be supposed that the alexithymic part of an adult personality is an extremely arrested and infantile psychic structure? Yet an adult has complete access to language. We may therefore presume that some vigorous mental process is at work, a process that enables people suffering from alexithymia to split word-presentations from their literal thing-presentations, at least as far as affect-laden ideas, experiences, and somatic messages are concerned. If this tendency dominated a person's mental functioning totally, we would be dealing with psychotic thought processes; I am suggesting for the moment that where gravely alexithymic people are concerned, we are faced with a nonpsychotic adult who in certain respects functions like a helpless, nonverbal child, dependent upon others for interpreting and coping with emotional experiences. I believe that something more than inhibited or arrested development or a neurobiological defect has occurred and that it is still active. My work with such patients has led me to recognize traumatic forms of relationship in early infancy and childhood (illustrated clinically in chapters 4 and 8) that appear to have contributed to the kind of psychic functioning that lies behind alexithymic symptoms and psychosomatic tendencies.

An infant's earliest external reality is, of course, the mother's physical presence and, above all, the impingement of the mother's unconscious. The latter includes not only her own inner world and the nature of her relationship to her own parents but also her narcissistic and sexual investment of her baby's father. A mother's tie to her partner is crucial, not only in influencing the oedipal structure that is to come but also in determining the narcissistic and libidinal roles that her child may unconsciously be called upon to fulfill for her. Accordingly there are specific ways in which a mother relates to (and may attempt to limit or control) her infant's body—not only its somatic functioning but also its vitality and affectivity. As I have already noted, many alexithymic-psychosomatic patients talk of their bodies as though they were foreign objects belonging to the external world, or as though they did not possess certain of their bodily zones and functions—in fact, as though these were unconsciously experienced as still belonging to the mother. The point here is that children may also conceive of their *emotions* as not being truly their own possessions. In that case the emotions are not the child's responsibility and may even be considered as existing only to the extent that the mother acknowledges them, much as though the feelings in question were her experience rather than the child's.

If a mother's way of relating to her nonverbal infant's bodily functions, gestures, and affective storms is of cardinal importance in the organization of early psychic life, it must be reemphasized that, as direct bodily communication gives way to symbolic communication and the acquisition of language, it is also the mother who first names the child's affects and thus provides the potential for thinking—or not thinking—about feelings. In the course of analysis analysands frequently depict their parents as idealized and all-important beings upon whom all security rested, yet at the same time as quite out of touch with the child's psychic reality. For example, the parents may be remembered as paying considerable attention to physical pain but totally uninterested in, or even condemning, any expression of mental pain. Sometimes a form of double-bind discourse seems to have attacked the affective aspects of the child's psychic reality: "I hate staying at Aunt Susie's!" "Nonsense. You know you just love going there!" If parents consistently reject what children are trying to grasp and then communicate of their emotional states of mind, and instead tell them what they feel and do not feel, or what they like and do not like, the children may end up confused about what is love and what is hate, about when they are sad and when they are happy, and indeed about whether feelings are allowable at all if they have not been dictated by the parents.

As time goes on, the family discourse continues to convey to children those affective experiences that are to be regarded as legitimate and those that are to be frowned upon or even denied access to conscious recognition. A very ill alexithymic and psychosomatic analysand said to me recently, "In our family it was forbidden to be sad or angry or in need of anything. I still get confused when you ask me what I am feeling—as though it were childish to have feelings!" A family milieu that holds that it is weak, foolish, or even dangerous to express emotion, that condemns either the psychological or the physical aspects of feeling states, may be laying the groundwork for a pathological ego-ideal with regard to affective experience (McDougall 1984). Any expression or even awareness of emotional reactions then tends to lower one's feelings of self-esteem.

As for the body and its different zones and functions, once again it is the mother who decides how these are to be named and what degree of libidinal investment, or counterinvestment, they are to receive. A severe lack of libidinal cathexis attached to certain bodily zones or to the somatic self as a whole, when coupled with parentally instilled alexithymia, runs the risk not only of impairing somatic and zonal functioning but also of allowing bodily pain as well as mental pain to be totally foreclosed from conscious awareness. This mechanism is reminiscent of one of the fundamental mechanisms that contribute to certain mystical states as well as to the maintenance of certain psychotic states such as catatonia and self-mutilation.

In cases of severe alexithymic disturbance, affective vitality, whether stimulated by instinctual promptings or by external solicitations, is immediately paralyzed, and perceptions that are likely to evoke keen bodily awareness or powerful affective reactions are either avoided or rapidly ejected from consciousness. In the analysis of such patients we are sometimes able to observe what occurs when they begin to recognize their affective states rather than ejecting them immediately. Affective flooding may then produce transitory episodes of depersonalization or of pseudo-perceptual phenomena in an attempt to deal with the emotional upsurge. (A clinical illustration of this process is given in the next chapter.) Such episodes create rough periods in the analytic adventure, of course, until such time as the tolerance for affect is increased and the analysand has created verbal representations and fantasies capable of containing the emotional storms and the free circulation of primitive affectivity through language. At this point analytical work proceeds along a double track: first there is the economic problem of retaining and experiencing strong affect without acting it out, and then there is the symbolic dimension that consists of uncovering or creating fantasies and metaphors, charged with affect, that are mobilized in the individual, sometimes for the first time in conscious awareness, by fleeting perceptions of internal and external events. The radical split between psyche and soma begins to heal, and thus the threat of psychosomatic disorganization is lessened.

Psychosomatosis

When patients face inner conflict and outer stress with no other mental mechanisms than psychic ejection of every affect-charged idea or perception (as in the case histories of Isaac in chapters 4 and 6 and Paul in chapter 8), and when in addition they produce severe or continual psychosomatic maladies, the form of psychic equilibrium maintained in this way deserves the name of *psychosomatosis.* This kind of mental functioning does not depend primarily on either repression or denial. In addition to psychosomatic phenomena, its major signs are therefore alexithymic manifestations allied with concrete or pragmatic ways of thought and operational ways of relating to other people. To these signs are frequently added an impoverished fantasy life and a paucity of dreams. It is my contention that the person caught in this kind of dilemma has no other recourse, in the face of stressful situations, than to attack any perceptions that risk arousing emotion. The gap thus created between affective arousal and mental presentations leads inevitably to the destruction of meaning. What other people expect or request does not make sense, and such sufferers therefore try to respond as concretely as possible to what is asked of them. And just as frequently they try to avoid emotional references as though they were admissions of childishness. Thus the world, and the people in it, become devitalized, and the exchange with others meaningless. Feeling is not disavowed; it no longer exists.

In one of his major papers on the subject of alexithymia, Sifneos (1974) made a similar observation but adduced different reasons to explain it. He noted that "what appears as a denial of emotion is in fact an absence of feelings . . . and this may be due to the existence of some kind of biological defect in [the patient's] brain" (p. 154). This may well be so. The defect may also prove to be a functional one, rather like an archaic hysterical manifestation, or indeed there may be an inherited fragility. The fact that in many instances alexithymic and psychosomatic symptoms disappear as a result of psychoanalytic treatment argues against the theory of neurobiological defect, whether innate or acquired, as a sufficient or necessary explanation. Nevertheless the psychodynamic and economic theory that I am proposing does not invalidate the neurobiological one and may be complementary to it. An inborn defect may affect the choice of symptom in the case of children who suffer early psychic trauma.

Alexithymia as a Defense Against Psychotic Fears

All psychological symptoms are attempts at self-cure, and alexithymia is no exception. Even though, as I have suggested, parents often actually teach their children to be alexithymic, we still need to know what fantasied dangers alexithymic sufferers are unconsciously protecting themselves against in continuing to maintain such devitalized relations with the world. Krystal's work with holocaust victims (1978a) demonstrates clearly that late onset of severe alexithymic symptoms serves to prevent the return of a traumatic state. My experience with patients who have, in a sense, been alexithymic since early childhood has led me to understand that unconscious fears concerning contact and exchange with others, coupled with fears of the damage that emotional states are thought to cause, are more akin to psychotic than to neurotic anxieties. Neurotic conflicts concern one's adult right to a love life and sexual pleasure, as well as pleasure in work, rivalry situations, and the pursuit of narcissistic satisfactions. When these adult rights are contested by the child within, neurotic symptoms and inhibitions arise as compromises. Psychotic anxiety, on the other hand, turns around the right to exist as well as to possess a separate identity without fear that it will be attacked or damaged by others. Deep uncertainty about one's otherness and the right or ability to maintain the privacy of one's thoughts and feelings is on the one hand the fear of implosion—of being destructively influenced, invaded, or possessed by another—and on the other the fear of explosion—of losing control over one's body limits, one's acts, and one's feeling of identity.

Psychosomatosis and Psychosis

My proposition is that psychosomatosis and psychosis reveal similar psychic structures and that this similarity is not limited to the dynamic force of the above-mentioned anxieties. Certain of the psychic mechanisms, such as alexithymia, that are employed to keep archaic terror at bay are also common to both states. This comparison may seem incongruous: few individuals appear more bizarre in public than those dominated by psychotic thought processes, while few seem so well adapted to external reality, and to comply so readily with what the world demands, as those who suffer from alexithymic and psychosomatic symptoms. The latter have created a *false-self adaptation* to others, and this wall of pseudonormality enables them to face the world in spite of grave inner distress concerning contact with others. There are, of course, important differences: in psychosis, thought functions in a delusional way; in psychosomatosis, the body functions in a delusional way. Psychosomatic symptoms neither make biological sense nor carry verbal symbolic significance, as is the case with neurotic and psychotic symptoms.

In a thought-provoking chapter concerning the fundamental elements that underlie schizophrenic conflict, Thomas Ogden (1980) states that he regards

> conflict in the representational sphere [between wishes to maintain a state of meaning and wishes to destroy all meaning] as the central schizophrenic conflict. . . . [In schizophrenia] there is an attack on the psychological capacities by which meanings are created and

thought about. . . . The schizophrenic unconsciously attacks his thoughts, feelings and perceptions, which are felt to be an endless source of pain. (P.166)

I find that something similar is occurring in alexithymic psychosomatosis.* In both states analysis frequently reveals that early psychic experience has led to confusion about one's body and one's mind and their limits, as well as to doubts about one's right to possess an individual body and an individual psychic existence. The latter includes inner liveliness and awareness of one's emotional states, in that affects and affectively charged fantasies permit children to possess a private world that need not be shared with the important adults in the outer world. But this pleasure (and the words to think the thoughts) may have been interpreted by the child as totally forbidden; there can then be no secrets, no separateness, and no private possession of one's bodily self.

Psychotics attribute to others their overwhelming affective pain and intolerable anxiety and proceed to create a neoreality in order to make continued existence tolerable and understandable. With the same aim in mind, alexithymics attack their psychological capacity to capture affect and use it for thought or as a signal to themselves. But instead of creating a neoreality, they simply drain external reality and object relationships of their meaning.

Two clinical examples illustrate these two psychic mechanisms. The first is a psychotic patient in psychoanalytic therapy at a time when he was driven into panic by any form of sexual arousal, who wrote the following note: "Doctor, I think you ought to know, they're putting sex hormones into my Wheaties." The second is an alexithymic patient in analysis (who also suffers from sclerodermatitis), who asked: "How can I know if I have any desire for this girl or not? All I know is that I get an erection when I'm with her." The alexithymic's erections were to him as mysterious—and as meaningless—as those of the psychotic patient

*There is a further form of psychosomatosis (not discussed in this book) in which emotion is rife and fantasy life extremely active but neither is contained in normal-neurotic structures. Instead they give rise to continual psychosomatic illnesses of a severe kind. Anxiety states and depressive episodes are both attached to feelings of being unable to cope with normal life situations. See McDougall, "Un Corps Pour Deux," in *Corps et Histoire* (Paris: Les Belles Lettres, 1986).

were to him. In spite of the different defenses employed, shades of the psychotic sexual fantasy of the "influencing machine" (Tausk 1919) may be detected in both.

In other situations the severely alexithymic sufferer's feelingless state approaches the schizophrenic state of apathy, but where the psychotic withdraws from external realities and relationships, the alexithymic makes a pseudoadjustment to these, often one that forces a hyperactive involvement with others and serves to mask the psychic catatonia. Both the withdrawal and the pseudoadjustment are techniques of psychic survival. But whereas the delusional thought and withdrawn state of the schizophrenic patient are obvious to the observer, all that remains to be seen of the profound internal struggle behind psychosomatosis (other than the alexithymic and psychosomatic symptoms) is perhaps the frequent observation of "stiffness of posture" and "rigid" or "wooden" facial expressions. I have noticed that several of my somatizing analysands refer to their attempts to "keep things in place" by tightening up their bodies and musculature, as though they are using the body in a stiff or wooden way to master the upsurge of strong or frightening affect.

It may be recalled that when Isaac (chapter 6) discovered in the third year of analysis that tachycardia and asthma attacks occurred in connection with homosexually linked excitement, he summed up these findings by saying: "But I close up everything against such ideas—my throat, my lungs, and my arteries." Such efforts to make the body magically impose order upon psychological disorder and threatening affect storms are clearly ineffectual beyond a certain point. These somatic defense measures must then be reinforced by vigorous psychological means, such as violent expulsion from the psyche of both the affect and its mental representation. This form of psychic functioning in my opinion contributes to the clinical factors so often observed by different research workers: insistence on the concrete, the tendency to addictive behavior, and the externalization of inner conflict, causing other people to react emotionally to the patient. These are all effective ways of discharging or dispersing emotion.

Another common trait derives from this same psychic mechanism—namely, the sudden affective outbursts, such as crying or flashes of rage, shown by many patients. Here the alexithymic defense breaks down, and I would suggest that what we are witnessing is an unconscious repetition of a pattern from the past. Some of my patients have been able to recall that these emotional storms were felt to be the only means by which they could hope to communicate something of their inner distress and psychic reality to the family, in spite of the alexithymic ideal that was promulgated. Such expressions of affect are, however, fixated at a childhood level and are therefore relatively undifferentiated, so that they are not readily available for thought about oneself.

The Paucity of Dreams and Daydreams

We might presume that the continual effort to cut emotional links—whether of a pleasurable or a painful nature, whether attached to instinctual promptings, to affectively charged fantasies and ideas, or to relationships with other people—is a major psychic activity in alexithymic and psychosomatic states. This capacity to attack and rapidly eject from the psyche both the somatic and the psychic poles of painful affect, frequently accompanied by an equally violent struggle against pleasurable affects, also affords an explanation for another clinical phenomenon associated with psychosomatosis: the marked poverty or even total absence of dreams and daydreaming (Warnes 1982). In normal-neurotic functioning, perceptual phenomena or the *day's residues* touch off instinctual impulses and become linked to significant objects in the inner world. These perceptions are repressed and stored to become the nodal points around which dream thoughts crystallize and eventually seek representation in the dream scene and its theme—an everyday observation in analytic practice. When ideas are rapidly eliminated from the psyche because of their affective charge, however, these potential dream elements are not available for further use, since they have been foreclosed. There is nothing left with which to make dreams.

In the analytic fragment quoted in the following chapter, some of the underlying reasons for the ejection of perceptually significant ideas are evident. Having no capacity for repressing these, the patient found himself invaded by what amounted to hallucinatory experiences like those of a small child who does not yet distinguish clearly between inner and outer reality. It is possible that everyday perceptions contain a potential hallucinatory quality for everybody, but filtering and repressing these associations—or eliminating them, as in states of psychosomatosis—avoids this outcome.

Alexithymic and Operational Forms of Relationship

The same mode of psychic functioning also throws light on the highly specific way many alexithymic and psychosomatic sufferers relate to others. Here again, any potential emotional links to others are attacked and destroyed so that the relationship risks becoming meaningless. The case of Mr. C. (chapter 2), who spoke "diabetic," is a clear illustration of this kind of exchange with others. The fragments of Isaac's and Paul's analyses show the rediscovery of the affective links to significant others during the analytic process.

This brings us to the important question of the therapeutic relation and the extent to which such patients are or are not accessible to psychoanalysis or psychoanalytic therapy. Countertransference reactions to patients suffering from psychosomatosis have been carefully documented by all workers in the field. Early on, I became aware that many of these patients—my own as well as those of younger analysts and students—while stifling all perception of their own affective states nevertheless frequently succeeded in arousing strong emotional reactions in those around them, including the analyst. I referred to this kind of interpersonal reaction elsewhere (McDougall 1978, pp. 247–98) as *primitive communication*—a form of communication in which words are used rather like cries and gestures, as an act intended to *affect* another human being rather than to communicate something. The Paris psychosomaticists have described the "poverty" of the patients' discourse and the feeling of "inertia" that pervades the sessions in psychosomatic treatment centers; Nemiah (1978) gives a succinct portrait of a psychosomatic patient.

> One frequently finds [alexithymic individuals] expressionless, stiff, wooden, and nearly gestureless during an interview. This rigid demeanor, taken in conjunction with the lack of emotional coloring in their speech and with their preoccupation with the small details of their daily existence, makes many of them seem dull and boring to the interviewer. . . . Such a reaction is not intended as a criticism, but should rather be considered as a diagnostic criterion for the presence of alexithymic symptoms. (P. 30)

Michael von Rad (1977, 1979) has published the results of several years' research into the comparison of words used by psychosomatic patients and those employed by psychoneurotic patients and adduces empirical evidence for the presence of alexithymic phenomena in the former group.

Analysts too come to discover that the words of their alexithymic and operational analysands (many of whom do not suffer from psychosomatic symptoms, let it be added) tend to produce in them the same difficulty in focusing attention on the patients' associations. The analyst comes to feel frustrated, inwardly paralyzed, and unable to function analytically, finally questioning the value of the analytical experience for these patients. The curious upshot of this kind of relationship is that in many instances consultants and analysts run the risk of becoming alexithymic themselves toward the patients in question! Certain therapists have even advocated avoiding phrases and questions that are likely to arouse nascent sparks of affect in these patients—a procedure that seems to me more dangerous than allowing the slow recovery of affective links within the therapeutic situation, when possible.

Why do the patients' words have this particular effect upon us? What exactly is happening in this kind of relationship? These are problems of countertransference and need to be understood if we are to avoid an analytic stalemate. Graeme Taylor (1977) expresses ideas that come very close to my own with regard to countertransference and primitive communications (McDougall 1978). I had written that we were faced "with a screen-discourse, impregnated with messages that have never been elaborated verbally, and that can in the first instance, only be captured by the arousal of countertransference affect" (pp. 257–58). In a paper on difficulties in the analysis of alexithymic patients, Taylor (1977) writes, "In my opinion access may be gained to the patient's inner life by considering the feelings of dullness, boredom and frustration as countertransference experiences" (p. 145).

Alexithymia and Projective Identification

The nature of this specific kind of transference-countertransference relationship becomes clearer in light of the psychoanalytic concepts of *splitting* and *projective identification* (Klein 1946, 1955; Ogden 1980). Projective identification is both an intrapersonal and an interpersonal phenomenon. It implies both an individual's capacity to split off from consciousness large segments of what has been registered psychically and a psychological process in which one person unconsciously brings pressure to bear upon another in an attempt to unburden the personal fantasies and problems that have been split off from consciousness. James Grotstein, in his masterly and comprehensive book *Splitting and Projective Identification* (1981), writes:

> Projective identification is an amalgam of concepts which can be confusing. When its purpose is defensive, projective identification aims really to *disavow* identification, and perhaps would be better called projective *dis*identification—the "I" wishes to split off some mental content, project itself into an object, and then sever any connection with itself. Moreover, like splitting, projective identification is both a benign defense which simply wishes to postpone confrontation with some experience that cannot yet be tolerated; but it is also a defense which can negate, destroy, and literally obliterate the sense of reality. (P. 131)

As Grotstein aptly points out, although clinically it may appear that one person "projects part of his I into the image of an external object for purposes of transactional or bipersonal manipulation, in point of fact we do not project into objects in the external world; we project into our images of them" (p. 133).

Nevertheless, in analysis we are frequently able to observe the way in which certain analysands, under the sway of splitting and projective mechanisms, do in fact bring psychological pressure to bear upon significant others, stirring up strong affect and other psychological reactions in them. Splitting off part of what they feel, such patients then seek unconsciously to control or regain contact with this lost part by experiencing it as an attribute of the other. In many cases, the other responds readily, jumping onto the projector's stage to play out the projected role (exemplified in Blanche's analysis in chapter 3). This kind of response can also arise as a countertransference experience.

It seems to me that severe alexithymic patients use splitting and projective identification mechanisms in this defensive way, but they are totally unaware that they have split off from consciousness large segments of their psychic reality, thereby expelling a series of fantasies and emotions in order not to feel them. Therapists in face-to-face interviews are well placed to study the ways in which patients' very gestures and postures may arouse strong feelings in the observer; those using the couch are perhaps even more attuned to the way in which patients use words, from the point of view not only of content but the under- or overuse of certain words, the richness or poverty of metaphor, and the presence or absence of an associative process arising from the interpenetration of primary and secondary thinking processes. It is my contention that alexithymic patients, in their unconscious but urgent need to keep a sterile space between themselves and others, use posture, gestures, and words to stir up considerable feeling in others and actually induce them to cooperate in keeping this distance.

In certain ways, alexithymic and operational modes of communicating and relating to others may be compared to schizoid withdrawal, in that both seek to maintain a state of inner deadness, as though to prevent invasion by tempestuous affective experiences. Certain psychosomatic as well as nonsomatizing alexithymic patients admit that they feel ill at ease with others or "go dead" in their presence and therefore tend to keep a prudent distance from impending encounters. Others have developed a false-self adaptation that allows considerable interaction with other people, although they sometimes say that they have "difficulty in thinking" when with others. In this kind of adaptation, the extensive use of projective identification is then coupled with an attack upon their own thought processes. Since these processes either eject or stifle affective experience they combine in creating an affectless exterior. Meanwhile those with whom they come in contact tend to be strongly "affected."

To illustrate the absence of thoughts and affects and the dependence on external stimuli displayed by alexithymic patients, Nemiah (1978) gives a striking example of the result of projective identification mechanisms in an interpersonal situation. The conversation is taken from a preliminary interview with a patient suffering from severe ulcerative colitis. The consultant is trying to find out what kind of thoughts the patient has when he is angry.

PATIENT: I have bad thoughts.

DOCTOR: For example?

P: I'm very—angry. Very resentful . . .

D: But what kind of thoughts do you have going through your mind when you're angry?

P: Thoughts? I'm just—I'm just plain—just plain angry . . . I'm trying to think what you mean by "thoughts" . . .

D: How can you tell that you're angry?

P: Oh, I know. I can tell because . . . the people I'm involved with—I can see how upset they get with me. (P. 29)

Nemiah notes that the patient hardly understands what is meant by thoughts and fantasies and is forced instead to rely on external stimuli such as the reaction of others. It must also be emphasized, however, that the patient himself has written the whole script and more or less stage-managed the show, the only way he knows how to react with others. After much hedging and reiteration that he is simply "angry," he intellectualizes in a typi-

cally alexithymic attempt to play for time and ward off or paralyze any thoughts that might potentially arouse emotion. In all
probability the patient is seeking unconsciously to paralyze the
therapist's mind as well as his own. Eventually he shows us that
by detaching from consciousness what he thinks and feels when
he is "angry," he ejects this part of his psychic reality in such a
way that the people he is "involved with" reflect it back to him.
They are his mirror.

No doubt this way of affecting others is a manner of communication that the patient learned in early childhood. Perhaps it
was then the only channel available for transmitting what he was
experiencing, but today it is achieved at the price of a loss of
contact with an important part of his own psychic experience, as
well as an impoverishment in the use and significance of
language—not to mention his grave physical illness.

What does feeling *angry* mean to this patient? The word is
drained of its meaning, devitalized and bloodless. Perhaps only
the patient's body, cruelly attacked by the constant hemorrhaging of his life-threatening illness, is capable, in its limited somatic
way, of expressing anger; it is an anger that is unstayed by the
mind, out of reach of thought. Anxiety is the mother of invention
in the psychic theater, and without it the patient invents nothing.
When anxiety itself is absent, as is so often the case, the therapist
may well feel that the patient is threatened with deathlike drives
that seem stronger than those on the side of life.

The characteristic way of reacting and relating that has such
a powerful effect upon others may enlighten the analyst as to
what is being ejected from the patient's psyche. Might we not
suppose that in the interview or treatment situation such patients, out of touch with an important dimension of their psychic
reality, manage to evoke in us their unacknowledged feelings of
helplessness and inner deadness? We are to experience what they
once had to learn—that their psychic survival depended upon the
ability to render inner liveliness inert. A mother who feels threatened by her baby's vivacity or overwhelmed by its storms of rage
or states of distress cannot fail to communicate to her infant those
gestures and cries that receive adequate attention and those that
do not. Babies, avid to discover and control the sources of plea-

sure and security, learn to hold back their spontaneous movements or, in states of unassuaged rage or fear, fall into exhausted sleep characterized by no dream life, only the search for nothingness. With certain patients we come to discover that this inner paralysis is intended to avoid primitive fantasies of implosion or abandonment or the return of a traumatic state of helplessness and hopelessness in which psychic existence, and perhaps life itself, was felt to be threatened.

Alexithymia and the Split Between Psyche and Soma

Thus we come to the conclusion that alexithymia is an uncommonly effective defense against inner vitality. Affects are one of the most privileged links between psyche and soma, between the instinctual center of life and the mind that must organize these life forces. That affects, intended to bring messages from the body or from the outer world to the mind, should become severed or paralyzed in their linking function as well as in their linguistic significance is a triumph of the mind over the instinctual and affective body. The creation of such a structure, while it has its roots in the earliest human transactions, is the work of a lifetime. It is evident that the more fragile the subject, the stronger is the defensive wall against collapse. Even though the maintenance of such a fortress may be costly in terms of physical or psychical disorganization, the patient may well fight fiercely against any threat of incursion into this solidly defended personality structure. In such circumstances, we must treat this massive construction with respect. It would be more than foolhardy to determine to knock doorways through it or to remove it at all cost. We need first to be sure that such patients are firmly determined to learn more about themselves, and even then caution is required. Much preliminary work may be necessary before these patients are able to recognize the nature of their defensive prison and the extent of their inability to experience and express their affects. Without insight into these serious symptoms, the suddenly liberated prisoner may be unable to gather up the fractured words, incapable of holding and using the hitherto strangled emotions, without pain and fear that may prove excessively disruptive to the psychic economy. Can the analytical situation provide a sufficiently strong and "holding" environment, so that the words that are missing or deadened may once more become alive?

In discussing the gravity of alexithymic symptoms, Sifneos (1973) once remarked that feelings are the most typically human feature of psychic life, and to have lost touch with them is a dehumanizing factor. I would extend this statement to say that the typically human factor—the one that distinguishes human beings most clearly from other animals—is the use of language and the symbolic communication of needs, wishes, and desires. It is through *words* that affects eventually become firmly linked to mental representations; it is words that bind the free circulation of primitive affectivity and render it available for thought—true thought, not operational thinking. Our subjective, sexual, and social identities are all stored in the form of emotionally impregnated words that have been gathered throughout our lifetime—first our parents' words, rich in affects of admonition or encouragement, and later the discourse of the society to which we belong. Without words we can neither think, except in a rather primitive fashion, nor think about what we feel. Our experiences then risk remaining as beta elements (Bion 1962a, 1970). At that point others must "think" for us, or our bodies will "think" in our stead. The psychic image of the body itself is made by words and enslaved by words. It is what we have done with the words, how well we use them to communicate with ourselves and with others, that determines what kind of human beings we have become—and what kind of psychoanalytic experiences await us.

Children learn early in life to be afraid of the emotional dynamite that words contain. Like adults, they tremble at the threat of humiliation or abandonment and fear words that express a potential loss of love or attack their sense of reality or personal identity. They rapidly learn to use words as weapons and to protect themselves against the hurtful words of others. Every schoolchild knows this little rhyme:

> Sticks and stones may break my bones
> But words'll never hurt me!

There's a magnificent piece of denial! The American poet Ogden Nash, with that intuitive insight into human frailty that characterizes all great humorists, has paraphrased this rhyme, expressing what every alexithymic "knows":

> Sticks and stones may break your bones
> But words can damn near kill you!

8

From Psychosomatosis to Psychoneurosis

The clinical notes that follow are taken from a lengthy analysis of a forty-year-old patient.* Paul was, in many respects, a typical psychosomatic personality in that he tended to be out of touch with his own psychic reality, particularly in its affective aspects. Since adolescence he had suffered from gastric ulcers and various skin allergies. These were not the reason he came to analysis, however, and in fact, at the beginning of our analytic work together, he gave little thought to the idea that these maladies might have psychological significance. He sought analytic help because of a feeling of failure both in his professional life and in his personal relationships. This fragment of Paul's analytic adventure is intended to illustrate the slow transformation from a psychosomatic state and way of mental functioning into a neurotic psychic organization. At the same time, it is my hope that this vignette will throw some light on the well-known difficulties such patients have in using dreams and fantasy. As we saw in the last chapter, the so-called alexithymic symptoms and operational ways of thinking and relating may serve as a massive defense against primitive emotional states, because of early psychic trauma.

The following sessions took place in the sixth year of our

*An excerpt from the analysis of the same patient was published in McDougall 1978, chapter 10, "Body and Language and the Language of the Body." The notes quoted here were taken two years later.

work together. For two years, Paul had had practically no digestive disturbance of any kind, nor had he mentioned further outbreaks of his various skin allergies. Much interpretive attention had been focused on the disturbance in Paul's psychic functioning from the economic point of view (Freud 1915a), enabling him to observe more closely his tendency to obliterate feelings and troubling perceptions as they occurred in his daily interchange with colleagues and in the analytical relationship. This type of intervention played a predominant role in the first session, described here.

Eyes that Attack What They See

Physically Paul is visibly much more relaxed than he used to be. He used to slink into my consulting room hastily, staying a careful distance away from me as well as avoiding any eye contact between us. Now he looks at me, and although he still rushes precipitately onto the couch, his whole attitude is distinctly less tense and odd than it used to be.

During last week's session Paul had developed a series of daydreams in which he imagines himself hollowing out "large black craters" in women's breasts, a theme inspired by a poster he saw daily, of a woman with naked breasts. This theme has been accompanied by another preoccupation, in which Paul perceives me as "smashed up" and "physically ill."

P: (as he lies down on the couch): Are you tired? If you only knew how anxious that makes me! I'm always terribly afraid of finding you looking worn out—don't know why. [Long pause]

It occurred to me that he may have had some fantasy about having attacked me and "tired" me on entering the room.

JM: You may remember that last week you imagined yourself digging black craters in women's breasts. Might this sort of activity make a woman look tired and worn out?

181

P: Now, that irritates me, because it has nothing to do with reality. I'm not the slightest bit interested in fantasies!

To have access to such fantasies and at the same time be obliged to contain and work them over in thought without acting upon them is in itself a frustration and a narcissistic wound for Paul.

JM: You see me looking worn out, rather like the other day when you found my face was "dislocated." Would these impressions arise in place of imagining or feeling something concerning me?

P: I sometimes "see" strange things just before falling asleep, and it terrifies me. [Paul rarely has any memories of dreaming.]

JM: As though there too you might avoid having fantasies, imagining just anything, like in a dream? Maybe if you refuse to let such thoughts come up, they appear in front of you like real perceptions?

Paul is refusing to recognize feelings and fantasies that are concerned with hostility and destruction toward women, not only because he feels such ideas are contrary to his ego ideal but because, if he allowed them to come into consciousness, he would be faced with having to contain their associated affects, and he has little affect tolerance. To limit himself to fantasies is intolerable, therefore, from both a narcissistic and an economic viewpoint. His pattern of mental functioning has been largely built upon immediate discharge reactions of various kinds, in response to unacceptable instinctual impulses. At the present moment he would prefer to see me looking "worn out" and "dislocated" than to become aware of his aggressive feelings, coupled with the interdiction to act them out.

P: But I've every reason to stifle my mad ideas. They cause me much greater panic than the things I "see." My ideas are truly horrible. Something important has changed, anyway. I can now look people in the eye, and I'm no longer afraid of their looking at me. It still troubles me because I see them all smashed up much of the time, but that doesn't worry me like it used to. So they're like that! Or is it *me* who makes them look that way?

JM: Like the way you sometimes see me?

P: [Long pause] Yes, it's exactly the same! *I have a destructive stare.* I'm just beginning to realize this—I massacre with my eyes whatever I look at. Mon Dieu, why do I do that? What do I reproach *you* with? Was I cross with you today or the other days when your face looked paralyzed and disjointed? [Long pause] Voilà, I've got it! I can't bear it when you tell me things—your interpretations. Oh! I hate them—*especially* if I feel that they are important and useful to me. Makes me feel ill at ease, you can't imagine. Really, I can't take it when you think of things first. [That is, he cannot tolerate the narcissistic pain this causes him.]

JM: As though you were afraid of being dependent on me? That I might possess something that you could need?

P: Exactly! Especially if it's something I could have thought of for myself. At those moments I'd like to tear you to bits.

JM: Like a small child who is hungry might feel furious to have to depend on its mother, depend on her breasts, in order to be fed? Would that make him want to "tear them to bits"?

Paul's fantasies about making "black craters" in women's breasts lent themselves to this symbolic interpretation. It should be mentioned that Paul was breast-fed by his mother for more than three years. Perhaps such a nursing experience renders this type of fantasy more concrete than with those who have no conscious recall of the breast-feeding situation.

P: You know, I think that's very true. And I hate you for that. Merde alors, why should I have to *need* you?

Paul's narcissistic fragility is evident here, as is its relationship to the problem of *envy* in the Kleinian sense (Klein 1957): the trauma of otherness, the dependence on the attributes of the other that one does not possess. The original difference between two bodies and the question of their interdependence is more global and induces anxiety that is more invasive than phallic castration anxiety, with its frustrating mutual dependence upon the desire of the other. In its archaic beginnings the "difference" —the experience of absence—has failed to become truly symbolic for Paul and thus to offer the reward of subjective identity in its place. Need objects inevitably become objects of hate as well as of love, for the small infant. The "breast" (I am using the term *breast* as a concept, not as a concrete part object) is, from the beginning, a bad and hated object from this point of view. As such it cannot fail to awaken the anguished fear that one might destroy this source of life.

Small infants under the sway of hunger, solitude, or fear cannot tolerate the slightest delay. What Freud named the normal hallucinatory satisfaction of infants is short-lived, and babies are rapidly overwhelmed by uncontainable affect that might be called rage or even hate. Freud was also the first to point out that, in this state, nurslings need urgently to get rid of this torturing image of the breast-mother with which such feelings are immediately linked. The longed-for breast (and all it encompasses) becomes an object of horror whose representation is ejected from the psyche together with its accompanying affect. In so doing infants risk at the same time destroying part of their awareness of the erogenous zones awakened by their need. Observations of tiny infants show that the baby who has waited too long for the feeding mother is overwhelmed by rage and distress and tends to refuse the breast even though hungry. Thus we see that the mother has a delicate task to accomplish in her primitive communication with her baby. Not only must she represent all the valuable qualities of the "breast-universe"—food, warmth, tenderness, liveliness, and so on—she must at the same time be the one who helps her infant get rid of the persecuting and hated breast that the baby cannot eject alone without great psychic damage. Thus at one and the same time the breast becomes an image of idealization and of persecution.

Dreams and Visions

In the following clinical fragment Paul reveals that certain factors stemming from early babyhood traumata are still in operation and likely to be projected upon anyone on whom he feels dependent. These factors also contribute to his avoidance of fantasy. I believe that these elements, linked to envy in this sense—the envious hatred born out of frustrating dependence on an object that seems totally out of one's control—contribute to the so-called psychosomatic personality. Such phenomena may, however, provide us with an explanatory hypothesis for the lack of dream life so often manifested in somatizing patients. According to Freud, dreams begin to crystallize during waking life around perceptions, thoughts, events, and the feelings they arouse. The *day's residues* in patients like Paul are likely to be rapidly ejected from consciousness rather than repressed and held in storage for the making of dreams. It is possible that many such people experience fleeting hallucinatory moments instead of dreams. The excerpts of Paul's analysis that follow illustrate such moments, in which perceptions of the outer world are altered in response to instinctual stimuli but do not receive a psychotic reconstruction of meaning to explain them nor a protective neurotic construction. Instead there are operational maneuvers to stifle nascent affect and to pulverize unwelcome ideas, which are thus repudiated from the psyche without compensation. This form of psychic rejection needs to be distinguished from denial and disavowal, which are defenses against neurotic anxiety; the rejection described here is marshaled to deal with preneurotic anxiety: narcissistic fears for bodily and ego integrity, terrifying sadistic fantasies linked to archaic sexual impulses, and the self-object confusions of the earliest mother-child relationship.

At the point in the session when Paul was beginning to distinguish between his way of looking and his fear of being looked at, it became clear that he foreclosed from consciousness all primitive erotic and sadistic impulses, so that his perception of others was correspondingly altered. Suddenly—and for the first time—he associated to his boyhood memories of his father in some of his father's more neurotic aspects, in particular his rigid control of instinctual impulses. Paul's father was known to be "strong and calm"; he paid "special attention to cleanliness." It is probable that Paul was clinging at that moment to the image of his father as "strong and calm" in order to shield him from the fantasied danger that he might make a sadistic attack upon the mother's body. Paul went on to describe his father's concern for cleanliness at the table and with regard to food and—what had impressed him most of all—a series of obsessional rituals around defecation and everything attached to it. These appeared to indicate the father's, and hence Paul's, anxiety linked to any anal signifiers.

> P: My father was so concerned about bodies and dirt that I could never imagine how my parents ever made love. My dad always issued grave warnings against the dangers of masturbation—and yet curiously enough he pushed me constantly to be "virile." I was never to forget that I was a "man"—I had to show interest in girls, in fact, had to screw! Like a masculine ideal that was beyond my capacities.

This portrait of Paul's father (which recalls, in certain respects, one of the internal fathers in Isaac's psychic theater, described in chapter 4) rather suggests that this father may have wished his son to live out heterosexual wishes in his place so that he might, through identification, participate homosexually. Such a hypothesis would not contradict the apparent signs of the father's neurosis and the image of false virility that emanates from Paul's descriptions. Whatever the external reality may have been, Paul felt himself propelled toward heterosexual relations to please his father, while at the same time he carried in his unconscious deeply archaic fears of the female body and sex—a dangerously attacking sexual image, with no clear representation of the father's penis as playing either an imaginary or a symbolic role in it. It is possible that Paul's apparently "normal" sexuality stirred up unrecognizable conflicts of a primitive order. When these were not experienced in an alienated fashion, they tended to be impregnated with virulent sadistic elements, such as the fantasy that his penis was a "white-hot pick" (McDougall 1978, pp. 404–5) and that his wife was impaled upon it.*

While Paul was attempting to come to terms with the idea that his parents must have shared a sexual life, since there were other children and he sometimes heard strange noises coming from their bedroom, I recalled that he had often spoken of his mother's outbursts of crying and that these always seemed mysterious to him. It seemed evident to me that his image of the primal scene, as it applied to his own parents, would include a fantasy of sadistic attack. While pondering this I leaned forward to ask Paul what he thought about it.

P: What's the matter with you? Mon Dieu, what's wrong? You moved suddenly.

JM: What might be wrong?

P: My first thought—just like that—was that you'd had a cerebral hemorrhage! I saw you quite clearly before my eyes, your face all out of joint and dislocated. Paralyzed for good. It was really horrible.

JM: If you behave like a virile male, as your father said you should, would I then run the risk of being physically destroyed?

P: Mon Dieu, if you only knew . . . the worst is that I truly believe it! I'm really afraid of destroying you and mashing you up. You're fragile and I have to be very careful of my thoughts about you. [Long pause] I wonder if you realize how great my panic is?

Paul firmly believes in the omnipotence of both his thoughts and his wishes. He is not able as yet to allow himself that transitional space for playing in which one can safely play around with ideas and fantasies and explore strong feelings without danger. He is still afraid of being unable (or even wishing) to contain and elaborate such thoughts and feelings without acting upon them.

---

*One year later Paul was tortured by an obsessive thought that he might "attack his wife with the ice pick." He had totally repressed the earlier fantasies and developed this transitory neurotic symptom instead.

JM: What might happen to me?

P: I'm scared to tell you . . . it's because of that poster—the girl with the beautiful bare breasts, and I was so frightened because I dug those big black craters—you know it's come true! I saw the poster again yesterday and *I saw the craters.* When I got up close I saw there were huge flies on her breasts—and I swear they made craters just on the nipples. I nearly fell over . . . everything spinning. All my old ideas came rushing back. Impossible to stop them. [We see here Paul's difficulty in *repressing* thoughts that should have become part of the day's residues and perhaps the material of dreams.] I started to bite those breasts, tear at them with my teeth, and they became all bloody and emptied out with great black craters in them.

Paul tosses his head from side to side as though to shake these images out of his mind. A simple external perception has suddenly come to confirm an inner terror and brought him perilously close to a psychotic moment. He mutters, "I saw them, I saw them!"

Paul's fundamental fantasy of the primal scene is a condensed oedipal situation reduced to the baby's mouth and the nipple. Everything that happens between this couple is potentially dangerous and disintegrating. In attempting to imagine his parents making love—and then thinking of his father's exhortations to have sexual relations—he has rapidly come back to the black craters in the nipples. We are tempted to surmise that Paul, as a baby, was never sure that he could throw himself with avid pleasure upon his mother's breast and that the nursing experience could be loving and good for both partners. Instead he appears to imagine himself as filled with sadistic hate and his mother as attacked and crying. There is little structure to the oedipal organization, except that in the present session the father begins to occupy an important position, even though his phallic attributes are largely expressed in anal and oral metaphors. Two years ago Paul imagined that his penis could cause dark brown shadows to fall on my breasts (McDougall 1978). Earlier attempts to analyze these primitive pregenital fantasies gave little new material, but this time there are the flies and his awareness of considerable panic. So I ask him, much as I would had it been a dream scene, "And what about those flies? Where did they come from?"

P: They're the kind of flies that sit on shit. Good heavens —the black craters—would they be craters full of shit? Have I thrown all that shit on them?

JM: Maybe just now you put all your shit in me and that produced a cerebral hemorrhage?

At this moment I feel that it is wiser to give a transference interpretation than to attach this primitive fantasy to an early oedipal notion. I also hope to join the theme of enviousness and to see whether the "nourishing breast" is imagined as being in my head, where Paul would once again want to attack me because of my psychoanalytical knowledge, which makes him so angry. But he surprises me with another fantasy dimension:

P: Yes, you're absolutely right. I know exactly what the cerebral hemorrhage means—it's the orgasm! Women's orgasms fill me with horror . . . always the same image of her inside in a state of liquification . . . everything black and shapeless and floating about.

Archaic Oedipal Elements Find Their First Expression

It is interesting to recall at this point a session two years ago in which Paul sought to fill my head with "disorder"—the disorder coming from an image of his own head as being "split in two." These thoughts had arisen following an incident of depersonalization Paul had experienced in a crowded street. At the same time it was impossible to attach his nameless terror to any coherent inner fantasy or to any sexual representations other than fluid, fusional, or unbridled images of part objects in terrifying conjunctions. At present there is remarkable progress in that he now has at his disposal a chain of pregenital sexual images, as we can see from the excerpts just quoted. Having access to these fantasies and being able to verbalize them helps Paul to stay the course of his instinctual impulses and give them nascent meaning that can be analyzed. The "disorder inside the head" was a prefiguration of his archaic sexual imagery that had not yet reached consciousness and gives us a glimpse of a first outline of early oedipal structure. With the "liquification" and "craters full of shit" imagery, one sees the beginning of a fecal-phallic representation of the father and his role in penetrating and limiting the maternal body, even though the representation may be at a very primitive level of body fantasy.

Paul's primal scene fantasy is also expressed in an archaic image of the baby at the breast in which the little boy attacks the breast-mother in devouring and fecalizing ways. Such imagery is no doubt drawn from the small infant's bodily experience of his erogenous zones. These erotic early experiences may be thought of as unifying factors that contribute richly to the consolidation of the body-image, but when there is a disturbed or frightening fantasy exchange in the early relationship, there is the risk that the small child will in fact lose touch with certain erogenous zones so that they become to some extent autonomous and indeed autistic. As we shall see later, one of the results of analyzing this primitive fantasy material is Paul's conclusion that he is "learning to defecate for the first time in his life"—that is, he allows his anal zone and its functions some psychic existence.*

Paul's new-found capacity to imagine leads him to replace a formless, irrepresentable idea of the female sex with one in which the woman's inner body space may be penetrated by a

---

*It is tempting to speculate on the possibility that respiratory sufferers and those who have psychosomatic disorders of the digestive and eliminatory system might also come to feel that they "possess" these zones and functions for the first time as a result of the analytic process. The vital functions require the mother's assistance to become invested for the infant as *pleasurable*. Their necessity in order to survive does not in itself suffice to guarantee adequate functioning.

paternal fecal phallus. Then follows his terror that this act will cause liquification and destruction—the "orgasm-cataclysm" that "fills him with horror." In fact, he is beginning to discover his early infantile sexual theories. From the time that these could be verbalized and worked through, he was able to create neurotic defenses rather than psychosomatic explosions.

Paul is thus leaving the terrain in which love relations are fusional and unlimited for another in which the object is differentiated and may be possessed, but to its destruction. This is the counterpart to the experience of primary identity in which one is but a small, though essential, part of a great whole (Lichtenstein 1961). Paul is moving painfully out of this morass, since he now is able to possess some objects of exchange—even though partial and limited to factors such as "taking" by looking or "giving" through one's feces. To protect himself from the fear of vengeful retaliation that such budding fantasy engenders and arouses in bodily experience, Paul had somehow managed to reject all such representations from consciousness and sustain an empty, nonfeeling, and sterile psychic space instead, thus enabling him to maintain relationships with others without too much fear, but with an inexpressible emotion of sadness and of being out of touch with others. The oedipal organization, largely reduced to a mother-image split in two through the projection of alternative feelings of rage and love, was neither containable nor thinkable for Paul. In the psychic silence that ensued, this total area of experiencing was inaccessible to verbal thought. It is only recently that he is able to support the "visions" produced by primary-process thinking that result from the dilemma of his painful conflict. The pseudoperceptions that now flood into his mind are something like lost dreams and perhaps similar to what the infant experiences.

Unable to recognize his powerful and painful emotions, Paul often said he saw my face as "dislocated" or "broken into different planes." This filled him with horror since he could not reflect on it. I experienced his "vision" much as I had once reacted to Picasso's famous portrait "Crying Woman," whose visage is also dislocated and severed into many planes as though split by conflicting emotions of hate and love. In this case it is the eye of the artist who perceives her face in this way and communicates his vision to us. It is no doubt one of the primordial psychological functions of the artist to communicate and render tolerable such painful visions and such ambivalent and violent feeling. Paul, on the other hand, has never been able to contain conflicting violence, let alone render it communicable even to himself, perhaps because he was not aided in this task at a time when it was crucial for him. For in fact it is the mother's task to render her infant's primitive emotional experience tolerable. It is she, the fundamental artist, who must give meaning to violent feeling and make bearable for the psyche all that is unacceptable and insupportable to the new human being. Owing to difficulties in the early relationship with his mother, this protective inner structure is lacking in Paul's psychic make-up. Among the results are a lack of distinction between inner and outer reality and a fear that violent and hostile impulses, by the very act of thinking about them, will be realized.

Paul's primitive and condensed oedipal organization, fraught with sadism and largely built around the presence-and-absence of the breast-mother, has been very little elaborated, giving him a persecutory vision of the external world. His capacity to expel troubling perceptions from the psyche, however, has enabled him to keep persecutory ideas at a distance. Grafted onto his archaic sexual fantasy is an adult sexual life of a false-self kind; the father, though lacking in symbolic significance in Paul's inner world, nevertheless incited his son to "virility" and thus to a certain phallic-genital compliance, giving rise to a form of pseudogenitality and pseudonormality.

A "double-bind" father may lead a child to cover up a fundamental layer of deadly anguish that can then achieve no psychic representation. We can summarize Paul's unconscious dilemma (and that of many others who resemble him) in these terms:

It is dangerous or even fatal for me to love a woman and to have sexual relations with her. Not only do I risk destroying her, but I too may be destroyed in return. Yet my father pushes me to be "a man," pushes me to kill my mother and also pushes me to my own death [a death that perhaps he is afraid of and wishes I would undergo in his place].

These are the terms of the double-bind message.

The father, in view of his own neurotic sexual fears, may have offered the son to the mother as phallic compensation, there to play the role of hostage in order to guarantee the father's integrity. In any case it became evident that Paul had created no solid defenses against phallic castration anxiety but endured unrecountable terrors in his sexual and love relations that constituted repetitive traumas of an "actual" kind in the sense that Freud gave to this term.

Paul's castration anxiety, of a global and primitive nature, is experienced as an ill-defined and cataclysmic danger—the liquification of the interior of the woman's body. It was not surprising that such preoccupations also reawakened in Paul fears for his own corporeal integrity, frequently represented in terms of falling to pieces, exploding, or dissolving. A series of hypochondriacal concerns that were distinctly different in character from his concern about his psychosomatic maladies now began to come to the fore. In several sessions he was waiting to catch viral influenza; he became convinced he was a victim of skin cancer; and then became preoccupied with ocular problems. The latter finally took over and aroused anxiety to such a point that eventually he produced genuine hysterical symptoms; I shall return to this important episode later.

Paul began the following session by speaking of a couple he had met and his feeling that the wife looked rather "bashed up," adding, "The very sight of this couple gave me a ferocious migraine." He went on to remark that I did not appear to be in very good health, either. Thinking he might be ready to link his hypochondriacal fantasies to his wish-and-fear of attacking women, I drew his attention to the fact that either his body or that of the woman was under attack.

P: Oh, là! Now you're the one who's getting it. But I mustn't even think such things, or you might really fall ill. I'm terribly afraid of such thoughts, you know. [He is still optimistically omnipotent, but he is nevertheless discovering his hatred for this destructive part of himself.]

JM: Afraid they might become magic and fulfill themselves?

P: There you go again! OK, let's plunge on. Why is it so terrible to imagine you with black craters in your nipples anyway? [He tosses his head from side to side again.] But I know why! It's because for me the breasts are the most beautiful, most soft, and most sensual part of the woman's body. I just can't bear to see myself attacking them. [His voice trembles and he seems to be on the verge of tears. This might well be considered as an approach to the *depressive position.* *] I feel as though I destroy everyone. Nadine—my mother—I look at them and I see them looking grotesque, deformed, aged. But with you it's worst of all. To you I mete out death. It's truly horrible.

Each time Paul feels I am "worn out"—that is to say, dying—he fears that in some obscure way he is the cause.

P: I really don't understand anything anymore. Why is everything erotic invariably full of horror for me? I want to make love and I imagine scenes of torture. Ow! I'm beginning to have terrible gastric pains!

We are back on familiar territory in which Paul's body and that of the Other are one and the same. If he has a skin cancer and I a cerebral hemorrhage, it is an identical event. So now the wheel has come full circle and Paul once again attacks the interior of his own body. But the long detour has permitted us to elaborate considerably the intervening areas of buried fan-

---

*This concept refers to a form of object relationship that is installed after the decline of the "paranoid-schizoid position." Among other features it is characterized by a fear of destroying the mother or losing her love because of one's sadistic impulses (Klein 1935).

tasy. This recent working through has in fact allowed him to attach new significance to his gastric malady. At the very least he is now capable of recognizing painful affect along with its accompanying fantasy, and indeed he seems more confident of his ability to contain such psychic experience without plunging into immediate action. In fact on this occasion Paul himself provides an "interpretation" of his gastric spasms.

> P: I harden up my whole body, tighten my inside, as though I wish to *prevent* such horrible thoughts—if I tense up enough maybe they won't come to mind. But that's a bit crazy—now let's see, what's wrong with these thoughts, anyway?

While he is exploring this idea he suddenly becomes aware that the sharp gastric pain has disappeared. He is astonished by this "miracle," and he begins to question this way of using his body to prevent himself from thinking. He recounts, for example, that certain women irritate him because he feels "penetrated" by their way of looking at him, as though they wish to invade and take possession of him. Quite frequently in these situations he suffers from sudden explosions of diarrhea. At a subsequent session, speaking of a colleague, he says, "She tears out my bowels" and adds "but I find it exciting to get rid of her, get her out of my system, in this violent way."

It would seem that Paul (like Isaac in chapter 6) has always tried to use his body or its functions to control or expel unacceptable thoughts and overwhelming emotion, rather than allow himself to be psychically "penetrated" by his emotions and their associated drive representations. He is still afraid of what might happen if he had free access to such thoughts. During this same phase of his analysis I noted the following "vision":

> P: There's a rabbit jerking up and down in front of me and some men are trying to force something into its anus. It looks terrified but doesn't try to escape. Look, the rabbit's wearing glasses!

At my invitation Paul provides associations to this fantasy. He says that the rabbit is wearing *his* glasses, and it knows that the men are actually doing something that is good for it. At this point he becomes anxious and breaks off to say:

P: But it would mean total confusion to allow just any thoughts to take possession of me. Disorganization—illness! I couldn't stand it—I'd go crazy.

This "disorganization" in Paul's mind indicates a creative movement. I am reminded once again of former sessions (McDougall 1978) in which Paul wished to pass on to me his "disorganization," hoping my "head would split in two." Even then, such a wish was a new and creative adventure in psychic experience for him, since it was at this time that he began to allow his affective experience to take mental shape; he became interested in these representations, even though he felt himself on the edge of a delusional experience. In fact he was crossing the frontier between pure bodily sensation ("something is shrinking in my stomach") and the translation of this somatic representation into an affective one capable of being named, symbolized, verbalized, and elaborated. At the present time it is the analytic situation and relationship upon which Paul is counting to act as a "protective shield" against being overwhelmed emotionally—a maternal function that may not have been within his mother's capacity in his early childhood. Paul now looks to the analysis to give structure and words to what he is experiencing, so that he may overcome the fear of going mad.

Such experience in psychic growing must inevitably use another person, in the same way that infants require someone to name their emotional states and put them into a context in which they can be utilized by the processes of thought. It is essential that a mother on occasion tell her child, "You are feeling sad . . . perhaps it is because . . .," when she perceives that the child is struggling with emotion and able only to act it out, not yet having the psychic wherewithal to reflect upon it and contain it. Words are invaluable containers! Should a mother instead deny her children's obvious emotion or insist upon affective states that they should be feeling rather than what they truly experience, there is a risk, as emphasized in previous chapters, that the children will grow up denying their affective lives and remaining out of touch with important sectors of their psychic reality— in fact, unable to think about emotionally important events in their lives.

Increasingly complex psychic elaboration now led Paul to linking corporeal reality to his imaginative life. As he found the courage to express his emotional experiences more freely, his somatic perceptions slowly became symbolic, while his somatizations decreased. But the going was hard. He was often overwhelmed by frightening "visions" of his body, or other people's bodies, torn to pieces or floating in infinite space. These aroused intense panic, but the panic experiences were of shorter duration. Anal-sadistic images predominated. He moved from metaphors of fecal attack, exploding bodies, and torn skin to fantasies of emptying a woman of her body matters by making love to her. In this way the anal-sadism began to take on an erotic tinge and led him (to his intense excitement and terror) to fantasies of amorously eating his partner's fecal matter or absorbing her body fluids in mysterious and affectionate ways. He would sometimes say that these erotic imaginings were making him crazy, but we were able to see the small child within him who was fascinated by all body zones and contents, his own and those of his parents.

P: A curious thing has happened. I'm beginning to *defecate* for the first time in my life. Truly a new experience. I've never been aware of defecating before. Where was I all this time?

It would seem that Paul's *I* did not possess or recognize as his own his body in its anal and urethral functioning. Either it belonged to someone else or it had no psychic existence. This experience comes close to being delusional. Through the slow construction of body dramas and zonal discoveries it became possible to reconstruct Paul's lost childhood fantasies. In particular, at this point, it was important to be able to link the anal product as a precious love-gift with its counterpart, feces as a sadistic weapon that might create havoc in one's own or the other's body. It became apparent that the anal-erotic gift was a highly forbidden link with his mother, and the anal-sadistic weapon was, at another level of fantasy, used against her, with the fear that she would empty him out ("tear out his bowels") and fill him with shame. It was also a revelation to Paul to realize that this intricate series of fecal fantasies found an echo in the immense importance accorded by his father to anal functioning. Thus we were able to explore the complicated mosaic of Paul's infantile sexuality with its interdictions, as well as his infantile narcissism with its delicate economic balance; both had been interwoven into his somatic self instead of being dealt with psychically. The underlying scenarios all related to the extreme danger that might result from any exchange between two people. From now on we followed two scenarios at the same time—the relationship between one body and another regardless of sex and the relationship between bodies of different sexes.

Consolidation of the Body-Image and Its Sexual Functions

The analytic material of this period, largely confined to fecal metaphors and signifiers, was accepted by Paul with great difficulty (as is true of most analysands). In classical fashion it led to symbolic chains such as anus-vagina-feces-sperm, or breast-nipple-eye-pupil, and from there to his inhibitions in the field of work, particularly his intellectual and creative activities. The important factor was that the anal part-object representation now had psychic existence for Paul. Since feces are, for every child, the fundamental unconscious representation of objects of *exchange* in the psychic space that separates one individual from another, our analytic exploration at this point no doubt contributed to the fact that Paul now found himself more at ease with his colleagues, friends, and family, and in a general way more at ease in his body. He came eventually to attach the anal-erotic exploration to his mother and her body.

P: I keep thinking of her and of my intense curiosity as a child—especially my wish to see her going to the toilet. I can imagine her now, as though she were defecating, and it is a tender image. She looks—how shall I put it?—*very feminine.* Suddenly her body is no longer disgusting to me.

Paul is able to accept the female genitals, but on condition that he add the anal product. He now permits himself to imagine these things, however, and thus prepares the ground for thinking about genital relationships.

P: I am thinking of a photo of my mother. I spent an hour hunting for it the other day. Mon Dieu, how pretty she was! Young, laughing—it was as though I'd forgotten *that* mother. Good heavens, I can see the photo in front of me, but something terrible has happened—*there's a mustache on her face!*

The screening function that would normally block primary-process thinking is once again in abeyance; a dreamlike activity suddenly takes the place of thought. On this occasion we see that condensation and displacement are both in operation: displacement upward of the anal-phallic object and the condensation of meaning that allows us to see that Paul is again completing the female sex organ with an anal derivative of the paternal phallus; he borrows a masculine symbol to put this on stage.

P: Oh, my poor mother! Why have I defaced you like that? And I've even made her hair all messy and curled.

JM: Does this remind you of anything?

P: Yes! A game I used to play with my sister—I would put a Hitler-type mustache on her face. But it isn't Hitler's mustache, *it's my father's.* Poor mother—why have I made you so ugly suddenly?

JM: As though your mother becomes "ugly" when an image of your father intervenes?

The sequences that followed this dream-vision enabled us to understand that from his childhood vantage point Paul imagined his mother as "dirtied" and "uglied" by sexual relations with his father. The anxious reactions attached to her bodily ills (her "dry skin," "infected spots," and so on) were engendered by the fantasy of her being filled by the fecal-phallic father, which gave rise to feelings of strangeness and disgust and the wish to reject all physical contact with her (while at the same time desiring it). Paul had not been able to construct an oedipal situation that could be imagined and thought about— and eventually undergo repression. This could have led to recognizing his jealousy of the parental couple, which in turn would have allowed him to create a true secondary identification to his father and renounce the fulfillment of his incestuous love for his mother. But none of this took place. Instead he was possessed of the envious wish to destroy the objects of desire that he did not possess. Instead of forming neurotic constructions to protect against oedipal distress, Paul had become a plaything of primitive forces that his ego did not control. He reacted to passing perceptions and situations that were apt to awaken his envious wishes and his terror of retribution, rather like someone who reacts with affect-shock to Rorschach cards: black immediately represents feces or death, red becomes blood or murder, and so on. It is possible that such psychic functioning is closely linked to archaic experience, as well as to the

phenomena of the actual neuroses, with their inexplicable outbursts of uncontrollable anxiety or sudden depression, mobilized by everyday events and perceptions of which the individual is unaware because they have been foreclosed from
consciousness.

It became apparent that, before his analysis, Paul had always
managed to render meaningless any perceptions likely to awaken
strong emotion. Consequently his somatic self alone was called
upon to react to the dangerous situation in question. The discovery of this psychosomatic defense was one of the fruits of his
analytic experience. His outburst of overwhelming emotion and
psychotic terror in certain sessions, equivalent to an anxiety neurosis, might also be considered as an archaic form of hysteria, but
one in which subjective existence itself, rather than sexual desire,
is threatened.

The Eyes Attack Themselves

A further fragment from Paul's analysis illustrates the "neu-
rotization" of his conflicts. He continued to have sudden "visions" and pseudoperceptions, but in the weeks following the
sessions just described he was able to examine them more
thoughtfully and with less fear that he was going crazy. Around
the same time he found the courage to tell me certain of his
thoughts that did indeed have a psychotic overtone to them. For
example, he noticed that his watch would suddenly go fast, and
he was convinced that the intensity of his feelings was responsible. The idea that his thoughts and feelings were "so powerful"
was terrifying to him. This was also the period when he became
aware of "blind spots" in his field of vision; his preoccupation
with this phenomenon, which he referred to as his "scotoma,"
reached hypochondriacal proportions, and he was sure he was
suffering from some serious eye disease. At the same time he
became increasingly aware of his capacity for "seeing" things that
had no external reality but corresponded to internal stress and
moments of anxiety.

P: I had a moment of madness when I came in just now. I saw your face broken up once more into three different planes, in three pieces. Yet I know it isn't true. It doesn't frighten me as much as it used to. It's just that *my eyes are sick.* That reminds me of my scotoma. Yesterday I finally went to see an opthalmologist. Would you believe it, he said everything was perfectly normal—no ocular spasm, and the retina is in perfect condition! But I keep seeing these black spots and the big scotoma is often there. Whatever he says, I don't see things the way I should.

From this point on Paul follows an associative discourse closely resembling a normal-neurotic one. He uses his body-images metaphorically. That is, he is beginning to "de-somatize" his approach to himself. He still has pseudoperceptions, but he now questions them.

P: I can tell what's going wrong by my way of seeing things nowadays—and I know that what I *think* I see is just a reflection of what I'm thinking, much of the time. Take this girl in my office—the one who flatters me so much. She really takes so much interest in everything I say that I begin to feel quite high on myself. So I often invite her to have coffee with me, and then the same thing happens with her as with you. Quite unexpectedly her face changes. Like when she suddenly criticizes me. She's really quite cute, but all of a sudden I see her looking like a gawky kid, dirty, unkempt, and sort of ugly. Even her gestures seem to me excessive and bizarre. It's really frightful and I have to get out rapidly at those moments, or else I'm swamped with anxiety—or like I told you, I might have a sudden bowel movement.

Paul goes on to talk of other women in his office, in particular one whom he finds unusually attractive. She has a small baby and he always refers to her as the "young mother," as though this factor were of specific importance to his feelings about her.

P: Ah, that reminds me of the young mother, the one I desire sexually. I can't stop thinking of her breasts and her fragility.

These phrases have also been used to describe Paul's transference preoccupations, and it is probable that his interest in the young mother includes that form of acting out that may be referred to as *lateral transference,* in which the patient projects onto someone in the outer world feelings that have been aroused in the analytic relationship. This may account for the following associations.

P: Her fragility—um—where was I? Funny, I've completely lost the thread of my thought. A void. Just as though I were up against a blank wall. Good God! *There's my scotoma back again!* [Sudden repression is followed by the reappearance of the hysterical manifestation.]

JM: What were you thinking of just before the scotoma appeared? When you said you felt as though you were up against a blank wall?

P: Haven't the vaguest. Don't even remember what I was talking about.

JM: The young mother who seems so fragile . . .

P: Oh là là! Do I dare let myself think just *anything* about her? Well, I see myself undressing her, and I'm biting her breasts, and I start to make love furiously to her, like a madman, and I sodomize her, and I eat her feces . . . I can't do this! If I follow your system of saying everything that comes into my mind I'll go quite crazy. Heavens—the scotoma has disappeared!

It is interesting to note that Paul's blind spot disappears at the very moment at which he allows himself to put into words some of his rejected and anxiety-arousing primitive erotic fantasies. What he once experienced as altered perceptions are now expressed verbally in the form of pregenital sexual wishes and fantasies. Behind his supposedly genital desire for the young mother Paul discovers the wish to eat her breasts and her body substances. Faced with the difficulty of keeping these archaic fantasies out of consciousness, he produces a hysterical symptom —he "sees" black spots in front of his eyes. In other words Paul does not wish to "see himself" in this light.

Archaic Hysteria and Its Transformations

It would perhaps be more exact to describe such symptoms as a primitive form of hysteria, a defense against pregenital libidinal wishes that have remained blocked and encapsulated rather than elaborated as fantasies to be subsequently repressed. These wishes stem from partial drives that would seem not to have become "genitalized" but to have remained in an embryonic state and therefore inaccessible to symbolic storage. The fact that Paul did not wish to see some portion of his psychic reality and the ensuing mechanism by which he avoided it—the production of blind spots in his field of vision—represents a highly significant change in psychic functioning: the attack upon the external world is now turned back upon himself. The "black craters" in the nipples have become black spots located in his own eyes— another clinical example of Klein's (1935) concept of "working through the depressive position."

The capacity of the ego to attack its own perceptual apparatus and functions is pertinent to our reflection on psychosomatic phenomena—and to the underlying significance of operational thinking and alexithymic defects. This fragment of Paul's analysis confirms my belief that the phenomena so often associated with the so-called psychosomatic personality pattern are not necessarily defects or a lack of psychic capacity but massive defenses against narcissistic or psychotic fears. Faced with what Bion (1970) describes as "nameless dread," one can construct a void in which terror can be kept at bay. In the throes of anguishing fantasies, such as those described by Paul in which he has not only had to accept his inability to protect his inner objects against destruction and death but also to support an intolerably bad narcissistic image, many people might well become alexithymic and operational in their psychic functioning. The alternative might seem like madness. Paul and many patients like him are truly afraid of losing touch with reality, of going crazy if they allow fantasy and feeling to invade their minds.

In the session just described, however, it may be seen that Paul is no longer faced with anonymous terror. He is now able to attach his painful affective states to mental representations; these begin to reflect common infantile sexual theories and their accompanying pregenital impulses.

The next session with Paul brought further confirmation of the hypothesis advanced here with regard to his scotoma.

P: Nadine is awfully aggressive to me lately. She reproaches me all the time for all the things I fail to do. It's really painful. I must admit that I never fulfill half of my projects and that I'm always breaking promises. But when she points it out in that relentless way of hers everything collapses inside me. Yesterday she started in ... [he gives details of his latest failures] and I tried not to listen but at the same time trying to give the impression of listening to her. And suddenly there was the scotoma again! A huge blind spot in my right eye. I realized that this often happens in her presence. But this time I made myself *think* about it—and I understood it all by myself. I knew right away what I was feeling— that I wanted to tear her up into a thousand pieces because I was so fed up with her complaints. And the scotoma immediately disappeared!

The situation here is on the borderline between pseudoperception with psychotic overtones and a process of "hystericalization" with neurotic overtones. The pseudoperceptions might be attributed to the work of an implacable, archaic superego agency that will not tolerate the slightest narcissistic wound and the neurotic creations—in view of their incestuous roots and their primitive expression—to a compromise between infantile sexual wishes and their interdictions. Paul can now permit himself to be in closer contact with his psychic reality, even if it brings him face to face with frightening fantasies and impulses, such as his devouring fantasies concerning the young mother and his sadistic fantasies toward his wife. The blind spots in his visual field are like a last line of defense against recognizing these primitive impulses, in both their narcissistic and their object orientation, and against the painful affects associated with them. He is nevertheless confused about what is and what is not real during this period. When he chooses to disavow his perception of his inner drives, rather than assume responsibility for his libidinal and death-dealing impulses and the fantasies in which they are embodied, the pseudoperceptions reappear. Toward the end of the session he says:

> P: But you know, when my wife persecutes me in this way I watch her carefully and her face is truly changed—she simply is not the same person and that frightens me.

On this occasion I recalled to him our recent sessions in which he had gained clear insight into the fact that what changed was not the external world and the people in it but his own vision of himself. When he was filled with unacceptable feelings of hate, rage, and destruction, his *I* did not want to recognize these feelings as part of him, since they did not fit in with his own ideal image. The image was so wounding that he preferred to feel it was the others who changed at such moments. (I found myself giving many interpretations concerning Paul's mode of mental functioning throughout this phase of his analysis. The dynamic content and exploration of the transference relationship were insufficient to advance his psychoanalytic process.)

Hallucinatory Experience and the Failure of the Ego

Paul's narcissistic fragility, common to many others faced with untamed affects and unacceptable fantasies, raises several theoretical questions. By what economic and dynamic means is the psyche able to manipulate the perception of external reality? What enables the *I* to submit to hallucinatory experience? Why has repression not worked in regard to the conflicts every infant has to face in learning to oppose the tendency to hallucinatory wish-fulfillment in times of frustration? After all, one of the primordial tasks of the ego is to *prevent* hallucination as a solution to inner conflict. What forces allow the maintenance of the confusion of inner and outer reality in subjects who are not dominated by psychotic thought processes?*

We have seen that the incapacity to dream and to daydream is often observed among psychosomatic patients (Warnes 1982). Quite apart from the fact that the apparent lack of capacity to dream or to pursue a private fantasy life is by no means reserved for psychosomatic sufferers, this missing dimension in the psychic life of people with a high psychosomatic vulnerability demands reflection. As we know, the day's residues that are not given any attention at the moment they occur are subsequently sorted through and repressed. They then serve as figurative elements for the creation of dreams to express inner psychic conflicts and wishes. The person who is ill equipped psychically to repress perceptions, images, and ideas that would otherwise inhibit functioning in the daytime may be obliged instead to eliminate them totally from the psyche. We might surmise that such a person not

---

*It is also interesting to speculate as to what developmental phase in childhood permits the distinction between inner and outer reality. I recall an incident when my grandson Joshua, almost three, had come with his parents to visit us. My daughter complained that Joshua had kept the family awake for weeks because "his room was full of monsters." I took it upon myself to attempt to allay Joshua's fears by telling him that the monsters belonged to him—they were only in his head and he could call them back when he wanted and even put them to sleep. He looked at me incredulously and pointed to his head. Then he promised he would try to sleep. I went off highly pleased with myself but was called back by Joshua within a matter of minutes. "Nana, Nana, come quickly; the monsters are coming out of my ears!" He could still see them. Obviously believing that I was crazy, he was trying desperately, as children always do, to fit in with my theory!

only would suffer from a lack of propitious images for representing on the dream scene the night thoughts that are seeking hallucinatory expression but in addition might also be subject to brief moments of hallucination. We might well wonder whether many daily incidents capable of mobilizing affect contain within themselves an eventual hallucinatory potentiality. Perhaps everyone's experience of the perceptual world has to be filtered, in some way or another, by selective psychic functioning, and obviously the most economical channel for such psychic experience is hallucination in dreams. The use of psychedelic drugs demonstrates the hallucinatory potential that follows from the breaking down of the selective filtering function.

This hypothesis does not, however, provide any answer to the question of why certain patients are unable to contain, and eventually repress, the bombardment of thoughts and affects mobilized by perceptions stemming from the external world or from the inner instinctual sphere. Without recovery of the lost material in the form of dreams, daydreams, sublimatory activities, or delusions, consciousness is deprived of potential enrichment. Among the possible factors leading to this sort of failure is the lack of distinction between inner and outer reality—in other words, the continuing belief in the omnipotence of thoughts and wishes. When patients believe that they have only to imagine something for it to happen, the two realities are immediately confused. Faced with such a dilemma, the subjects must henceforth avoid feeling and fantasizing in order to protect themselves and both their inner and their outer objects from what might befall them.

This brings us back once more to the experience of early infancy, in which the caretaking parent who causes the infant to feel rage, frustration, and hatred is also the one who provides her baby with gratification, pleasure, and appeasement. In the relentless search for comfort and pleasure, the infant eventually creates a unified image of the mother, which implies at the same time the acquisition of a unified image of the self—not only of the body as a whole, including its sensitivity to libidinal stimulation, but also of the psyche as a container within which it is possible to retain and work over contradictory emotions of love and hate, centered on the person of the mother. In patients like Paul this inner structure is missing.

We are led back to speculations about the factors that favor such an impasse in psychic functioning and the breakdown in the mother's role as a filtering or protective screen for her infant. External reality is an abstract entity that has to be *constructed;* it does not exist per se. The early relationship between mother and infant plays a fundamental role in this aspect of ego functioning.

Considering the difficulties that Paul experienced in mastering his view of the external perceptual world, as inner psychic pressures constantly infiltrated his perception of it, his recognition that it is he who "changes," and not his wife, when he is in narcissistic pain is an important step forward. Until he could verbalize his feelings of rage and his destructive impulses toward his wife and finally join these to fantasies of envious attack against all women for what he felt they possessed and he did not, he was likely to reexperience his affective storms as pseudoperceptions in which it was the object that aroused him that changed. To this series of fantasies were eventually added Paul's discovery of the archaic libidinal wishes implied in his "attacks" upon women's bodies, which enabled us to understand that the "blind spot" now served to obliterate the woman as a sexual object along with his complicated desires toward her.

The Primitive Oedipal Organization Becomes a Phallic-Genital One

The following fragment illustrates clearly the way in which the foregoing material allowed access for the first time to the analysis of true oedipal material.

Paul has given much thought to his scotoma and has finally acquired the certain knowledge that he alone is responsible for producing his varied pseudoperceptual phenomena. In this session, he tries to discover what it is about the woman's body that makes him so anxious.

P: I am at my most fragile when I make love—the woman becomes terribly dangerous at those moments, and I am only just beginning to realize this fully. I become very vigilant . . . Huh! A blank—I don't even know what I was going to say. Ah yes, the woman—oh là là, I'm sliding down dangerous slopes in talking about this. I really must try not to think about it.

JM: So you're having recourse to your scotoma once more? Each time you come up against a frightening thought or feeling, you draw a blank over it—like the woman's sex being a dangerous slope?

P: Voilà! But it goes even further than that. The scotoma makes me anguished enough—and I'm sure that it's a way of not seeing, that is, not *knowing* something. But the trouble is I don't know what. At such moments I'm filled with a most terrible anguish, like a frenetic primordial dread.

JM: Faced with the woman's body when you make love?

P: Yes, yes, of course—but especially just after making love—I simply *can't look* at the woman; *she becomes a vampire.* [Long pause] I'm thinking of that film of Polanski's about the vampire-killers. It upset me for weeks. I'm really afraid of the woman when she turns into a vampire.

JM: Yet you were the one who had daydreams of eating up women who attracted you sexually—like the young mother, you remember? You wanted to eat her breasts and her excrements. Do you think that the frightening and destructive side of your own fantasies could make you afraid that the woman is going to vampirize *you?*

P: Oh, I don't know about that! God, I've got palpitations just thinking about it, exactly the same palpitations that I get now when I make love—or even thinking I'd like to. That happened during the Polanski film, when that man carried off the pretty girl. Tiens! *The vampire was a man!*

JM: Are you the vampire, then?

P: [laughs with astonishment and delight at this discovery]
       Of course—it's me!! How come I never even thought of
       it? I'm sure all this has to do with my sexuality.

In Paul's fantasy, making love is equivalent to destroying the partner. In Polanski's film, vampirism is represented as an erotic act; the vampire in question desires
ardently to vampirize a pretty woman who attracts him,
and the homosexual vampire wishes to vampirize a young
man.

P: You know, that handsome vampire who chased the
       pretty girl, he looked strangely like my father. I was
       very struck at the time—and I followed all his move-
       ments with the greatest of interest.
JM: The movements of the couple?
P: Yes, that especially. It's just such a couple that I always
       imagined my parents to be. I never could bear even to
       think of their lovemaking. I was sure my mother would
       be destroyed. That he would hurt her by making love
       to her. You know my father was a bit disturbed men-
       tally—a vampire, always sucking on people. But where
       am I in this?

Thinking of his many oral-erotic and oral-sadistic fantasies toward women, I encourage him to see just where he
is in his relation to his father.

P: It's too horrible—I see myself vampirizing my father's
       penis; it has a very alive gland and look to it. I can't bear
       it [he covers his eyes with his hands]; this image makes
       me dizzy and I have to lower my eyes. There's a jet of
       sperm—I can't stop these images. What is happening to
       me?
JM: The other day you described your father as sexually
       dead, and you had an image of his sex as totally lifeless.
       Now it seems that you allow it to come to life and to
       give sperm.

211

The penis-breast equivalence in Paul's associations and fantasies is important in that for the first time in the analysis he now attaches the exciting breast-images to his father's penis. Perhaps he is coming closer to imagining a penis that can nourish and complete a woman rather than one that can only destroy. In any case he comes back to his own sexual fantasies and his destructive role toward women. These underlying thoughts are doubly frightening to Paul from the point of view of homosexual impulses: if his father's penis is "alive," on the one hand he will desire it libidinally, and on the other, he will wish to destroy it out of envy and jealousy.

P: Why do I see my father's penis as so evil? Why is all pleasure for me turned into poison? I can see those black holes in the breasts again—just like dead holes, as though they had been stung by hornets. Yes, that's what they are—poisonous bites into the nipples. [Long pause] I believe I have always associated eroticism with death. Sometimes lately I'm afraid to make love to Nadine—I get an image of those hornet holes—and I suddenly lose my erection. Otherwise I would be making love in that dead hole!

We see here all the condensation, as in a dream, that has taken place in these images. The black craters in the breasts are in themselves a condensed and metaphorical fantasy of the primal scene in archaic terms. The "dead hole" is now the vagina and is imagined as having been torn in the woman's body by the penis. Paul's psychic imagery is becoming organized in typically hysterical fashion.

JM: As though you wish to avoid being the hornet who attacks the breasts or who goes into the dead hole?
P: Absolutely! I'm the hornet! I'm the one who is dangerous to her—even my eyes can destroy her. The vampire—the male vampire! That's some part of me. Yes, it's true, I wanted to be that implacable vampire in the film.
JM: The man who reminded you of your father?

P: Yes, yes. Do I have destructive wishes toward my father also? I've never felt anything like that before—nor any wish to be like him!

This rivalry with his father has been a notably lacking element in Paul's oedipal structure.

P: I've never been afraid of my father—he's just a paper tiger, really. But this mysterious sperm flowing from him—it creates a strong feeling of desire and also makes me very afraid. [Long pause] You know I can see more clearly these days. Tiens! The night after my visit to the opthalmologist I dreamed I was being pursued by the police—and I had to take off my glasses so they wouldn't recognize me.

It would seem that Paul allows the "police" in, at last, to play some paternal and law-giving role. He becomes aware that he has something to hide: he must take off his glasses, because his visual troubles are all marshaled against his recognition of archaic sexual and aggressive wishes. But he is becoming able to face these primitive impulses now, insofar as they involve his father.

P: Those changing faces of the women, they're two parts of myself that change really, but I can't seem to bring them together. Maybe it's the same with my father? You know I'm no longer afraid of people—neither men nor women. *I'm no longer blind,* I must get this clear, because I'm sure this has to do with my scotoma.

Thus we arrive at the beginning of Paul's oedipal analysis. His psychosomatosis, inaccessible to verbal thought, has gradually become an analyzable psychoneurosis.

9

Theater in the Round: Thoughts on the Economy of Narcissism

We now leave the theater in which inaccessible affect seeks to go on stage in the form of psychosomatic maladies. The preceding chapters dealt mainly with disturbance in the psychic economy of affect. The next two are concerned with the narcissistic economy. Disturbances in self-esteem and in one's image of oneself can cause painful conflict in the attempt to protect a stable and reassuring self-image and thus maintain psychic homeostasis in its narcissistically oriented as well as its object-oriented libidinal dimensions. Both narcissistic and libidinal investments, of course, are necessary to psychic health.

It should be emphasized that people with so-called narcissistic pathology, while they may seem concerned with only themselves and their mirror image, are actually suffering from a serious depletion in their narcissistic reserves. Their self-image tends to be either gravely damaged or fleeting and in danger of disappearing. The mind's *I* then reflects either a persecutory or a misty, unclear image. This painful situation leads some subjects to cling to themselves and their inner worlds in an attempt to ameliorate the image or protect it from being lost altogether. Others suffering from the same uncertainties use other people as their mirrors, with similar aims in mind.

The fundamental dramas of people who suffer in this way are expressed in scenarios in which different reflections and aspects of themselves appear as players. I have likened their psychic creations to the theater in the round—there is always an exit, but neither the actors nor the audience appear to be aware of it while the play is proceeding.

The Changing Analytical Scene

The last fifteen years have seen considerable research devoted not only to the clinical problems of narcissistic disturbance but also to the theoretical concept of narcissistic libido and the complex questions to which it gives rise. The attempt to conceptualize the clinical problems has led to the creation of a new clinical category, the *narcissistic personality disorder*. There is little doubt that our clinical confusions and theoretical dissensions are reinforced during those periods in the history and development of psychoanalytic thought where clinical observation seems to be at odds with established psychoanalytic theory, or appears to be dealing with hitherto unencountered phenomena. The abundant literature on narcissistic problems, while it reveals widely divergent interpretations, appears to agree that today's analysands present a different form of suffering or indeed psychic structure than those studied in the first half-century of psychoanalytic research. The patients of today, with their "psychotic parts," "narcissistic shields," "grandiose selves," "operational thinking," and "alexithymic defects," seem strangely dissimilar to the "good classical neurotics" of the *Belle Epoque*.

Is there, in fact, a "new" or "modern" analysand? Or indeed a new or modern narcissism? (Hanly and Masson 1976) Might it not be more appropriate to speak in terms of a new *demand* made upon psychoanalysis, to which today's analysands are seeking a response? The nature of the symptoms, and the way in which psychological suffering is experienced and expressed, appear to have changed over the years. This development would not have surprised Freud, who predicted that certain neuroses that were rife in his time were destined to disappear. Specifically, he had in mind those neuroses whose roots lay in a radical refusal, on the part of both family and society, to recognize the existence of the sexual drives. His prediction would appear to have been fulfilled, particularly with regard to the dramatic hysterical symptomatology, so common in Freud's time, that was directly linked to sexual repression and is so rarely met with today. Instead, our patients complain of their incapacity to love, their feelings of profound dissatisfaction in work and social relationships, their sense of alienation from society, or their ill-defined states of emptiness, depression, and anxiety. It is perhaps important for future research into narcissistic problems to emphasize the diverse and contradictory hypotheses that might be adduced to explain such phenomena in both dynamic and economic terms. An attempt to develop global theoretical explanations for such complex and evolving phenomena may run the risk of oversimplification.

Even factors foreign to personal psychic structure afford partial explanations of these apparently new symptoms. The length of analytic treatments in today's practice is but one example. In marked contrast to patients of Freud's time, whose analyses were relatively short, today's analysands, as well as their analysts, tend to pursue personal analysis for a period of years. This fact has changed not only the analyst's way of listening to patients and the expectations of the analytic experience, but also the nature of the patient's analytic discourse. The longer time span allows unsuspected narcissistic and psychotic anxieties, hidden behind neurotic structures, to come to the fore. In lengthy analyses neurotic and psychotic character outbursts, addictive behavior, psychosomatic manifestations, and aberrant sexual impulses are all quite likely to reveal themselves, perhaps only temporarily, when the analysand is faced with unusual stress. The potential for affective flooding and consequent perturbation in the narcissistic economy is not limited to narcissistic personality disturbances. All patients may display any of the above behaviors in sporadic fashion, even those who are not chronically disturbed in their narcissistic relationship to themselves or to others. Some patients, of course, live in an almost constant state of psychic unease in that they experience the demands of external reality and the very existence of other people as a continual and potentially trauma- tizing threat to their psychic equilibrium. (Such was the case with Angela, a fragment of whose analysis will be presented in the next chapter.) The vulnerability of the human psyche is such that we are all likely to suffer from occasional narcissistic personality disorders, and even from critical narcissistic hemorrhaging in self-esteem when faced with unexpected internal or external catastrophes. It is my contention that people must maintain their narcissistic libidinal homeostasis as best they can in the face of internal and external pressures, and that their ability to do so is largely determined by the nature of the libidinally invested ob- jects they have preserved in their internal psychic world.

Narcissistic Versus Neurotic Disorders?

When narcissistic fragility and the symptoms to which it gives rise are dominant features of the psychic structure, it is a moot point whether our theoretical and clinical conception of narcissistic disorders is advanced by opposing them to neurotic disorders. From a theoretical viewpoint the concept of two libidos of different quality, evolving separately, presents many metapsy- chological difficulties. My own views are closer to Otto Kern- berg's than to Heinz Kohut's theoretical conceptions in that Kernberg does not accept the notion of narcissism as a libidinal impulse detached from internalized objects and object-libido and that he makes room for the importance of early traumatic experi- ences likely to mobilize rage and hatred with which the small child cannot cope (Kernberg 1975, 1976).

From a clinical standpoint, I am equally dubious about the value of a sharp delineation between narcissistic personalities and neurotic personalities. Whenever we designate personality dis- orders as obsessional, masochistic, schizoid, or narcissistic, we are in fact referring only to a dominant feature, or a dominant defensive element, in the overall structure of the personality. In fact analysts rarely think of an analysand as a personality structure. Each patient is an intricate personality, endowed with unique internal and external object constellations and a specific psychic economy developed to deal with his or her own system of internal relations and identifications. Our hope is to understand this mental mosaic even though (or perhaps because) our understanding is necessarily filtered through our own intricate network of libidinal investments and narcissistic defenses. Even if certain character traits are considerably more accentuated in some patients than in others, our essential interest is directed less to relieving one overloaded defensive wall in the psychic edifice than to grasping the unique and delicate balance of psychological forces to which a patient has had recourse in structuring his or her ego and intimate self.

By what system of weights and balances, of essential beliefs and identifications, does the analysand protect this libidinal homeostasis, in either its self or its object orientation? The narcissistic economy, in order to maintain the sense of personal identity and to regulate self-esteem, must deal with a constantly fluctuating fantasy of the self, a process that involves exchange with internal and external objects as well as a continuing intimate relationship to this inner self. Through what pathways may the constant oscillation of narcissistic and object-oriented libidinal investment be traced in the course of a psychoanalysis? What specific means does any given analysand use to preserve the link between the inner self and the outer world? Finally, what forces threaten this essential link, whose obscure origins are hidden in the prehistory of every person?

In my attempt to answer these questions it will be seen that my interest in narcissistic problems is not in categorization but in a deeper exploration of the twofold function of narcissistic libido in preserving identity feeling and self-esteem, both in relation to the external world and as a defense against the loss of inner object cathexes. Clinical observation should enable us to follow the continual oscillation between self representation and object representation and to understand more clearly their mutual interdependence and their importance for maintaining psychic stability. From this vantage point, we may be better equipped to understand the mental pain and anguish that ensues when this constant movement is blocked or the psyche's delicate equilibrium is overthrown.

Reflections on Kohut's Theoretical Position

The above reflections lead me to a critical consideration of Kohut's research work into narcissistic personality disorders. I do not deny the value of nosological research. Defining a category or depicting clinical phenomena by the gifted use of metaphor frequently renders us more sensitive to certain important clinical data. It may even reveal a whole dimension of psychic life that has previously passed unnoticed. Such discoveries become self-evident to any attentive observer. Who, before Freud, was aware of infantile sexuality, and who, since then, could deny it? It could be said with justice that Kohut, prophet of the "new narcissism," has certainly rendered this service to the observation of narcissistic disorders. Whether or not one agrees with his theoretical deductions, his clinical acuity points up common denominators among the innumerable manifestations of narcissistic perturbation.

Building a theory requires the creation of metaphors capable of communicating the essential discovery behind the findings in question. *Id, ego,* and *superego* are Freud's personal poetry; *internal objects* is a brilliant figure of speech that conveys Melanie Klein's intuitive perception of psychic reality. In the same vein, we may admire the aptness of Kohut's references to *self-objects, grandiosity,* and *mirror transference.* They communicate, in condensed imagery, complex clinical phenomena which we may hitherto have overlooked or for which we lacked the evocative phrase that could further reflection on them. There is, of course, the ever-present danger that gifted metaphors may seem so satisfactory that they become reified; if they are treated as though they designate real things, their usefulness is hampered. A theory, by definition, is a system of assumptions that has not been proved; its utility lies in its ability to enable us to think more clearly and more concisely about the clinical problems and theoretical impasses that confront us.

Nevertheless, it is important in any research field to articulate one's findings with the basic theoretical doctrine of the discipline to which one purports to contribute. Although Kohut, like all workers in the field, is bent upon understanding the mysteries of the human psyche, he suggests that his explanatory hypotheses are superior to those contained in what he calls "traditional psychoanalysis." While this estimation of his concepts does not invalidate them, it may limit their usefulness in the advancement of psychoanalytic research. If Kohut's models of the "self" and of "narcissistic health" herald the constitution of a new paradigm (Kuhn 1962), this would seem to have been achieved at the expense of many of the classical Freudian paradigms. I shall not review here the many thoughtful criticisms that have been made of Kohut's somewhat lighthearted treatment of the basic tenets of our metapsychology, to which he nevertheless claims adherence (Stolorow 1975; Hanly and Masson 1976; Stein 1979), but I would question a conception that minimizes the value of the libido theory, the role of the oedipal organization, and the far-reaching effects of infantile sexuality yet claims to be extending basic conceptualizations and developing fundamental paradigm shifts. The clinical phenomena that result from disturbance in the narcissistic investment of the self give rise to a wide spectrum of psychic ills, and indeed we might wonder whether there are any analytic treatments in which narcissistic factors do not play an important role.

Furthermore, Kohut's wish to discard the economic model of psychic functioning does away with the potential explanatory power of this concept, particularly in regard to narcissistic pathology. As Kohut himself frequently points out, narcissistic pathology includes a wide variety of behavior patterns through which direct discharge or immediate dispersal of painful affect is sought in place of psychic elaboration. In fact, Kohut uses the economic model while claiming that it is of no use. The Freudian concept of libido as the reservoir of instinctual "energy" capable of being invested in a multiplicity of objects, including the self, is of course, as Kohut suggests, open to question. But so is Kohut's concept of two libidos—one self-oriented, one object-oriented—each with a separate evolution and source of energy, such that disturbance in one may leave the other untouched.

For those who believe, as I do, that the "subject" comes into psychic being only with the "object"—that is to say, that the nascent sense of self exists only in relation to the apperception of Another as different from the subject—Kohut's conception presents problems. I suggest that the appearance of "normal" object relations in people with narcissistic personality problems is spurious. We frequently deal with patients who, while they manifest no overt neurotic symptoms in sexual or social situations, display pragmatic forms of relationship that cloak a manipulatory or addictive use of others under the guise of normality (the patients I have referred to as normopaths). Such patients do not recognize the poverty of their libidinal or erotic investment in others or in their own love lives, and perhaps for this reason, it may escape the attention of the analyst as well. The failure to recognize narcissistic problems may be due to the subtle disguises that mental conflict borrows when its source lies in the primitive nature of early object relations and archaic sexuality. Freud postulated, with reason, that human sexuality is essentially traumatic. If this is conceded, then psychological problems may be regarded as unavoidable, even though their expression will vary from one society and one epoch to another.

The Trauma of Otherness and Its Pathogenic Potential

Narcissistic pathology has its roots also in the inevitable trauma of otherness and the obligation to assume separate identity. I suggest that when the self-image is markedly pathological, we are faced with anxiety of a global kind that precedes, and is perhaps prototypic of, later castration anxiety; such conflict is first linked closely to the difference between two bodies and later to the anatomical difference between the two sexes. Both discoveries entail considerable narcissistic pain, but the earlier trauma involves tensions regarding primitive sensual wishes that the infant is incapable of elaborating and resolving for itself. In the lack of distinction between inner and outer and between one body and another, narcissistic and sexual aims coalesce.

It is perhaps pertinent to point out once more that narcissistic symptoms may follow two distinct and, in appearance, widely different forms of expression. Certain persons, in their attempt to combat primitive castration fears of a narcissistic order, seek to create a continuing series of narcissistic object relations with the hope of repairing the damaged self-image and stemming the rising tide of panic whenever they are threatened with separations and other anxiety-arousing situations. Such a system of relationships includes what Kohut has aptly named the relation to self-objects, a relationship to another who is considered and treated as part of oneself. No doubt this form of relating approximates the primitive oneness with the Other that the infant experiences in its relation to the maternal universe—the need for another to be fully responsible for dealing with tension and with all that is too painful or too exciting for the infant to retain and work over psychically. This accumulation of affect is discharged by the very fact of the other's presence and, in Bion's terminology, the other's capacity to "contain" it (Bion 1957, pp. 43–64).

In contrast to those who feel they can function only under such circumstances, others, with the same basic need to avoid the loss of the sense of self, are compelled to defend themselves ardently *against* the fusional danger that narcissistic relationships imply. They tend to create an elaborate series of narcissistic defenses and to maintain a distance from the rest of the world, for fear of losing their self-limits and feeling of identity.* These people show a tendency to self-sufficiency and disavowal of almost all dependency needs. Desires, whether sexual or narcissistic in nature, tend also to be treated lightly and their force denied. Such people often engage in love relationships that are temporary or, if stable, are profoundly delibidinized. Once again, under the

---

*This theme is developed at length in J. McDougall, "Narcissus in search of a reflection," in *Plea for a Measure of Abnormality* (New York: International Universities Press, 1980).

appearance of normality, the individual may be engaged in a struggle with or flight from libidinal wishes as though they were imbued with the threat of destruction or of deathlike slavery. This avoidance of close contact with others, under the cover of superficial conformity to social standards, may also include flight from what Kohut has named the demands of the "grandiose self" —ego ideal and superego exigencies of such an order that no response would ever be adequate. Unlike Kohut, I suggest that this defensive battery has been constructed from infancy to protect the subject against extremely primitive libidinal object-oriented goals and fantasies of which the subject is unconscious. In analysis these reveal themselves to be attached to the archaic objects of early infancy as well as to the part-objects of pregenitally conceived sexuality, telescoped and confused with the individual's own self and body. The analytic fragment in the following chapter is a relevant illustration of what I have called *archaic sexuality* and of the way its terrors are held in check by narcissistic character defenses.

Two Solutions to a Fundamental Conflict

The terror of patients who protect themselves narcissistically from too close an involvement with others is frequently expressed as a fear of being bewitched or of becoming hopelessly addicted to one's love objects. This description recalls in striking fashion the sexual and love relations of patients who actively seek to fulfill urgent narcissistic needs in their sexuality. Their search for the other is less concerned with desire than with the psychic economy of need that underlies addictive behavior and deviant sexual organizations in which sexuality is used like a drug. While one kind of patient with narcissistic problems seeks such relationships constantly, the other continually reinforces the barricades against such enthrallment.

Both personality structures have their roots in the narcissistic sexuality of infancy, and each tries in hidden ways to maintain or recreate the primitive tie to the mother. For the self-object seekers, this object is sought in the external world. Those who defend themselves against the danger of the wish for a fusional self-object, on the other hand, live this fusion in fantasy only. The involvement (whether decathected or compulsive) of such patients with their sexual and love objects may give the impression that they have no difficulty in their capacity to love or to have satisfactory sexual relations. From a normative point of view, they may appear to have no neurotic problems and thus to substantiate the view that object libido and narcissistic libido are capable of separate and independent existences. Only the intense illumination provided by analytical experience can highlight the psychological impoverishment that so often underlies compulsive object-seeking or superficial encounters. In fact, we are faced with psychic organizations designed to seek or to avoid relationships that follow the primitive mode of love—a fantasy of fusion. The two structures are exemplified by the two patients below:

SANDRA: Alone I simply cease to exist. Nothing but a void. There has to be someone there for me to feel alive.

SABINE: When I'm too long with other people I lose my limits; I'm only truly myself when I'm alone.

Patients like Sandra, who use others as self-objects in order to confirm their narcissistic value and feeling of identity, have been the subject of numerous analytic writings. Those like Sabine, who use their self-sufficiency to protect themselves against external reality with its demands, disappointments, and unexpected catastrophes, have received less attention in psychoanalytic literature, perhaps because they appear to be delivered from the dangers of object-dependency. The theory of their psychic functioning seems to me more complex than that of patients who are addicted to their objects, however. Their sexuality is secretive and obscure or marked by indifference (sometimes hidden, sometimes proudly proclaimed) toward all love relationships and sexual adventures. Their devitalized sexual life is rarely compensated by neurotic symptoms but revealed in character traits, and it stamps all their relationships. The subject's role in the maintenance of this decathected world and the veiled gratification received from it remain impalpable. This evanescent quality also permeates the analytic relationship, expressing itself as an absence, an apparent lack of transference affect, much as though the analyst were part of the analysand or the analysand an extension of the analyst—the type of transference relationship described in detail by Kohut (1971).

The Archaic Sexual Roots of Narcissistic Disturbances

My own clinical observation leads me to the conviction that the narcissistic transference relationship is more fully accessible to analysis once the instinctual roots that have rendered such massive defenses necessary become visible. The significant objects of the archaic libidinal substructure are scattered throughout such patients' lives, as they are throughout their analytic discourse. These objects are so fragmented, condensed, or devitalized that they are often buried within inanimate objects; the libidinal fragments therefore are invisible in the patients' lives and inaudible in their associations. The profoundly repressed archaic sexuality concerns a "body-sex"; castration anxiety attached to this representation may be felt to endanger the body as a whole or the psychic integrity of the self.

It must be reiterated that the earliest psychic trace of the recognition of the difference between the two sexes originates in the discovery of the difference between two bodies and this contributes at a later stage to the manifestations of phallic-oedipal castration anxiety in both sexes. The close sensual relationship of the mother to her nursling contains a paradox: the maternal body, thanks to its libidinal investment, is better armed than that of the infant against the force of the death impulses (whether these are conceived in terms of expressions of aggression and rage or as the magnetic pull toward inertia and nirvana). The mother's maternal function must include her desire to mobilize in her baby the will to live, protecting it against the danger of returning to marasmic inertia. At the same time, it is in moments of separation, when the mother does not act as a sheltering rampart and magical extension of the infant itself, that the first fragments of independent psychic activity are set in motion.

If this primitive sensual relationship may be considered the fundamental condition of psychic survival, it must also be recognized as the earliest prototype of both the sexual life to come and the narcissistic self-image. During that primordial phase of psychic structuring, there is no other agency than the mother herself and her unconscious—that is to say, her interpretation of her baby's needs—that can transform the small biological body into an erogenic one. Should this primitive communication fail (Castoriadis-Aulagnier 1975; McDougall 1978), and should she prove unable, because of her own anxiety, to fulfill her role as a protective shield against excitation—for example, by showing either excessive or insufficient investment of her baby and its body (Fain 1971)—there is a risk of fragility in the psychic structure with which the tiny infant will face the universal traumata of human psychic life: the discovery of otherness, the difference between the sexes, and the inevitability of death. Such fragility, while it is likely to increase psychosomatic vulnerability or psychotic potentiality, may also mobilize narcissistic defenses capable of protecting the adult-to-be against psychosomatosis and psychosis.

In the latter case, this underlying fragility gives rise to character defenses that, far from being frail or unstable, are frequently unshakable. Narcissistic autarky encloses within its precincts invaluable inner objects, but their state of condensation and fragmentation, imbued with archaic drives, requires a certain vigilance with regard to contacts in the external world. This precious psychic capital must be protected, and the danger of encountering people likely to be perceived as compulsive need-objects must be avoided, for objects of need are at the same time potential objects of primitive hatred. Those who have succeeded in constructing a narcissistic fortress between themselves and others protect not only their own selves and inner universes but also the others, who unwittingly draw them toward a relationship felt to be potentially death-dealing for both. In the unconscious, this relationship bears the stamp of the elemental violence that makes up the archaic sexual substructure of the human being.

In the next chapter I give a clinical illustration of these themes. At the same time, this analytic fragment may demonstrate my divergence from Kohut's theoretical standpoint. The patient in question presented the signs, symptoms, and character traits, as well as the "mirror transference," that Kohut considers paradigmatic of a narcissistic personality disorder. She did not feel that she had any sexual problems, nor was she aware of suffering from the neurotic symptoms she observed in her friends. Her suffering was of another order: she frequently felt empty and hopeless about her life and questioned the value of continuing to live. At the same time she expended frenetic energy in protecting herself from close or continued contact with other people. In his introduction to *The Analysis of the Self*, Kohut writes, "Such persons have thus learned to distance themselves from others in order to avoid the specific danger of exposing themselves to a narcissistic injury" (1971, p. 12). I have no criticism of this formulation other than its inadequate reference to the instinctual conflicts that lie behind such projections. In my clinical experience, the potentially wounding and persecutory external world that surrounds the fragile narcissistic self-image draws its projective force from the nuclei of the early, fragmentary sexual objects and the primitive fantasies that lie deeply buried within the barricaded self.

10

The Narcissistic Stage and the Role of Archaic Sexuality

Angela, a pretty woman of thirty-four, lived alone with her little boy but maintained friendly contact with his father. Psychologically she dwelled in what one might call a narcissistic retreat, in which she needed to be alone much of the time because people "wore her to shreds" if she spent too long with them. She nevertheless took immense pleasure in "observing" others and talked about them rather as though they were Martians whom she must try to understand. Intellectually gifted, Angela spent much of her time writing essays and plays of a historical or philosophical nature. She made little attempt to get her essays published, and with much reluctance allowed the plays to be put on by friends in a small experimental theater in Paris. She said she had no need for a public, for the pleasure of producing sufficed. Similarly she had "no need for sexual relations, either," although she was not frigid and had had passing adventures with different friends.

This attitude did not hide any strong homosexual conflicts. In the course of her analysis, her latent homosexual preoccupations revealed themselves to be similar to those of most neurotic-normal patients. More exactly, Angela spoke of her men and women friends as though they were barely distinguishable from one another. They had no sex, no age, no names. Although she was constantly afraid they would take up too much of her precious time, she was attached to them in the following terms: "I just love watching them; it's like going to the theater." If by chance the friends suddenly invited her to "go on stage" herself —to give advice on a question or to talk about herself—she was filled with panic. Her anxiety was so great that she had the impression she no longer even understood what people were saying to her.

In similar circumstances she would sometimes forget the existence of others; her thoughts would be a thousand miles away, and at these times a sudden interruption not only terrified her but made her feel she had been painfully invaded and bruised: "I totally lose my touch with reality; the unexpected word is just like an unanticipated sexual demand. With men friends I am careful not to behave in too feminine a manner. Love affairs make me lose my limits. I don't need that." Angela disliked music for the same reasons: "It penetrates you, upsets everything, overrides your boundaries. The African music some of my friends like—I just have to leave." In the same vein Angela suffered "atrociously" from the cold and felt she was unable to think when she was cold. At the same time the thought of being warmed by the contact with another's body filled her with horror. Once, when she had to decide between these two anxiety-arousing situations, she chose to be cold and adduced the following explanation for her choice: "The temperature difference between two bodies not only makes me anxious, it disgusts me beyond measure."

In sum, any closeness with another person, whether psychological or physical, threatened Angela's sense of narcissistic integrity and aroused her fear of "losing touch with reality." I sometimes wondered if her carefully maintained detachment from other humans contributed to her rare qualities of observation and her strong perception of human foibles and frailties. She saw through people's self-deceptions and mutual illusions with astonishing acuity. For someone who appeared to inhabit the rarefied air of another planet, her reflections on well-known public figures—thinkers, politicians, artists—never failed to surprise me with their perspicacity. As the analysis progressed she became capable of turning this penetrating eye upon herself: "It is painful for me to feel so separated from the rest of the world and so inaccessible to passion."

In spite of her unusual and fascinating analytic associations, Angela's analysis left me profoundly unsatisfied. She was there yet absent, giving an impression of impalpability that was increased by her strangely unreal way of talking about her bodily self, as though she lived next door to her physical envelope rather than within it. She was like a disembodied mind. Her analytical discourse recalled the reflection once made to me by the mother of a psychotic little boy: "Sammy talks all the time—and yet he never, ever talks about anything real." This kind of communication is in sharp contrast and in a sense in counterpoint to the operational or alexithymic way of talking and relating, discussed in chapter 7. The latter appears emotionally devitalized, cemented to the actual and the factual, and seems to reduce life itself to a series of external events. Yet in a strange way, in patients like Angela the seeming nonexistence of others is somewhat similar to that revealed by operational or alexithymic personalities. I have suggested in earlier chapters that we are witnessing here a primitive defense against overwhelming pain.

The First "Embodied" Associations

The following excerpts are from the first sessions in which it became possible, after three years of analysis, to grasp in Angela's associations a fleeting reference to her body as an object of libidinal investment. And with this reference came the first glimpse into the organization of her childhood sexual fantasies and her early oedipal imagery—in other words, the evolving core of her neurotic difficulties as opposed to her narcissistic conflicts. During these first years, my various interventions, intended to throw light on this missing dimension in her psychic life, had met with little response. My voice "upset" her because she "suddenly became aware that we were two distinct persons"; my words "penetrated her like foreign bodies which [she had] to take time to digest," a crystal-clear image of mirror transference as described by Kohut (1971). I had of course formed a number of free-floating hypotheses about her psychic structure and libidinal economy, and in particular some notion of what her sexual fantasies might be. Her "horror of music," for example, was evocative of a sensitive recoil from the mother's voice as well as from the primal scene, now displaced onto music and African rhythms. I was eventually able to understand that for Angela my voice was experienced as an unconscious symbolic equivalent of the breast, and my words, an unconscious symbolic equivalent of the phallus. Instead of carrying the possibility of bringing meaning to the oedipal scene, whatever I said hurt and confused her. Her air of being a disembodied spirit, inhabiting an ill-defined space, and her continual fear of "losing her boundaries" and her contact with reality, or of melting into other people, called forth the image of a fragile child as yet uncertain of her body's capacity to "contain" her (Bick 1968): a body image that was permeable, unstable, perhaps in the end unknowable.

Angela claimed that she never looked at herself in the mirror, and if by chance she caught her own reflection, she rarely recognized it as her own. Her massive denial of her corporeal self as an object of narcissistic interest was coupled with an equally forceful refusal to recognize bodily states such as hunger, thirst, pain, or illness. Though hungry or thirsty she would manage to remain unaware of these biological appeals for hours on end. When I once asked her if the same obliteration of body needs applied to elimination, she replied quickly that she managed to forget it so totally she could never remember having performed it at all during her waking life. Of her sexual desires and erotic bodily self she made no mention. She did, however, offer me learned dissertations on sexuality as a topic of reflection, in which she would explain how mistaken Freud had been to have based his whole conceptual system of psychic structure and psychopathology on the libidinal impulses. The fear that analysis might expose her to "erroneous interpretations of this kind" had prevented her from undertaking a personal analysis much earlier. (Angela had sought analytic help following an acute period of depression that had led a close friend of hers to insist that she come to see me at least once.) "I don't need that kind of Freudian analysis; I have no sexual problems. My difficulties lie in quite another direction," she explained.

Angela's Clothes Become Libidinal Objects

Curiously enough, this ethereal and other-worldly way of experiencing herself ran counter to a manifest investment of bodily interest to which she never made reference: Angela always dressed with extreme care and elegance. In summer she was frequently arrayed in nothing but white—well-cut pants suits, long skirts with white embroidered blouses, handmade silk shirts with matching scarves, never discordant yet often strikingly different from the fashion of the moment. Even though somewhat disembodied she apparently wished to be attractive, to draw attention to her bodily self as an object of libidinal interest. But for whom? Was it possible that she was merely a "body-object" of contemplation, or an erotically invested body for herself alone? One might hold that this concern with dress was part and parcel of her narcissistic self structure. But what could that mean if it was detached from any inner object representation? Was such an investment in physical appearance conceivable without some object-libidinal tie, even if hotly denied by Angela herself, or to all appearances unconscious?

One day, to my surprise, Angela states that she nearly missed her session because she has not had time to wash her clothes. In the midst of her ethereal associations, this fleeting reference to her physical body, though limited to the clothes that touched it, creates an effect as astonishing as that of a delusional thought in a well-constructed dissertation.

I invite Angela to tell me a little more about washing her clothes. She seems surprised by this request but replies by saying that she spends one to several hours each day doing so—she, who leaves all other household chores to a full-time maid, would not dream of leaving her such a delicate task. I comment that washing her clothes appears to be highly important to her and ask what she thinks about it. Her first response is a rapid denial.

A: No! It doesn't interest me particularly—ah, how shall I put it, well, I can never wear the same garment two days running. I don't feel right.

After a long pause Angela continues:

A: You know I really enjoy washing my clothes; it's no problem, it's a real pleasure. *Really!*

Since we have never been so close to Angela's bodily reality before, and since her discourse has a hint of neurotic intensity, I ask if she can tell me more about this idea, and I begin to take notes.

A: Well, it's as though I have dead cells on my skin . . . [Angela begins to murmur under her breath as she has often done in the past when her feelings seemed to her incommunicable.] . . . worse than dirt . . . [Her voice fades away completely as though the thought she is communicating has disappeared also. After a minute's silence she takes up the theme of washing once more.]
A: You know, I really enjoy cleaning my clothes; it's no problem.

Struck by her insistence I tell her she seems rather emphatic about this daily pleasure and ask her whether she would feel in any way upset if she were prevented from her ceaseless washing. (I was clearly running after this significant fragment of embodied reality, with its hint of repressed fantasy content.)

A: Oh yes! I get terribly upset—in fact, quite panicked whenever that happens.

She goes on to give details of the precautionary measures she takes when going to stay with friends or on long boat trips. With only a small bowl of water she manages to wash everything every day. Angela then falls silent as though my questioning bothers her, but I pursue this promising line of inquiry.

JM: This feeling of panic when your precautions fail—what do you think it's due to? What do you imagine at those moments?

A: Er . . . well, I've never given it any thought . . . Tiens! I've just thought of something, something I haven't remembered in years. When I was about three I had threadworms. They showed me the potty full of them. Tiny, white, horrible! To think that all those things were living inside me, and I didn't even know it!

Her words bring to mind the innumerable times she has told me of her terror of being "invaded" by others, her fear that they, or I, might "take possession of her." I have often asked myself why she should harbor such anxious thoughts about the loss of subjective identity when she is with others. I write down that people and threadworms seem to take possession of Angela in identical fashion. Is there an unconscious link between people and worms? After a moment's silence she continues.

A: Yes, the used clothing! That's what it's like. Just like the worms. Horrible!

My own associations began to gallop ahead. I was particularly struck by the transposition of the scene of horror. What had once been on the inside (the worms) now occurred on the outside: Angela's clothes were in some mysterious fashion impregnated with the worm-horror. Did her clothes represent someone who might touch her skin? Make her dirty? Cover her with "dead cells"? Perhaps it had to do with her parents, who died when she was young? It is a fact that Angela feels them to be very alive inside her, "as though soldered together," she would say—wonderful, precious, highly idealized, "grandiose" images. We had worked out that an important part of her need for solitude was the feeling of being alone with them as she had felt herself to be in childhood, before their deaths. Once when I asked her about them as a sexual couple she replied that the idea was absurd. They were ethereal beings, sexless and bodiless. Angela's oedipal structure appeared to be a near total blank.

The next day's session:

A: It's really odd. I've thought about yesterday's session for hours. Washing my clothes is no simple pleasure. I've washed things frantically all my life. All my childhood is wrapped up in this. I must get to the bottom of it! It's not just a fear of dirt; what is even more intolerable is the *shape of clothes* once they've been worn. Sort of stiff and rounded out. Reminds me of the time I broke my arm when I was a child. It hadn't bothered me until they took the plaster off, and then the horror of that sight, the plaster cast all rounded out—I thought I was going to vomit. As long as you don't see it, you aren't aware.

JM: You aren't aware of what?

A: Well, the clothes. You're fine inside them, they sort of melt into your body, envelop you. But once off, especially the next morning, it's as if they've been changed during the night. Ugh! I have to wash them right away.

My fantasy during yesterday's session comes back to me: the clothes that take the place of people, "that melt into your body." But these "people-clothes" are "changed during the night." Are they the mother, dirtied, changed by her relation to the father? And what about Angela's comment, "As long as you don't see it, you aren't aware"? I repeated these last words and added, "the clothes which touch our bodies and envelop us—but afterward are changed?" As though Angela too were thinking of maternal metaphors, she replies vivaciously:

A: That makes me think of my mother's skin. I loathed it, couldn't bear her to touch me. Luckily she was not the kind of woman to pick children up all the time. The idea of being enveloped in her arms gives me a feeling of disgust.

JM: As though she were dirty?

A: Tiens! Like the clothing!!

JM: Our clothes are a bit like the mothers of our babyhood. Our mothers choose our clothes, put them on us when we're little; and in a way they remain associated with her.

A: Clothes, once worn, are all rounded and sloppy-looking. [Angela traces in the air a form that looks more like a wine jar than a garment.] Ugh! Just like my mother's detestable body. [She again draws the rounded form in the air, this time making me think of a belly—and Angela's little-girl stomach full of worms.]

JM: This rounded shape that you trace in the air—it looks more like a body than a piece of clothing. A body full of worms? Like little Angela's stomach? Or babies in her mother's stomach?

A: Ugh! The idea of pregnant women revolts me. I hate to see them, and the thought of touching a pregnant woman's stomach . . . well, that's something that's never happened to me anyway. Why should I even think of it?

JM: Your mother was pregnant several times when you were little.

A: [in an almost inaudible whisper] All that . . . too horrible . . . [She again gestures in the air, but this time as though brushing away a painful thought.] And to think that I never wanted to become pregnant; it took me years to accept the idea of having "that" growing inside me. Exactly the same feeling as the threadworms. Ugh! Growing inside me. I had to do everything possible to make sure that "that" wouldn't get into my body. [Long pause] Is it my mother, pregnant, that I can't bear? As

though I have to wash it off? Yes, all those things that
wiggle around inside—filth! When I was little I believed
that women caught "that" by eating something that was
alive. Did I think they ate worms? [Long pause] When
I say *worms* I think more of those worms that eat corpses.
That's quite different.

JM: What are they like?

My own imagination had run to the thought of Angela's
dead parents. I wondered for the first time if her severe anorexia
of childhood and her adult disgust with food in general might
hide a fantasy of having ingested her dead parents, or the content
of her mother's abdomen—the babies, clearly linked in today's
session with threadworms. Was there also a father-worm somewhere on the horizon? Angela's associations to threadworms and
other worms that eat corpses might point in this direction.

A: I always imagined those worms like earthworms. I used
to love watching them come up out of the ground, all
pink. Much less disgusting than those ghastly threadworms! They don't wriggle about all over the place. And
they're always on their own *("toujours solitaires")*.

In French the word for a tapeworm is *un vers solitaire,*
"a worm on its own." This term therefore has particular
resonance for a French-speaking child, and I ask:

JM: A tapeworm, then?

A: My goodness, yes! Our cook once told me that tape-
worms could come out your mouth, and that once she
had put a saucer of milk out to catch one and when it
came out she cut its head off. Oh yes, I remember now
that I was just as afraid of getting a tapeworm as of
getting the stomach worms. I kept well away from everybody for fear of catching them. It was dangerous
even to touch people. Ugh, I'm thinking of a time when
I had to wash my sister's hair. She'd asked me to do it,

and it was pure torture. [I wondered, but did not say so, if her little sister were also unconsciously equated with a "stomach worm" from the mother's body.]

A: Now that's the same horror as the pregnant women. I just tremble at the idea that they might put their arms around me. But my mother would never have done that. Even to hear women talking about their pregnancies makes me feel ill. [Long pause] It's shameless, somehow —this sensuality. Horrible. Makes your head spin. [She begins to murmur.] Anguish . . . can't think of this . . . feel lost. . . .

Seeing her distress and the vague movements she is making, I invite her to try to pinpoint this sudden rush of anxiety.

A: When you're forced to participate like that . . . then you become "that." You get mixed up in their story.

The Emerging Oedipal Organization

Angela shows me once again how difficult it is for her to remain distinct from others, particularly when they speak of subjects that upset her or touch her too closely. At these moments she is penetrated by their words in a way that attacks her feeling of identity. This is an obvious threat to her narcissistic economy, but as we shall see it represents at the same time the threat of being invaded by primitive sexual fantasies. An archaic oedipal organization is beginning to emerge, with the primal scene still encapsulated in the mother's body. In her imagination Angela is "wedded," as she once expressed it, to her clothing. It now seems feasible that she is "wedded" to her mother's body, which contains the "worm on its own," the "father-worm," and their mutual fruit, the tiny "stomach worms." It is only when Angela is *separated* from this maternal substitute in the form of clothing, when she perceives that the garment-mother-body, swelled out with pregnancy, is no longer part of herself, that she is filled with disgust for everything to which she aspired to be joined, much as though there were an unconscious fantasy of having incorporated all the precious maternal contents. She now hates what she once envied and desired.

A: I cannot bear the self-satisfaction of pregnant women, nor their incredible lack of sensitivity toward other people's feelings. When I was pregnant I never made the slightest reference to the fact—particularly in front of women who had no children. Yes, it's that forced participation in the pregnant woman's pleasure that is unbearable to me! [Angela expresses surprise at this discovery.]

JM: Do you think you might also be referring to your own mother and your feelings as a little child?

A: Certainly not! I never envied my mother—and besides, why would I have felt that I had to participate? I wonder why pregnant women involve one in their pregnancies, anyway?

JM: It seems that *you* join in actively in this participation— your eyes seek out these rounded shapes, your ears take in the words of these women, with particular acuity . . .

A: Yes . . . it's true that I'm sort of . . . fascinated. But then I'm fascinated by everything I watch, provided I'm not involved.

JM: And with the pregnant women you are involved?

A: When I come to think of it, I do, somehow, feel deprived . . . as though they possessed something . . . maybe also as though I were being kept at a distance . . . I remember how unhappy I used to feel when my sister received something I didn't get. I'm always very careful never to do that to anyone else, especially careful not to talk about my child to anyone without children.

We see here, in her reference to her child as well as to her own pregnancy, that Angela takes great pains not to incite envy in others, no doubt a way of mastering what might well have been a series of traumatizing and envy-arousing events in her own childhood. Today she believes that she is beyond all envy, all desire, and even needs.

JM: We might wonder whether you felt yourself to be "deprived" and "kept at a distance" by your own mother, with her babies growing inside her . . . her rounded belly, like those rounded garments. Could this be linked to the idea that she had nothing whatever that you could envy—except those worms?

A: How disgusting! Well, I got clear of it, anyway! I always believed that I was my father's favorite. We were a world of our own, he and I. In his office he taught me lots of things. Flesh, bodies, and insides—all that belonged to the other side, the kitchen quarters! In his rooms everything was quiet and calm. Only the intellectual things counted. I was the most favored member of the family.

JM: Yet it was not to you that your father gave his "solitary worm"; and all those "baby worms" were growing in your mother's stomach, not in yours.

A: But my father had nothing to do with all that! . . . Oh dear, what have I said? I've never thought . . . makes me feel giddy . . . can't really think of it . . .

Angela makes vague movements in the air, and her voice becomes almost inaudible. I think to myself that the attempt to imagine the sexual relation of one's own parents is often accompanied in analytic sessions by a feeling of giddiness or confusion, as though the little child of the past were struggling between the desire to participate in this scene and at the same time trying to observe it or to make it stop—a complicated anxiety made up of envy, narcissistic mortification, and the fear of losing one's own identity.

A: The four children—my mother made them all by herself. Otherwise . . . well, er . . . it's just unthinkable. That reminds me that there's something worse than pregnant women, and it's those who talk about their lovers and their sexual lives. Like people possessed. The idea of being devoured by such feelings would terrify me. They seem to live solely for the other one—as though they were filled with his being. It must be horrible. I shall never be possessed of another person like that.

Once more we see that Angela can identify with the genital mother only in a climate of horror. The "rounded" woman, turned in upon herself, enclosing those "worm babies" that she "caught" through the mouth—and that come out through the anus—these and other elements of Angela's childhood sexual theories are becoming visible and capable of verbal expression. There is now a further element to be added to this already full mother, the women "possessed . . . filled," by their sexual partners. Hidden inside the mother's roundness, there is still place for the solitary father-worm that takes possession of her. This worm, according to the cook, goes in through the mouth, but he also comes out that way, at which moment his head will be cut off.

The oedipal couple is a vermiform fantasy!

The Two Worms

To deal with this archaic and condensed primal scene, Angela had built up defenses that were equally archaic. It is not surprising that she was a seriously anorexic child. In attempting to deal with her primitive fears she found, as most humans do, that external reality one day fortuitously confirmed her fantasy and provided her with a mental representation of her early sexual anxieties—the threadworms miraculously revealed as the hidden fruit of her own body and, added to these, the stories of the cook that provided a fantasy to deny sexual wishes toward a genital father. Her fantasies of sexual desire as well as her desire for children of her own were counterinvested in the form of phobic objects. From now on Angela "knew" what she was afraid of, and against what enemy she must defend herself. A repressed knowledge, maintained on the basis of a false splitting (Meltzer 1967) into good and bad objects: the two worms. The father-worm had a slightly better chance of being idealized than the numerous little "stomach worms." On the "kitchen side" Angela was able to pile up the smells, sights, and body-contents, like so many wriggling worms. On the "office side" was the worm on its own, the now disembodied father, pure spirit, with whom Angela was destined to make a profound identification. Her family romance created the certitude that her mother had fabricated her wormlike children alone, whereas Angela, only true child of her father, had sprung, like Minerva, from his head.

The long-repressed fantasies of her childhood sexual theories began to emerge: the mother is changed, rendered dirty and disgusting, by the absorption of the father. Angela, still very young during her mother's succeeding pregnancies, was as yet little differentiated in her narcissistic self-image from her mother's image or her mother's body. She had been exposed very early not only to the fear of losing her bodily and emotionally intimate relationship with her mother, but also to the fantasy danger of being "changed and dirtied" in turn. Her childhood memories all tend to show that in fact she became autonomous at an unusually early age in regard to her reliance upon and her attachment to her mother, as well as to the control of her bodily functions.

During the year following this session, we were able to piece together memories that suggested a childhood psychotic episode. Angela remembered that her mother constantly force-fed her and that her father taught her strings of words she would recite on command. She felt invaded and possessed by both parents. This double source of force-feeding no doubt contributed to the fact that when she was eighteen months old she practically refused all food and also gave up talking. (The mother was also pregnant at this time.) According to the family stories, it was her grandmother who proclaimed that the child would starve to death if she were not removed from her parents for a time, and she did in fact take the little girl away with her for some weeks. As a result, Angela began to eat and to talk normally once again, but she remained an aloof child, and family legends present her as unusually precocious in development and independent of others.

This early-acquired autonomy from the adult world seems to have run parallel with the encapsulation, at an extremely primitive level of fantasy, of Angela's childlike sexual fantasies at this period. The precocity of her defenses, no doubt constructed to deal with anxiety-arousing images of her mother and her mother's internal problems and pregnancies, is also manifest. Her anguish is associated with an earlier phase of development than that of classical castration anxiety and the phallic-oedipal crisis. Angela is unconsciously at grips with a world in which inside and outside are confounded, in which sexual objects have not become genitalized and are thus capable of invading her body at any moment and through any one of her different sense organs. They might be called sexually archaic self-objects. With regard to her childhood sexual wishes, which at the same time terrify her, she has maintained defensive solutions that utilize splitting backed up by massive disavowal; these have helped her remain unaware of her envious attitude toward her mother during her pregnancies and have protected Angela herself against any knowledge of her equally envious position with regard to the penis and the male world. What is important here is not so much the archaic representations of these desired objects, nor the infantile sexual theories attached to them; the latter are in fact quite banal. I should like to emphasize the primitive mechanisms involved in this way of relating to one's sexual self and to the object world, and the effects of such a relationship upon a fragile narcissistic self-image. The danger of invasion—both desired and feared—associated with such an archaic primal scene and its related fantasies is ever-present and risks becoming actual at any moment, through all the body's openings; touching, looking, hearing, and speaking all become potentially dangerous and disorienting in space and time. Angela was therefore obliged to keep a careful distance from others, to maintain invincible narcissistic walls around her, for fear of being touched, colonized, devoured, and emptied out by other people's drives. When such defenses failed she was threatened with the loss of her body limits and ego identity, arising from her own archaic sexual wishes, unconsciously projected onto the external object world.

With regard to Angela's two worms—the "solitary worm," metaphor of her father's phallus, and the "stomach worms," metonymic of her mother's power—the little girl hidden in the adult in her heart of hearts desires them both and must continually protect herself against her devouring wish to take possession of them. In order to defend herself against this mortal danger to her narcissistic integrity, she must forever wash her clothes—the clothes she loves so much and that do duty for a physical self with libidinal desires. In addition, this activity also gives her a feeling of "reality." Encapsulated in her clothes we find the link between Angela's archaic sexual organization and her narcissistic personality structure.

It is perhaps of anecdotal interest to add that a few weeks after the analysis of the material that first came to light in these sessions, Angela met the man who was to become her first lover, an indication of considerable change in her psychic economy and in the underlying structure of her "narcissistic disorder."

It is my hope that this analytic fragment demonstrates the extent to which the narcissistic ramparts of the personality, and the symptoms that arise from them, are fundamentally linked with the unconscious fantasy of the primal scene in its most primitive and condensed form. I hope to convey as well the extent to which any blocking of the perpetual oscillation between the two poles of libidinal investment, the constant swing from narcissistic libido to object libido, will result in narcissistic perturbation. The analysis of narcissistic symptomatology will frequently lead us to the fragmented and archaic sexuality of early infancy. If we neglect this primordial link between the two libidinal expressions, we run the risk of finding ourselves in a clinical as well as a theoretical impasse.

11

Neosexualities

Beyond the archaic, scarcely verbal sexual fantasies of the last chapter, we come now to those comparatively sophisticated creations known as sexual perversions. Like sexual fantasies, sexual deviations have an underlying archaic significance, but it has been overlaid by a genitalized scenario that combines many themes and psychological aims into one highly condensed whole. In this and the next chapter I discuss the many functions of *neosexualities*—for they are indeed new versions of human sexuality—and the way in which, in order to fulfill their functions, they must not only deal with the well-known neurotic anxieties but also keep at bay fears and fantasies that might be called psychotic.

What Is Perversion?

Before exploring the structure and psychic economy of perversions, we must first identify the objects of our research. This is not a simple matter. What acts do we designate as "perverse"? Who is a "pervert"? One might well reply that everyone knows the answer: a pervert is someone who does not make love like everyone else. Apart from the complex question of how everyone else makes love, the word *perverse* clearly carries a pejorative innuendo—one that may tell us more about the person who is speaking than about the person who practices this sexuality. Even if the so-called deviant makes sexual use of objects (mirrors, whips, fecal matter, or partners of the same sex) that seem inappropriate to the nonperverse observer, it is hardly justifiable to label the sexual deviant according to his or her sexual practice alone, even if this act is considered a symptom. (Would we say of someone unable to sleep like everybody else, "Bah, he's an insomniac, you know!"?) The person whose sexuality is different may disturb us or threaten us in some way, however, and the analyst must therefore bear in mind that to concentrate uniquely on a patient's sexuality is an artificial approach that ignores the rest of the personality. The aim of this chapter is to examine the role that perverse sexuality plays in the total structure of the personality and in maintaining psychic equilibrium in the face of unconscious anxieties.

If we take exception to the term *pervert* as giving partial and indeed biased information regarding another human being, we must nevertheless define what we mean by *perversion* if we wish to study its role in a given patient's psychic economy. But the pejorative meaning lingers. Etymologically *per-vertere* means no more than a movement of returning or reversing. Any dictionary will inform us, however, that this movement is invariably in the direction of evil. An attempt to escape from this implicit value judgment may be detected in the current use in analytic writings of the term *deviation* (Stoller 1979). But this term in turn presents an equivalent inconvenience etymologically, and one that runs counter to clinical truth. *Deviation* (*de via:* another route) suggests that perverse sexuality is nothing other than the choice of a different path to the same end pleasure as that sought in so-called normal sexuality. If the supposed aim of heterosexual relations is orgasm, then deviation would signify that a sexual perversion leading to orgasm in no way differs from any other form of sexual relationship except that it follows a more complicated route. In that case nothing would distinguish sexual perversions from erotic foreplay. Even if love games share certain features with some of the sexual perversions, such a lack of distinction would leave us with a highly simplified conception of the dynamic meaning of these inventions that I designate as neosexualities.

In fact perverse sexuality is but one manifestation of a complex psychic state in which anxiety, depression, inhibitions, and narcissistic perturbation all play a role. It is no simple deviation on the road to sexual satisfaction, but rather an intricate organization that must fulfill multiple needs, giving neosexualities a dimension of particular compulsiveness.

What are these needs? What is the significance of a sexual act in which anxiety and suffering are rarely absent? What might predispose a person to this kind of invention? What finally is the role of a neosexual invention in the libidinal and narcissistic economy of its author? To explore these questions, I shall take as my starting point certain of Freud's fundamental concepts concerning sexual aberrations.

Freud's Concepts of Perversion

For Freud, perversion existed whenever there was an abnormality of object (homosexuality, pedophilia), of zones (avoidance of the genital organs), or of aims (seeking pain), as well as any situation in which orgasm was subordinate to ineluctable external conditions (fetishism, voyeurism). These descriptions, of course, imply a concept of sexual normality, defined by Freud as "the union of the genitals in the act known as copulation" (1905, p. 149). In the same essay he wrote that "the pathological character in a perversion is found to lie not in *the content* of the new sexual aim but in its relation to the normal" (p. 161). The notion of normal sexuality as defined in the Freudian approach raises many questions. Donald Meltzer (1977) discusses the problem of Freud's "normative attitude" and points out that Freud gave rather exclusive value to genital heterosexuality, as though it were the only aspect of infantile sexuality that deserved to survive into adult life. Meltzer emphasizes the fact that in adults, nonneurotic and nonperverse sexuality still takes many forms.

Even while appearing to subscribe to a notion of "normative sexual behavior," Freud also held that the disposition to perversion was neither rare nor particular but merely a part of the so-called normal constitution (1905).

Freud's early formulations tended to treat perversions as simple vicissitudes of the sexual drive and as fixations to earlier libidinal stages. The modifications in the later structural model led to the concept of the superego as the inheritor of the oedipus complex and considerably enriched the understanding of perverse structure in oedipal terms. But it was perhaps the case of the "Wolf-Man" that forced Freud to explore in greater depth the problem of perversions. During this analysis Freud discovered that part of the answer to the enigma of their invention was to be found in the complex situation of the child faced with the primal scene and the emotions to which it gave rise. In other papers (1919, 1924, 1927, 1938a), Freud had already acknowledged the fact that sexual perversion could no longer be considered a mere fragment of infantile sexuality that had escaped repression. The celebrated dictum that "neurosis is the negative of perversion" (1905, p. 231) may be regarded as a somewhat inadequate statement, although it loses none of its pertinence in relation to *neurotic* structure.

For Freud it was abundantly clear that difficulties in resolving the oedipus complex were the source of both perversions and neuroses, and clinical experience over the ensuing half-century has confirmed this finding. We might say that neosexual inventions are, at one level, an attempt to short-circuit the multiple effects of castration anxiety and to maintain, camouflaged within the sexual scenario itself, the hidden incestuous links to infantile sexual wishes (McDougall 1978, pp. 21–86). The oedipal constellation is of course centered on the privileged role of the father-figure. The mother-image, in her primitive aspect as breast-mother or the primordial environment, does not form part of this constellation in classical Freudian theory. Although the libido theory gives considerable importance to the earliest mother-child relationship, Freud did not delve into the problematical questions of the infant's archaic sexual experience and fantasies and their potential effect on the later oedipal constellation. Moreover, he tended to idealize the early relation of the baby at the breast, in particular that of the mother to her son. In Freud's view, man's object of desire was woman, whereas woman's desire was for a male child. Freud seemed loath to conceive of the mother–nursling relationship as other than a good one and indeed wondered whether this period might not be the basis for the myth of Paradise. Although he recognized that the "object" is born in moments of hate, he left no place for the idea of a "not good enough" mother, whether in the infant's mind or in the historic reality of the maternal psyche. If the fantasy of Paradise finds its origins in the nostalgic experience of the babe at the breast, it seems feasible that the fantasy of Hell might find its roots there, too. The idealization of maternity in Freud's writing tends to overshadow the importance of the genital woman whose desires are not limited to her child, whether male or female.

The idealization of maternity frequently serves to mask the hatred and destructive envy that the child in the adult inevitably carries toward the breast-mother. The early mother image plays a continuing, essential role in the unconscious of all neosexual creators. The idealized maternal image not only suggests that the mother is devoid of sexual desire but also contains an implicit denial of the importance of genital differences. The belief that the difference between the sexes plays no role in the arousal of sexual desire underlies every neosexual scenario (McDougall 1978).

Infant Autoerotism

Freud's position regarding autoerotism deserves attention. My reflections on this aspect of Freudian theory are inspired by the view of Laplanche and Pontalis (1967) that the Freudian conception of human sexuality implies the "perversion" of the sexual drives from the very beginning of life. Of cardinal importance in Freud's theory of sexuality is the concept of *anaclisis,* which refers to a vitally important psychological dependence on another. This concept holds that the libidinal drives are based upon the instinct of self-preservation and only secondarily find their own direction and object. If for the baby the mother's milk is the earliest object of need, it is the breast that becomes the earliest object of sexual desire. Thus the mouth fulfills a double function; it is at one and the same time an alimentary and a sexual organ. The importance that Freudian theory gives to *autoerotism* as prototypic of human sexuality is frequently overlooked. For Freud the original model of the future sexual relationship is not to be found in the act of suckling, the instinctual aim of which is self-preservation, but in the autoerotic activity of thumb-sucking, the instinctual aim of which is libidinal pleasure. This emphasis places the accent on the child's autonomy, not only with regard to the feeding situation but above all in respect to its original sexual object. The mother's breast is recreated in fantasy in the activity of thumb-sucking, which is manifestly a pleasure-seeking and not a biologically necessary activity.

Presumably, this normal "deviation" of thumb-sucking that is the foundation stone of human sexuality may be inhibited by the mother's attitude to her baby's early autoerotic activity, especially if, at a later stage, the rituals of urination and defecation are equally divested of their libidinal and autoerotic potential. This idea poses a potential line of research that seems to me particularly pertinent to any exploration of the primitive basis of perversions and their relationship to genital autoerotism. Clinical observation has led me to the conclusion that the person who finds a neosexual solution to sexual conflict has rarely had any experience in childhood of normal masturbation. Normal masturbation is always manual, from the earliest baby experiences of genital play (in the terminology of Spitz 1949, 1962). With neosexual creators one gets the impression of a serious rift between hand and sex, as though all manipulation of the genitals had become severely inhibited from a very early age, so that the infant appears to have been driven to inventing other means of obtaining autoerotic satisfaction and appeasement. Spitz's observations of the mother-baby relationship and its effect on normal infant masturbation are revealing. He points out that when the early relationship is a disturbed one, the normal genital play of nurslings is replaced by body rocking, violent head banging, and games with excrement. This field of research into the origins of sexual perversions seems to have remained largely unexplored. We may envisage forms of masturbation in small babies that could already be designated as "perverted" or "deviated" from their normal genital aim.

The primordial deviation from the nursing relationship to thumb-sucking, which may be considered one of the corner-stones of the human sexual edifice, may be blocked from the beginning for certain infants, who then will be pushed to invent-ing some form of neosexuality in order to maintain both an intact body-image and an erogenous one. Infants may also need such autoerotic creations in order to stave off the turning back upon the self of primitive sadism, in which normal autoerotism is transformed into autoaggression. One triumphal result of all perverse sexuality lies in the eroticization of this particular manifestation of the destructive drives (Stoller 1976).

The Neosexual Scenario

It is my contention that neosexualities must deal with a double set of problems, not only those connected with the oedi-pal conflict but also those belonging to the realm of primitive sexuality—that is, the child's earliest conceptions of the sensual world, with its archaic internal and external stimulations and frustrations. In the enactment of the neosexual scene, the con-flicts at both levels must be adroitly disavowed. Neosexualities then serve not only to maintain libidinal homeostasis but narcis-sistic homeostasis as well. The overriding importance that these complex sexual creations may acquire in a person's life are inti-mately linked to the fragility of the psychic economy as well as to the varied purposes that the erotic act might be called upon to fulfill. This thesis will be exemplified in the clinical illustrations that follow.

The person who creates a perversion has in a sense rein-vented human sexuality in its genital and heterosexual aspects. By changing the aims and objects, he or she creates a new primal scene (McDougall 1978). This invented sexual reality is not achieved without cost. The act that sustains the new sexual theory is heavily weighted with anxiety and experienced as possessing a compulsive force beyond control. Even though the compulsiveness and the anxiety become eroticized in their turn, neosexual inventors always have the impression that they neither choose nor master their sexual manifestations. "It is as though a spell had been cast upon me," a fetishist patient once said. "I am certain I was born this way," confided a lesbian patient who would invite couples to her home and watch them making love. The person concerned usually feels lucky to have made a miraculous erotic discovery. Sometimes such analysands reveal their conviction that they have discovered the true secret of sexual pleasure and that others, lacking the courage to try it, envy their perfect solution. The "perfection," of course, lies in the fact that the creator of the neosexual invention has written all the rules as well as dictated the role of the partner. Nothing is left to chance. The rules are iron-clad, and the slightest change in the situation or in the response of the partner may release intolerable anxiety. This fragility is allied with the tendency to attribute to society a part of the subject's own internal reality, a projection that resembles psychotic thinking. "It's shocking that they sell these little whips openly in leather shops; it's intended to incite people to sexual excesses," explained one young man who paid prostitutes to whip him. "All men are basically homosexual," said another who was himself homosexual, "but they lack the courage to admit it." In fact the authors of neosexual scenarios are constantly on the lookout for external confirmation of their universality. It is perhaps this very vigilance that enables people to find, with such astonishing ease, partners willing to play the desired roles in their personal erotic theaters.

The leading theme of the neosexual plot is invariably castration. The drama may be fantasized as a maternal or paternal punishment of a phallic kind, a form of narcissistic castration, a pregenital castration, or even a threat to the whole body and life itself. But the triumph of the neosexual scenario lies in the fact that the castrative aim is only playfully carried out, and many of the principal themes are carefully concealed: the wish to castrate the partner, for example, is hidden beneath the need to repair the other. The fear of being castrated oneself is symbolically acted out to prove that castration does no harm; far from being castrated, one is instead completed. We might add that if this were not the dominant fantasy, we would no longer be in the world of deviant sexuality but in that of psychosis. Whether the scenario requires the act of whipping, lacerating, or strangling (the sex organ or the body as a whole), whether it requires that oneself or the partner be forced to lose control (of the sphincter or the orgasm) or to be humiliated or to humiliate the partner—in every case the unconscious meaning remains the same. These are all substitute acts of castration and thus serve to master castration anxiety in illusory fashion, at every conceivable level.

We must necessarily assume that these unusual inventions, which usually come to light in adolescence, represent the best available explanation or sexual theory that the child was able to find in order to deal with overwhelming conflicts and contradictions. The parental dialogue concerning sexuality, along with the model of a sexual couple that the parents formed in the child's eyes, are of major etiological importance. In the course of analysis many of the strange details of these erotic scenes reveal their historic and often pathetic roots in the inventor's personal past, particularly when overwhelming feelings of narcissistic pain have been added to castration anxiety. The following cases illustrate the way in which traumatic parental attitudes in childhood were able to be contained in a neosexual scenario in adulthood.

A young man who compulsively sought homosexual partners every night was erotically satisfied only when he had obtained on his penis some trace of a partner's fecal matter. Another analysand would whip himself in front of a mirror, the acme of his sexual excitement being his glimpse of the marks of the whip on his buttocks. What do these scenarios represent, and what is the source of their erotic power? There are many gaps in these theatrical erotic scripts to which even the author has lost the clues. In these instances, the hidden significance was partially reconstructed in each case during the course of the analysis.

The man who needed to see traces of fecal matter to reach the height of sexual excitement brought pertinent childhood memories. As a little boy he had been forced by his mother to go out in the park, where other children were playing, with his soiled underpants tied around his head. The maid, a girl cousin, and the other children would join in the hilarious humiliation of the little boy. In addition, his mother gave him frequent enemas. In his memory these acquired an erotic overtone, in contrast to the drastic punishment of the soiled underclothing. Nevertheless, this intimate contact with his mother through the enema was also experienced by the little boy as a form of phallic-anal castration. One solution was to soil his underpants in advance rather than submit to this maternal castration. The narcissistic mortification engendered by the soiling was felt to be a just, albeit intolerable punishment for the unconsciously eroticized anal relationship with his mother. In the adult's sexual play, the same painful humiliation had become the object of his sexual desire and the cause of his orgasmic response. What was originally an object of horror for his mother became the motivating factor in his sexual arousal, but the height of his triumph came with the fact that it was another person's fecal matter that was now rendered visible. The partner became the one to submit to the fantasized castration and narcissistic mortification he had once experienced.

The patient who whipped himself in front of the mirror dressed for this scene in women's clothing. To his intense humiliation as a child, he had always been dressed in delicate, effeminate attire and made to wear his hair long, while all his playmates had their hair cropped. The fantasy that accompanied his adult sexual scenario was one in which a little girl was publicly whipped by an older woman. Her imagined humiliation brought him to an orgasmic climax. She was the person he had once been, and all the world was now witness to his castration and his humiliation. In this way he triumphed over the supposed desire of his mother to turn him into a girl by making his castration the very condition of erotic excitement and the attainment of orgasm.

Other themes were of course eventually grafted on to these erotic childhood scripts and in turn served to contain anxiety—not only castration anxiety and narcissistic pain but also the unfathomable rage of the child dominated, excited, and humiliated by the controlling image of the mother. It was essential that this violence become playful—and therefore harmless—by being held within the neosexual act. Such destructive desires come to the fore only with difficulty in the course of analysis, since they have been profoundly modified owing to their dangerous quality. Disavowed or repudiated from the psyche rather than repressed, they are directed against the parental objects or their part object representatives, all of which have been fragmented and damaged in the internal world of psychic representations. Such fragments tend to come into the analytic discourse disguised by primary-process thinking, as in a dream. They are played out in the neosexual scenario in a way that conceals their meaning. The role of the partner in the sexual act—a role the partner is of course willing to play and is perhaps unconsciously in collusion with— is thus a complicated one.

The Partner

The sexual partner is required not only to embody the idealized image that the subject desires but also to incarnate all the reprehensible elements that the subject does not wish to acknowledge. In every neosexual production, valued as well as dangerous parts of the self are in this way recovered, mastered, or rendered innocuous. Thus we come to understand that in order to reverse an intrapsychic conflict the subject seeks an attempted solution in the external world. The partner, by participating in and enjoying the act, furnishes proof that the intrapsychic stress has no need to exist, that castration is harmless, that the genital difference between the sexes is not the source of sexual desire, and that the true primal scene is the one presented in the neosexual scenario. It is this magical resolution of internal tension and psychic distress that gives to the compulsive search for partners and the reenactment of the scenario the quality of an urgent need. Sexuality thus acquires an addictive quality, as though it fulfilled the function of a drug. The role of the other (or the objects that represent another) is to facilitate the disavowal and dispersal not only of phallic oedipal guilt and castration anxiety but also of more primitive anxieties, the fantasies of having attacked and destroyed the internal objects. The fantasy need to castrate the other—or to complete oneself at the other's expense—consequently demands the aim of reparation, an illusory reparation of the original objects and an expression of archaic sexuality in which body parts and substances are exchanged as reparative items.

One further highly important dimension, among the many demands made upon the neosexual act, must be taken into consideration. The constant danger presented by sadistic and destructive impulses is frequently countered by maintaining a state of paralysis, or inner deadness, as a magical means of protecting the self and the inner objects from damage. This interior state of death creates a feeling of emptiness that is sometimes more frightening than the agitated inner excitement connected with castration anxiety and fears of disintegration. The neosexual act is then called upon to block it out. Thus the act and the role of the partner serve as lightning conductors to protect against neurotic and narcissistic as well as psychotic fears. Although there is an important distinction to be made between neosexualities such as fetishism that are usually attached to heterosexual relationships and the different homosexualities, some of which do not qualify as neosexualities, the role of the partner or partners in homosexual relationships particularly highlights this proposition. (The significant difference between male and female homosexualities is not dealt with here.)

Dreams of two homosexual patients illustrate the intricate double aim of the sexual act. The first illustrates the way in which the sexual partner is required to deflect oedipal anxiety so that the dreamer's narcissistic image may be maintained intact. A man of thirty-five sought analysis because of professional problems as well as considerable anxiety arising from sporadic homosexual activities that frequently followed heterosexual adventures. The homosexual relationships required a partner who would mistreat him and insult him while he performed fellatio on the other. The dream came in the fifth year of analysis, by which time the analysand was almost relieved of his compulsive need to seek homosexual partners and was in fact engaged to the young woman who later became his wife. In moments of crisis* his homosexual fears and wishes would again come to the surface, but they would be expressed in dreams rather than acted out. This dream allows us to see much of the unconscious significance formerly concealed in the act. It occurred just before my vacation and at a time when the newspapers were filled with reports of Israeli-Arab hostilities. The patient, who is Jewish, had had several dreams and daydreams in which an Arab figured as the castrative father.

> I dreamed I was trying to park my car; I'd found a super spot just the right size. At that moment an Arab driver came up, I don't know where from, and took my parking place. I was furious and ran after him but he pulled a knife on me. I was panicked, but then I noticed suddenly that his knife was very handsome. Its form intrigued me. I told him how much I admired it, and I began to stroke it gently. The Arab gave a big smile and offered me the knife. I grabbed it eagerly and asked if I could have the little purse attached to his belt as well. He gave me this, too. It was divided into two parts —just like the money purse my fiancée wears. Suddenly the Arab cried out loudly and fell into a canal filled with mud. He was carried away by the current. I listened to his cries with disdain and said to myself, Well, I knew he would have to die anyway. Now I'm rich and can go on vacation wherever I want, without being afraid. Just as though, with the knife and purse, I didn't need anything more.

This dream contains all the central elements of the neurotic oedipal conflicts that are concealed in the homosexual drama. The latent meaning of the dream is evident: the incestuous son attempts to move into the place of the Arab-father. They dispute

*One might wonder whether neosexual solutions are not always discovered during a crisis, something like a daydream that might surge forth in times of extreme tension or painful emotional experience, revealing the power of certain representations to deflect attention from mental pain and unresolvable conflict. The chain of elements would be the following: painful affective crisis, incapacity to find a solution, sudden dreamlike scenario, dispersal of tension through some form of orgasmic or other psychic discharge. These disparate elements would henceforth remain attached.

the right to this maternal space, but the father, as one might imagine, is better armed than the son. (In his actual childhood, the patient believed that his father was weak and unarmed against life.) He threatens the son with his powerful phallus, which at the same time represents the instrument that will castrate him. Faced with this forbidding father, the son finds a magical solution (today a dream one, but in the past it had indeed been his erotic solution to the fantasied threat). He gives up the desired place, and his new desire is centered on the beauty of his father's knife, which forbids him access to this "super spot." Stroking it, he is able to seduce the Arab-father and deflect his attention from the threatening situation. The father smiles, cries out, and is carried away by the (dirty and dangerous) sexual current. He falls into the mud, where he will die.

Thus the son erotically overcomes his internal persecutor, just as he did in his homosexual scenario, in which the figure of the persecutor was projected on to the partner. In the guise of "repairing" the other (in fact, this patient often claimed that his acts of fellatio were beneficial), the patient repairs himself in profiting by the other's loss, as the dream reveals. He is also freed from the analyst (it is she who is going on vacation, and not the patient) and is at the same time liberated from his dependence on the abandoning and castrating mother. He also frees himself from his fiancée, who holds the purse strings *(la bourse),* a sign that she possesses access to the father's fertile power. (In French the word *bourse* is also the word for testicles.) Possessed of the father's weapon and the precious *bourse,* he can now do whatever he wishes.

This patient had often bragged about his homosexual adventures and the erotic excitement he felt in seducing his partners to do what he wanted. But he had come to understand that the important control of the orgasmic release of the partner meant a symbolic castration of the other, which would satisfy him for a brief time by giving him the feeling of more virility. The dream sequence in which he calmly assumes that the partner will die stirred up considerable anxiety in his associations and a suspicion that his sexual adventures had always hidden a murderous wish. This insight played an important role in his analysis for many months and allowed him at the same time to reconstruct certain of his repressed infantile sexual theories.

The metaphors expressed in the dream are rich in significance. The Arab-father dies by anal expulsion. His falling into the mud signifies on the one hand falling victim to sexual desire, which is equated with being carried away by a "vagina-anus" in a shameful and dirty act. This fantasy was linked to the exciting theme of humiliation that played an equally important role in the sexual scenario. The dimension of humiliation so frequent in neosexualities is almost invariably associated with anal eroticism and the mastery of bodily functions. These in turn are linked to genital, narcissistic, and oedipal fantasies and feelings of castration at each level. In this patient the exploration of these factors, along with the essential discovery of the murderous aggression concealed within his affective relations to his partners (as well as the parental imagos), produced a radical change in his libidinal economy. After lengthy elaboration of his hatred of men and, concomitantly, his hated image of himself, he was finally able to understand and accept his infantile sadism and see it as part of the primitive sexuality that had never been integrated into his adult erotic life. Instead it had produced an equally ferocious and archaic type of guilt that forced him to seek punishment compulsively. (All of this forms part of the Kleinian concept of elaborating the depressive position.) Following this phase of the analysis, the compulsive element in the patient's homosexuality began to weaken, until eventually his homosexual activity lost all interest for him. His phallic image of himself had become an internalized one and no longer needed to be sought in the external world.

The second dream bears more directly on the important question of the need to repair the other while at the same time denying the interior state of deadness, a sort of psychic catatonia that is less elaborated than true depression and closer to the narcissistic fears and psychotic fantasies associated with early object relations than to neurotic anxieties around the oedipal situation. Sophie, a young homosexual woman, had been able after seven years of analysis to resolve a persecutory side of her character as well as to modify certain virtually psychotic ideas related to her body-image. This psychic change resulted in greater stability in her work as well as in her amorous relations. Condemned in the past to restless seeking of new partners, she had at last been able to maintain a relatively stable relationship with the same woman friend. Like many homosexuals of both sexes she was totally uninterested in personal orgasmic pleasure. As she put it, her unique erotic pleasure consisted of procuring pleasure for her partner; we find once again the fantasy of Karen in chapter 1, that there is only one sex for two. The dream came at the moment of a definitive break in the two-year relationship that Sophie had maintained with her friend.

> I am on the flank of a dried-out valley, and I too am parched and thirsty. On the other side of the valley I see Beatrice, but she is locked inside her own house. Furious at being so far away, I plunge into the dry valley. Everywhere I stumble over dog excrement, but as I go on further the valley becomes fresh and green, plants growing and water running. Suddenly I am in the basement of Beatrice's house, and there are trees, flowers, and fruit growing here, too. I reach out to pluck a fruit, but it slides away from me where I cannot get it and I begin to weep with rage.

We see in these dream images Sophie's need to bring her partner fresh water, greenness, and life, whereas she herself was unable to taste the fruits of her erotic love. She is the thirsty one, but the other is to be given those things of which she is deprived. All these elements of fantasy were concealed in her love acts. Her lovers were all "broken people," as she called them, with many psychological problems that she would try to understand and to solve for them. If she did not have the conviction that she was "repairing" her love-objects, she would be overwhelmed with feelings of being dangerous and inwardly dead. Then she would have serious car accidents and indulge in alcoholic orgies that put her life in danger.

In the second part of her dream the patient attempts to kill her friend with a revolver. If she can no longer be the means of reparation, no longer offer her own life as a gift to her lover, then she has no identity and no valid reason to exist. She thus finds herself back in her childhood relationship to her mother, a depressed woman who was unable to allow her daughter the slightest liberty of movement. As a baby the patient could sleep only in her mother's arms; as a young girl she had to keep her bedroom door open so that her mother, from the parental bedroom, could watch her with the aid of a mirror. Her friend Beatrice had become this controlling but essential person. Speaking of her, Sophie would say, "Our relationship is a constant anguish, and I have to struggle to prevent her from destroying me; yet without her I don't exist. It's either life with her, or death alone." In these desperate terms she gave expression to the infantile breast-mother relationship, but one in which the infant is called upon to bring life to the mother. Only in this way could she find some meaning in her own existence and survive psychically. Not only one sex for two and one body for two, but indeed, one life for two!

With homosexual analysands suicide may not be an empty threat, supported as it is by the unconscious wish to kill the object of desire when the latter is felt to be an object of vital need. This fantasy is successfully kept at bay by the inner state of deadness. Faced with the horror of the empty feeling that results, the patient chooses almost any path of escape. This pathogenic aftermath to a failure in separation and individuation is prototypic of what later becomes phallic castration anxiety. Unless the subject chooses to kill the depriving and controlling object of such desperate need—that is, kill the partner who gives some meaning to life (a psychotic act and a rare solution)—he or she will frequently choose suicide when the pain of being abandoned is overwhelming.*

---

*Five years later Sophie did, in fact, put a tragic end to her life. She had left analysis two years earlier because Beatrice returned to live with her and they moved from Paris. A further separation led Sophie to her suicidal act. In an attempt to deal with the pain and incomprehension I felt at Sophie's death, I chose to present this material at the Sixth International Congress of Psychiatry in 1983. ("Developmental Aspects of Affect Pathology," *Psychiatry*, vol. 4 [New York: Plenum, 1985], pp. 369–74.)

Eroticism and Death

Some sexual innovators prefer to be the sole actors in their erotic theaters. There are several reasons for this choice. It may be that no one wishes to play the role that satisfies the demands involved, or that the subject, for megalomanic reasons, wishes to play all the roles, thereby obtaining total freedom from the dangers of dependency. Others, with the same narcissistic needs, cannot tolerate the slightest deviation from their prefabricated plot—any difference between the wishes of the scenarist and the desire of the partner is experienced as a castrative or even mortal threat—and therefore must act alone. There may also exist a deathly fear of erotic exchange with another, implying anxiety stemming from the psychotic* rather than the neurotic pole of neosexual structures. The fear is of one's own destructiveness along with terror of the inner deadness that the other can so readily produce by refusing to play the designated role. Sometimes there is an equally great fear that engaging in the erotic stage play with a partner would result in death or in the loss of ego identity, which is a psychic equivalent to death.

A fetishist patient whose case has been published elsewhere (Stewart 1972) acted out in strict solitude a scenario in which a woman forcibly administered a boiling enema to a young girl. With certain accessories the patient would give himself this painful enema, but he always insisted that he was a sadist since in his fantasy he played the role of the sadistic woman. One day he decided to act out with a real partner the erotic drama that for twenty years he had played alone. In a sex shop he had found a provocative advertisement with an address and telephone number. On dialing this number and timidly describing his request, he was assured by a deep-voiced woman that she "would administer meticulously and with severity the required punishment." The patient reacted to these words with a temporary loss of memory for the next hour or so. When he recovered his wits, he

---

*I am not referring here to that psychotic use of the sexual relationship which leads some persons to seek and accept any form of sexual contact in order to find their body limits and achieve a feeling of personal psychic space as proof that they truly exist.

had wandered miles from the site of the telephone and felt as though he had awakened from a nightmare. All he could remember was the woman's voice and words and the dangling telephone receiver that he had forgotten to replace. He said simply, "I had made a rendezvous with my death."

Certain literary works have evoked this atmosphere of flirting with death that is so often a part of neosexual fantasy. Tennessee Williams's *Suddenly One Summer* recreates this atmosphere in the story of a homosexual who is drawn, by his attraction to a band of hungry boys, to a horrifying but inevitable death. Truman Capote's *Other Voices, Other Rooms* deals essentially with the same theme. Throughout the work of Sade, death is always on the horizon of the sexual climax. In all these cases it would seem that the subject can hope to be recognized as an object of desire only through submitting to some inexorable law —such as it was interpreted in childhood—that requires that this privilege must be paid for by giving up one's life.

12

Scenes of Fantasy, Delusion, and Death

Parental Images and Neosexualities

Numerous psychoanalytic texts have described the typical parental images presented by analysands who have created new forms of sexuality. These family portraits are so similar that one might readily believe the patients were all members of the same family (McDougall 1978, pp. 53–86). The mother, adoring and adored, is a highly idealized image, often described as an accomplice in excluding the father from her relationship with the child and sometimes as having actually favored the child's sexual deviation in latency and adolescence. The father is remembered as weak, totally absent, under the mother's thumb, or possessed of character traits that make him appear worthless or contemptible. Consciously, the child, boy or girl, wishes neither to identify with him nor to be loved by him.

In the course of analysis, however, these strongly drawn portraits reveal their counterparts. The imagos are totally split. Behind the idealized mother we discover the witch-woman, castrating and castrated; behind the despicable father is a godlike one with an idealized and uncastratable phallus. The avoidance of the oedipal conflict, the counterfeit castration, the refusal to give symbolic significance to the difference between the sexes and the generations, the rejection of the phallus as the symbol of desire for both sexes, the disavowal of the primal scene—all these factors are clearly linked to the internal objects and the clash between them hidden in the unconscious.

The parental couple consisting of an adoring mother and a worthless father is not, of course, the exclusive property of those who have reinvented human sexuality. The new primal scene and the neosexuality cannot be fully explained by oedipal frustrations and the need to protect the libidinal and narcissistic cathexes of the inner object world. It is frequently said that behind every perversion are hidden bisexual wishes, but again this feature is in no way specific to neosexual inventors. The unconscious wish to possess the privileges and organs of both sexes exists in everyone and constitutes an important element in satisfactory heterosexual and love relationships; in neurotic people this same factor is a fertile source of symptoms. As far as neosexual innovators are concerned, it would be more precise to say that this bipolarity in sexual identification is forbidden and becomes a source of deep anxiety. They have been unable to identify fully with either one or the other sex. Instead there is a factitious identification resembling a caricature rather than a sexual identity, such as the caricature of femininity displayed by transvestites or the false virility flaunted in sadomasochistic practices.

Parental Attitudes and Neosexualities

Children who are destined in adolescence to invent neosexualities are also attempting to make sense of what they have heard and understood from family discussions about sex. We discover in their analyses as adults that there was an urgent need to understand incoherent communications concerning the body and the genitals of the child's own sex as well as those of the opposite sex. The necessity to invent a theory arose initially from the fact that what the child heard ran counter to what society (and other children) seemed to believe. The adolescent or adult sexuality to come will embody the childhood theory.

The mother's reflections on sexual differences and the role of sexuality in the parental couple are usually remembered—or interpreted—as being hostile to the father, to his sexual wishes, and to male sexuality in general. While it is undoubtedly true that many a deviant act conceals an identification to the mother's desire to receive the penis (in homosexual relations or in symbolic ways in the form of fetishistic objects), at the same time there is a second identification of an unconscious nature, to the mother's castrative attitude toward men and specifically to the father and his penis.

Those who become homosexual also appear to have been indoctrinated with the mother's negative attitudes toward people of the opposite sex. The boy has frequently heard that girls are dangerous, dirty, sly, and out to capture him; the girl learns that men have only one idea in their heads, to seduce, defile, or mistreat her, or to entice her into sadistic rape that may well cause her death. Who would want to engage in heterosexual relations presented in these terms? The mother then becomes the only acceptable love object. Her discourse on sexuality is received as incontrovertible truth, particularly when the father becomes an accomplice to this sexual attitude by his distance from the child or by active mockery of the child's sexuality and future manhood or womanhood. The depression that invariably comes to light in the analyses of these patients is frequently linked with the father's devaluation or nonrecognition of their sexual identity; his denial of their intrinsic value as human beings becomes a source of narcissistic mortification that will also seek compensation later in the neosexual scenario.

The oedipal structure is the blueprint for every child's conception of adult sexuality and its symbolic extensions into a view of society as a whole. Thus the model affects not only the child's future sexual pattern but also future social interchanges of all kinds. In the children with whom we are concerned here, this structure is clearly distorted, in part as the result of parental discussions and exhortations about the sexes and sexuality. Since these communications differ from normal cultural communications concerning sexuality, such children run the risk of confusion in their sense of sexual identity as well as their place in the family structure. It is then that they feel propelled to invent a theory in order to render their place and role coherent.

It could be said that these children have become the prisoners of their parents' unconscious fears and wishes. But not all prisoners seek to escape. Children's incestuous wishes lead them readily to believe that they are the mother's privileged sexual object and that their destiny is to fulfill her wishes. At the same time, both boys and girls wish to believe that they are upheld in their envious desire to castrate the father and magically take possession of his phallic power. The eventual loss of these illusions becomes a powerful force toward constructing the neosexual myth and its accompanying scenario. Thus the deviated objects and aims of sexual desire are already in place in the internal world, drawn from early fixations and aided by deviant parental communications. Such children repudiate the oedipal myth, with its universal status based on sexual differences and the social laws of the society to which they belong. In this way they escape from the maze in which they find themselves by creating a private mythology reserved for their exclusive use and in which they alone will establish the laws that uphold it. Faced with seemingly meaningless reflections on sexuality, they manage to find a meaning of their own.

The Dangerous Phallus

The neosexual inventor's discovery of a personal solution is invariably felt to be a triumph over the parents and their injunctions and contradictions, as well as a confirmation of the subject's right to some form of sexual life. The inventor is still not free of the contradictory internalized images, however; the inner conflict continues, often at considerable cost to psychic equilibrium. The damaged image of the symbolic phallus creates continuing havoc. If adults are to enjoy their sex lives without excessive guilt or anxiety, the phallus, symbol of power, fertility, and life, must also come to represent, for both sexes, the image of narcissistic completion and sexual desire. The analysands who concern us here harbor within their psychic realities a disintegrated phallic image, whose different fragments are given mysterious or dangerous significance. Nevertheless it is important to emphasize that these very fragments that take the place of the phallus in the unconscious have their structural value for the personality. Should a symbolic phallic image be entirely missing, psychotic confusion about sexual relationships would ensue. With no theory—even a mythical and deviant one—about the father's penis and its role in relation to the mother's sexual organ and erotic life, the child may be faced with a vision of the mother's body as a limitless chasm. Her body becomes an omnipotent and malevolent object, likely to form the nodal point for delusional sexual beliefs or in certain cases (as with Isaac in chapters 4 and 6 and Paul in chapter 8) for psychosomatic vulnerability.

In neosexual organizations the phallus, disinvested of its symbolic oedipal value, becomes divided into a persecuting, sadistic penis and an unattainable, idealized one. The first must be constantly avoided and the second constantly sought after, in whatever imaginary ways the subject has been able to devise. The fantasy of being a castrated man—invariably assimilated to an unconscious representation of femininity—is readily observable in the analyses of patients of both sexes. But this fantasy (common to many neurotic patients as well) is in deviant sexuality used by both sexes to conceal a more dangerous one, that of being inhabited by a destructive or potentially poisonous internal penis. This fantasy may be experienced as a threat to one's personal integrity or to that of others. It is important to recognize the powerful effect of this unconscious representation. One of its roots lies in the damaged image of the father, but eventually in the case of the man, it is felt as a threat to the subject himself and drives him to seek a compensatory "good penis" in the external world—that of another man or a "fetishistic penis" that he can add to his own in order to transform it into a penis capable of performing the sexual act.

This internalized "bad penis" fantasy may also give rise to hypochondriacal fears. A fragment of the analysis of a neurotic patient with obsessive homosexual fantasies illustrates this type of problem. The patient had a long history of back pain stemming from both somatic and psychological sources. One day he brought to analysis a dream in which a surgeon opens up his back to find the cause of his continual pain and discovers, in a state of putrefaction, a gigantic penis, which he removes. The manifest wish pertains to the analysand's desire that the analyst remove this source of malady. In point of fact the working through of the different fantasy elements and associations that the patient brought to his dream considerably modified his homosexual obsession, and within a matter of weeks his back troubles had also disappeared.

The fantasy of the dangerous internal penis may also be thought of as threatening the partner in the sexual act. One fetishist patient, in order to become sexually excited, beat his girlfriends in a ferocious manner. He always managed to find partners who desired this treatment, in accordance with their own erotic fantasies, but he was invariably overwhelmed with panic at the moment of penetration, because he feared hurting them with his penis. The analysis revealed that his penis was at that moment transformed in fantasy into a sadistic object imbued with fecal qualities.

For the woman as for the man, the unconscious fantasy of a penis with fecal and anal-sadistic characteristics frequently comes to light, but with this difference: both the appearance and the somatic functioning of the whole body are subject to hypochondriacal anxiety. This kind of fantasy comes perilously close at times to assuming delusional proportions (McDougall 1964).

The only way out of the impasse for people who harbor such a representation in their internal worlds is to transform the harmful and frightening qualities of this fantasy penis into an external object possessed of valuable and reparative qualities, at which moment it can become a source of erotic arousal. The fantasied reparation may be attached to the self-image or to that of the partner, but in either case it is a manic illusion and as such it can repair only provisionally the depression and anxiety caused by the fantasied damage. Thus the fetish that repairs the subject while at the same time protecting the partner becomes increasingly precious and obsessive. The continual acts of fellatio, when they are intended to appease internal persecutors, become more and more compulsive; the exclusive pursuit of anal intercourse or the giving of painful enemas, when intended in unconscious fantasy to get rid of the dangerous internal penis, becomes increasingly urgent and necessary to the subject's peace of mind. Many such patients are afraid that they may become obliged to spend their entire lives in pursuit of their inexorable erotic scripts.

The Fantasy of the Poisoned Mother

Another important and common fantasy deserves attention, that of the mother poisoned by the father's penis because of its supposed fecal and urinary qualities. This fantasy is frequently added to that of the injury of the mother during the sexual relation. Henceforth any stirring of desire toward her body or her genitals provokes a catastrophic reaction in male patients. In female patients, the same fantasies lead to quasi-delusional beliefs about their own bodies and to a compulsive drive to repair their own or the partners' bodies. The belief that the mother is damaged is accentuated by children's projection of their own archaic anal and oral sadistic impulses toward her. For various reasons these archaic drives, which are primitive fantasies of love relations, have failed to find a creative solution in the early maternal relationship. The failure may be due, as Bion (1970) put it, to the mother's incapacity for "reverie"—that is, her inability to identify with what her infant is experiencing and to contain her baby's ferocious affects until such time as she can transform them into constructive feelings and fantasies and thus prevent the infant from being overwhelmed with rage and distress. However this may be, the patients that concern us here were often compelled, as children and even as adults, to remain close to the real mother, to protect her against the slightest criticism or attack and to show themselves loyal not only to her person but also to her judgments, her tastes, her ideals, and her prejudices. Frequently the sole escape from this impasse is the neosexual creation, and then only on condition that this invention be capable of containing and dramatizing all the inner conflicts involved, of satisfying the reparative demand, and of maintaining in repression the true significance of the neosexual act and the true relationship to the partner.

In the light of these considerations we are able to understand the dynamic power with which these heterodox models of the sexual relation are imbued. At the same time the neosexual invention must be capable of standing up against the weight of external reality and the social opinion that may oppose it. The belief in the invention, along with the fantasies concerning the sexual body and the objects or acts held to be the cause of sexual desire, must be endowed with feelings of certitude. The Freudian concept of a split in the ego provides one theoretical explanation of the way in which a focalized psychosis may be maintained in someone who is not otherwise psychotic, but it still leaves unanswered many questions regarding the neosexualities and their psychic economy.

The Origins of Neosexual Constructions

If we wish to gain a better understanding of the origins of neosexualities, we must look beyond the false or fragmentary parental communications on sexual identity and sexual relations and attempt to reconstruct the earliest mother-infant bodily communications. The first difference of which the infant becomes aware is not between the sexes but between these two corporeal entities, and the earliest anxieties therefore involve global body damage. The mother's voice long precedes her words. Her way of nursing, rocking, caressing, and otherwise handling her infant all contribute to the earliest traces of erogenous experience. In this first sensual exchange between the two bodies, the mother's unconscious reactions to sensuous arousal are already being transmitted, and the infant is beginning to form a sexual identity (Lichtenstein 1961). The psychic representations of the erogenous zones and bodily functions are acquired in direct relationship to the mother's body; little by little the biological body becomes a psychological and erogenic one.

At the beginning of the infant's life, the psyche, in hallucinatory fashion, treats the objects of need and of pleasure as though they were self-engendered. This primitive megalomania then gives way rapidly to the recognition of an "elsewhere" responsible for the production of satisfying and gratifying experiences. From this time on the infant becomes an indefatigable scientist in search of the sources of pleasure and the avoidance of unpleasure. Henceforth the psyche functions under the dominance of primary-process thinking; the sources of pleasure and pain are no longer self-engendered but are considered to be entirely in the power of Another. This Other can decide whether the subject is to experience pleasure and gratification or unpleasure and pain. Everything that happens to the infant is understood as being in accordance with "her" desires. We can already detect here the primitive roots of what may be transformed by psychotic thinking into an "influencing-machine" fantasy of sexual excitation (Tausk 1919)—that mysterious apparatus, out of the subject's control, that procures sexual or cruelly painful sensations.

This belief in the magical power of the Other is present in many neosexual creators, although a healthier part of the psyche questions such beliefs. Thus the analyst may frequently hear analysands claim, while speaking of their own ego-syntonic inventions, "I am the victim of a spell" or "It is not I, myself, engaged in perpetrating this act—I'm like a robot, programmed in advance, powerless to do anything about it." The Other is responsible, and the subject is liberated from any feeling of personal guilt or responsibility.

In the earliest stages of psychic life, every infant responds to what its mother wishes for it, consciously or unconsciously. Castoriadis-Aulagnier (1975), in her thought-provoking book on the roots of psychosis, refers to the continually "speaking shadow" that every mother projects on the small physical being that is her child.

> The mother asks this little body that is cared for, pampered, and nourished by her to try to conform to the fantasy-shadow that she casts upon it. This "shadow," which is but a fragment of her communication to her baby, represents for her conscious ego what the child's body represents for her unconsciously; a certain way of being, certain qualities, and a future are all unconsciously desired for this child. . . . Thus what every mother wishes for her child will inevitably become that which the child asks for and expects from her. (P. 136; my translation)

A mother may make inappropriate and unjustifiable demands on her infant's body and mind without being aware of it. One of my patients gave her three children, from babyhood onward, frequent enemas (see chapter 4), not because they seemed physiologically necessary but in order to get rid of an intolerable feeling that she herself was "dirty." In the same way an infant may become a counterphobic object to protect the mother against anxiety or depressive states. Robert Stoller (1968), in his exhaustive research on the problems of sexual and gender identity, has proposed the hypothesis that the mothers of sexual deviants may well have utilized their children as transitional objects. The mother's communications are permeated with her own psychological viewpoint, which is transmitted to her child since it is she who is responsible for giving her child the words for the body zones and functions, just as she alone can teach her child to name and recognize different affective states. She is the ultimate arbiter of those thoughts that are to be accepted as permissible and those that are "unthinkable." Thus a mother may easily transmit to her child a body-image that is fragile, devoid of eroticism, alienated, or mutilated.

Clinical observation confirms that those children who become sexually deviant in adulthood have created their erotic theater as a protective barrier against a damaged corporeal image and against the loss of the body-representation as an entity and with it the loss of a cohesive sense of ego identity. They thus avoid the danger of experiencing the body and its sexuality in psychotic fashion—that is, as an object over which they have no control because it is in the power of someone else. Neosexual creations propose what is basically a delusional theory of human sexuality and the origins of sexual desire, but one over which the subject has mastery and toward which he or she retains a modicum of doubt. The certitude that accompanies psychotic beliefs is on the whole absent or at least denied by another part of the personality.

Linked to the early oedipal organization and the mother's verbal communications is the development of children's autoerotic activities, to which reference has already been made in chapter 11. Their evolution depends entirely on a mother's willingness to permit her infant to become detached from her through recreating psychically some memory trace of her, allied with an autoerotic act such as thumb-sucking. This early form of internalization allows the child to maintain a measure of independence from her body and presence. But certain mothers violently oppose these infant inventions.

The first true autoerotic act is the child's sucking a part of the body or some other available object that gives the infant a "hallucinatory" breast. Melanie Klein (1945) has posited that this hallucinatory phenomenon can only take place if there is a libidinal investment already attached to an internal object. This concept seems satisfactory, not only in the interests of theoretical coherence but also in view of clinical facts, even though the internalized "object" may be nothing more than a fragmentary memory trace of the Other and the shared experience of satisfaction associated with it. The observational research of René Spitz (1949, 1962) brings some confirmation of Klein's theory, as does the research of certain psychosomaticists (Fain 1974).

These observations demonstrate clearly that certain mothers, although unconscious of the fact, can allow no early introjection of their image, nor can they tolerate any object that may be utilized by the infant as a substitute for themselves. They offer their own bodies instead of leaving some space in which the infant can find the first substitute objects or activities (the transitional phenomena of Winnicott's theory) and thus constitute a personal autoerotic and narcissistic psychic capital. A mother-child relationship that forbids this activity favors the creation of psychosomatic illnesses in early infancy, of which one example is infant insomnia. Such babies can sleep only in their mothers' arms; separation from the mother and hospitalization are often required to safeguard their lives. Some mothers use constant and sometimes violent physical means to restrain their infants' normal autoerotic manifestations, perhaps because of severe anxiety concerning their own sexual impulses. Excessive or violent reactions to any form of autoerotic invention may set in motion the serious psychosomatic malady known as rumination or merycism (McDougall 1978, chap. 9), which also endangers the child's life. Ruminating babies might be considered to have created an extremely precocious autoerotic perversion.

My own observations (1978) have led me to remark the frequency with which psychosomatic illnesses occur in patients who have constructed organized neosexualities. In chapter 5 mention is made of differentiating factors that may produce a psychosomatic rather than a neosexual outcome. Psychosomatic sufferers who have not created a deviant sexuality frequently describe identical disturbance in infantile autoerotism, in particular a lack of normal manual masturbatory activity in childhood and adolescence. It is possible that the mother-nursling relation is marked by similar bodily contact and affective exchange. Both neosexual and psychosomatic patients report a higher-than-average frequency of body-rocking and infant insomnia, along with dermatological and respiratory problems. These phenomena appear to arise from early disturbance in the cathexes of the body and the construction of narcissistic links between psyche and soma, as well as from a premature breach in the all-important hand-sex link that leads in infancy to what Spitz (1949) named "genital play." The small child who vigorously pursues autoerotic gratifications in spite of these fractured links between body and mind and between hand and genital will be obliged to invent other sexual activities and other zones of excitation. The retention of urine, fecal games, incessant stroking of the body, seeking painful sensations, head-banging, rocking, and other similar acts are all attempts to make the body feel alive and able to be represented psychically as an entity with limits as well as pleasurable possibilities.

These activities then fulfill one of the primary functions of infantile autoerotism, that is, they become a compensation for the object's absence and the painful affects that accompany this loss. There is little doubt that with those who become erotic innovators, normal infantile autoerotism has been deviated well before the oedipal crisis and that the elements of the future neosexual creation are already in existence. The distance that separates the subject's hand from the sexual organs is in a sense the measure of the distance that exists between the narcissistic self-representation and the representation of the sexual identity. The autoerotic quest of infants to render their bodies erogenous serves more than instinctual and object needs; it is also a search for proof of their psychic existence and of their capacity to maintain a feeling of personal identity although separated from the Other. The phrases used by analysands when discussing their perverse acts exemplify this aim. "It's the only time I have the proof that I truly exist and that my life has some meaning," said a fetishist when talking of his sexual practices. An exhibitionist remarked, "While it lasts I feel real, and afterward I am calm for a long time." Sophie (quoted in the preceding chapter) frequently said, "Beatrice makes me suffer, but it's either life with her, or death alone."

Thus in different ways these patients seek compulsively in the external world an object, act, or person capable of helping them evade the existential doubts and emptiness or deadness in the inner psychic world. The neosexual act must embody a narcissistic-phallic representation to combat oedipal and narcissistic castration anxiety. At the same time, the fetish, partner, or part-object represents a primary maternal object to combat the state of inner death and the subsequent awakening of destructive impulses and deathlike drives.

The Creation of the Neosexual Erotic Theater

As we have seen, so-called perverse sexuality can be satisfactorily understood neither as a mere regression nor as a simple deviation of the sexual drives. It is a neoreality created by the child's psychic labor in order to come to terms with the unconscious problems of both parents. The parental problems are of two orders: unresolved sexual conflicts, which are frequently reflected in the children's memories of parental communications, and profound narcissistic anxieties that impel both parents to attempt to repair their narcissistic wounds or control narcissistic fears by limiting and controlling their children's developing sexuality.

Children's own discoveries of erotic games that escape parental vigilance are a challenge to both of the internalized images and imply a measure of freedom from their introjected prohibitions. Above all, in finding a solution to the puzzle provided by the parents' devious communications on bodily and sexual matters, children succeed in giving meaning to the enigma of sexual desire, thus allowing themselves some sexual expression and the possibility of future erotic exchange with others. As time goes on, these sexual acts are eventually called upon to fulfill other functions. In addition to deflecting castration anxiety and neutralizing the anguish that stems from archaic sadistic impulses, they have value as a means of discharging the accumulated tensions mobilized by all the narcissistic injuries and reality frustrations that human beings suffer. It is evident that an invention capable of fulfilling such diverse functions must be solidly constructed from infancy on and that such a structure will scarcely be modifiable in the years to come, unless the experience of analysis leads to a richer erotic life. The secret erotic game of childhood becomes for the adolescent his or her adult sexuality. At the same time the subject discovers that his or her sexual expression, although appearing to be the only true one, does not resemble the solutions of others. Then begins the ceaseless searching for partners capable of playing the required role in the erotic theater. For some neosexual creators there is the discovery that they are condemned to erotic autarky and must henceforth assume the imposed solitude that it implies.

The Basic Functions of Neosexuality

How may we best sum up the dynamic and economic dimensions of this complex organization in order to understand its vital function in the eyes of the subject who has created it? If in the Freudian metaphor perverse sexuality may be regarded as the "positive" of a neurotic organization, it may also be described as the "negative" of a psychotic one. The structure shares the characteristics and defenses of both neuroses and psychoses. The act resembles an erotic daydream, but it is a dream carried out in reality. Its realization implies a manipulation of sexual truth and external reality as a defensive maneuver to repair the self-image and in this respect resembles a psychotic construction, although a highly focalized one.

A deviant sexual symptom may be distinguished from a neurotic or psychotic symptom in several ways. First, acting takes the place of mental elaboration and working through. Second, the act is consciously eroticized, which is not the case with neurotic constructions nor with delusions. Third, there is a specific form of relationship to the sexual object; the latter, though frequently treated more as a condition than a subject, is unconsciously called upon to fulfill multiple functions. Schematically we could say that neurosis indicates a defense that has failed with respect to the libidinal drives, while psychosis indicates a defense that has failed with regard to the sadistic drives. The first is a struggle to safeguard one's sexuality; the second, a struggle for life. The neosexual construction represents a twofold defensive attempt: to find a compromise solution on the one hand to neurotic castration fears and on the other to psychotic anxieties concerning the loss of ego identity and the risk of being propelled by violent or suicidal impulses. Fear of castration, of ego fragmentation, and of death must find their place in the new scenario, there to be enacted and eroticized without danger. The act must therefore sustain three fundamental illusions: that castration and oedipal prohibitions are powerless threats, that sadistic violence causes no harm either to oneself or one's partner, and finally that the dreaded state of inner deadness stemming from early psychic traumata in infancy does not exist.

The dynamic and economic implications of neosexuality may be summarized in this way: those who succeed in creating a neoreality in human sexuality and in putting it into action have discovered a roundabout means for disavowing the oedipal conflict and have thus short-circuited psychic elaboration of castration anxiety; at the same time they have found an intricate way of disavowing the problems of separateness and infantile sadism, thus avoiding psychic elaboration of the depressive position.

It is evident that this structure is forced to carry considerable dynamic weight as well as to stand firm against inner and outer realities. Painful mental representations and affects demand constant discharge through the magical act. Its compulsive and repetitive nature is characteristic of what I have named *action symptoms*, that is, psychic organizations that attempt to resolve the conflicts in the inner world by some form of action in the external world. This obligation to act indicates a certain failure in symbolic functioning as well as an inability to contain painful emotional states and to use fantasy constructively. It also points to frightening internal object relations against which protection is sought in the relation to external ones. Neosexualities avoid the necessity for dealing with the psychic pain of anxiety or depression that might otherwise overwhelm the subject's capacity to metabolize it. Thus once again, action takes the place of containing, feeling, and thinking.

As we have seen in the preceding chapters, the externalization of internal conflict is not limited to neosexualities. We find the same means of maintaining psychic homeostasis in the character neuroses, for example, some of which may also be described as *character perversions* (Arlow 1954, 1963, 1971). People with "perverse" character symptoms also find themselves compelled to repeat endlessly the dramas and deceptions in which they use others to play out their inner scenarios. Since the authors are usually unaware of this prefabricated drama, they frequently attribute to others the suffering that results. The eroticization is still present but totally unconscious.

The Concept of Addictive Sexuality

Related to the same economic organization for dealing with libidinal and narcissistic conflicts are the addictions. It has been proposed in the preceding chapters that people suffering from character neuroses use others like a drug and that many sexual deviants use sexuality—their own orgasmic prowess or other people's—as an opiate. From this point of view I am tempted to speak of addictive sexuality to emphasize not only the negation of the partner as a separate individual but also the compulsive, archaic, counterphobic aspects of neosexual creations. The analyses of such patients reveal that the compulsive counterphobic dimension of the sexual act becomes considerably modified as the analytic work progresses, while at the same time intense phobic reactions and symptoms come to the fore for the first time in the analysands' memory. When they do, it is a decisive and delicate moment requiring careful interpreting. A detailed study of these clinical aspects goes beyond the aims of this chapter, however.

It should be pointed out that nondeviant sexuality may also display addictive and compulsive qualities when the sexual relation is principally utilized to disperse painful psychic states or is carried out with a partner who does not exist as a separate and libidinally invested object. The other again serves the function of a drug or becomes a container for dangerous parts of the individual, which may be mastered by gaining erotic control over the partner.

Behind all addictive organizations (Krystal 1977) lies the archaic breast-mother, that is to say, a part of the mother that was not able to be internalized; her function then becomes equivalent to that of an addictive substance—the "drug-mother." This fundamental weakness in psychic structure, as we have seen throughout the different psychic theaters discussed in this book, is capable of producing a series of psychological disasters. The subject runs the risk of being constantly obliged to make an object in the external world do duty for one that is damaged or symbolically absent in the inner psychic structure, and even in the world of imagination. The inability to develop constructive fantasies or to dispose of a store of repressed fantasies implies a profound prohibition of the freedom to fantasize. The magical dependence on external objects for repairing fantasy damage tends to perpetuate the fear of omnipotent wishes and thoughts and to block the psyche from functioning in more creative ways. This fact suggests, as already indicated in chapter 3, that the maturation of transitional phenomena has been arrested and that pathological or transitory objects have been created in place of true transitional objects and activities. Consequently there is an inability to play with one's thoughts and fantasies, and the self-regulation of psychic tension and painful affective states is rendered more difficult. A stumbling block has been placed in the way of giving significance to that which is missing or absent. Only one rigidified fantasy persists, the one that directs the quest for the addictive situation.

Constructed of neurotic and psychotic defenses, this way of mental functioning is also suspended between fantasy and delusion. The original fantasies that give rise to the creation of neosexual acts are the result of precocious infantile creativity. The child's specific sexual theory has arisen in response to two major aims: the avoidance of oedipal interdictions, with their demand that the difference between the sexes and between the generations be respected, and the avoidance of archaic anxiety linked to the destructive drives and the feared state of inner death. This fantasy creation, almost too successful in deflecting the diverse threats in question, is maintained, petrified for life (or should one say for death?). When the addictive dimension is prominent, the neosexual scenario (and the sexual quest of some nondeviant heterosexuals) immediately seeks a stage whenever internal or external pressures threaten to attack the psychic equilibrium of the subject. Since there is no freedom to fantasize, some manipulation of external reality is required to prevent a drastic loss of narcissistic equilibrium. Delusion consists of believing in the objective reality of one's fantasies. But as Freud (1911a) demonstrated in his study of President Schreber, even the creation of a delusion is an attempt at self-cure. It fulfills the wish to recreate a world in which one can continue to live and a neoreality in which one can believe, in spite of the collapse of the internal world.

From the economic viewpoint, however, delusions do not fulfill the same function as fantasies. The person who imagines perverse scenes during intercourse or masturbation is not undergoing the same experience as the one who is acting out organized neosexual or addictive scenarios. Fantasies that are sufficient unto themselves play an important role in the narcissistic economy, whereas delusions always imply some manipulation of one's representation of the external world and its objects. In fantasy the object is not directly touched and therefore can in no way be damaged, nor its force depleted. Delusion on the other hand is constantly demolished by the impact of reality testing and must, just as constantly, be repeated. The compulsive, repetitive aspect applies to all addictive sexualities. The person caught in this web of illusion will always choose the magical act, and its painfully compulsive quality, rather than face anguish and internal persecutors.

In sum, neosexualities as well as nondeviant addictive sexualities are created in response to a complex psychic situation. From a dynamic point of view they require secret scenarios that combat oedipal conflicts as well as those belonging to the realm of archaic sexuality. Castration anxiety must be mastered by turning it into a sexual game with invented aims and objects, while primitive sadism must be compensated by the illusion of reparation of either oneself or the partner.

From the economic point of view, most neosexual creations have a drug-like quality; they are used to escape from painful psychic states and to repair rifts in the feeling of identity as well as to satisfy instinctual impulses. These erotic theater-pieces are therefore constantly required to maintain libidinal as well as narcissistic homeostasis. This attempt at self-cure allows such creators to maintain erotic contact with themselves as well as with others while at the same time avoiding a state of emotional flooding that might otherwise precipitate acts of self-destruction or violence to others.

Although neosexualities may frequently be regarded as a form of addiction, their inventive and theatrical aspects that make up the scenario and provide an imaginary answer to the riddles of desire and the problem of otherness may be regarded as a creative process. As long as the dimension of reparation is maintained, deviant sexuality is able to avoid a psychotic solution to the conflicts, and Eros triumphs over death.

Epilogue

Illusion and Truth

> It no longer staggers me to discover that I behave toward myself like a mean mother and a disgraced father . . . nor to know that I am inhabited by a madman, a tyrant, a saint, and a sexual maniac.
>
> *Patient in the third year of analysis*

Psychoanalysis is a theater on whose stage all our psychic repertory may be played. In these scenarios the features of the internal characters undergo many changes, the dialogues are rewritten and the roles recast. The work of elaboration leads analysands to the discovery of their internal reality and their inner truth, once all the different parts of themselves and all the people who have played important roles in their lives have had a chance to speak their lines. Accounts are settled with the loved-hated figures of the past; the analysands now possess them in all their aspects, good and bad, instead of being possessed by them, and now are ready to take stock of all they have received from those who brought them up and of what they have done with this inheritance. Whatever their conclusions may be, they recognize their place in this inner universe and claim that which is their own.

The analysis is declared terminated when the analyst and the analysand agree to stop seeing each other, but the analysand must fully realize that the work they have undertaken together is by its very nature unfinished. Both analyst and analysand are aware that certain inner characters have remained anonymous, that others with whom important dialogue has been established may still jump from the wings and force their way once more upon the mind's stage.

With regard to all the voices that have remained silent, we are faced with a complex question that engenders anxiety: Were they silent because the analyst refused to listen when they clamored for attention? They were always there, whispering behind the scenes in the preconscious mind. Was the analyst negligent or distracted? Or were they speaking a language that the analyst did not understand? Might they have been speaking in Rhinencephalon? Asthmatic? Diabetic? Or Cardiac? In other words, how may we evaluate the different factors that contribute to the outcome of a psychoanalysis? Are shortcomings in analytic treatment due to unconscious dissimulations, weaknesses in our theory, or the vicissitudes of countertransference interference? The last element certainly constitutes one of our greatest stumbling blocks: every analyst is keenly aware of the risk of listening too closely to his or her own inner beliefs and expectations, knowing that these may deflect the analytic discourse and transmit to the patient problems that belong to the analyst.

The psychoanalytic enterprise of decoding the inner dramas nevertheless comes to an end. The actors take off their costumes and return to their dressing rooms. We are permitted to hope that, from now on, our patients will have gained sufficient understanding of the fundamental themes that occupy their psychic repertory to recognize them when new life circumstances remobilize them. It is hoped that the patients will then be able to continue the work of elaboration begun in the consulting room and speak to these inner people, but using their own words and moved by their own affective reactions. For the formal termination of an analysis ushers in the beginning of self-analysis. It should permit those inner characters who have remained in limbo to come on stage, as well as allowing patients to rediscover in themselves the close identification that their mind's *I* has made with each internal object, in both its good and its bad aspects. It is important to recognize within oneself the roles of Oedipus, Jocasta, Laius, Antigone, Narcissus, Hermaphrodite, and some of the sinister Furies. But the *I*'s acquisitions are not limited to myths and dreams. We must not lose sight of the fact that inner psychic reality is created on the rock of anatomical and external realities and the truth of infantile desires. The psychoanalytic adventure will be forever torn between these two poles, a compound of reality and illusion.

Who then is *I?* And who is speaking within us each time we say "I think this," "I believe that," "I dread, desire, or detest this, that, or the other"? How may we determine the part played by illusion in the rediscoveries and constructions that are revealed in the space created between two people's *I*—that is, created by an agency called the ego that is made of words and a psychic stage that comes into existence through a dialogue?

The analyst might be likened to the stage manager of Luigi Pirandello's celebrated *Six Characters in Search of an Author,* in that he or she seeks to maintain a space that is ready to welcome all the internal inhabitants of each analysand's secret theater, as well as to capture the lost and wandering characters playing roles in the external world that go unrecognized by the mind's *I* as part of its own personal cast. The *I* needs its creations as well as its illusions and in this respect recalls the touching character of the Father in Pirandello's play, who pleads for the reality of his particular personage after the stage manager has reminded him rather sharply that he is nothing but a creature of illusion.

> The Father: It's just that I would like to know, Sir, if you see yourself, as you are now, as being the same throughout the years that you once were, with all the illusions that you formerly nourished? . . . Do you not realize that "he" whom you feel yourself to be at this moment, your reality of today, is destined tomorrow to appear to you nothing but an illusion?*

The *I* who presents itself to each individual as being the veritable self, with its pleasures and pains, its force and frailty, its capacity to love and to hate, to work and to play, its right to succeed—and also to fail—in its many projects, its possession and acceptance of the infantile *I* within its precincts—all these factors

*From *Naked Masks: Five Plays* by Luigi Pirandello, edited by Eric Bentley. Copyright 1922, 1952 by E. P. Dutton. Renewed 1950 in the names of Stefano, Fausto, and Lietta Pirandello, and 1980 by Eric Bentley. Reprinted by permission of the publisher, E. P. Dutton, a division of New American Library.

contribute to the *I* that reveals itself upon the analytic stage. Indeed, this *I* is more like a portrait than a photograph.

What does the analyst hope will be the outcome of each psychoanalytic adventure? Perhaps something like Gertrude Stein's famous remark when she saw the portrait that Picasso had made of her. She had complained that she bore no resemblance to the portrait in its initial stages, and Picasso replied that with time she would. When faced with the finished painting, she exclaimed, *"Pour moi, c'est je!"* ("To me, that is I!").

Bibliography

Arlow, J. 1954. Perversions: Theoretic and therapeutic aspects. Panel report. *Journal of the American Psychoanalytic Association* 2: 336–45.

———. 1963. Conflict, regression and symptom formation. *International Journal of Psycho-Analysis* 44: 12–22.

———. 1971. Character perversion. In *Currents in psychoanalysis,* ed. I. M. Marcus. New York: International Universities Press.

Bick, E. 1968. The experience of the skin in early object relations. *International Journal of Psycho-Analysis* 49: 484–86.

Bion, W. 1957. Differentiation of the psychotic from the non-psychotic personalities. In *Second Thoughts* pp. 43–64. New York: Jason Aronson, 1967.

———. 1962a. *Elements of psychoanalysis.* London: Heinemann.

———. 1962b. A theory of thinking. In *Second thoughts.* London: Heinemann, 1967.

———. 1970. *Attention and interpretation.* London: Heinemann.

Breuer, J., and S. Freud. 1893–96. *Studies on hysteria,* standard ed. 2. London: Hogarth Press, 1955.

Castoriadis-Aulagnier, P. 1975. *La violence de l'interprétation.* Paris: Presses Universitaires de France.

Charcot, J. M. 1888. *Leçons du Mardi de la Salpêtriere.* Paris: Delatray et Lecrosnier.

Dayan, M. 1981. Causalité psychique et interprétation. *Topique* 27: 93–122.

Engel, G. 1962. Anxiety and depression withdrawal: The primary affects of unpleasure. *International Journal of Psycho-Analysis* 43: 89–97.

Fain, M. 1971. Prélude à la vie fantasmatique. *Revue Française de Psychanalyse* 35: 291–364.

———. 1974. In *L'enfant et son corps,* eds. M. Fain, L. Kreisler, and M. Soulé. Paris: Presses Universitaires de France.

Freud, S. 1898. Sexuality in the aetiology of the neuroses, standard ed. 3: 263–85. London: Hogarth Press, 1962.

———. 1900. The interpretation of dreams, standard ed. 5: 509–622. London: Hogarth Press, 1953.

———. 1905. Three essays on sexuality, standard ed. 7: 125–245. London: Hogarth Press, 1957.

———. 1911a. Psychoanalytic notes on an autobiographical account of a case of paranoia, standard ed. 12: 9–79. London: Hogarth Press, 1957.

———. 1911b. Formulations on the two principles of mental functioning, standard ed. 12: 219–20. London: Hogarth Press, 1957.

———. 1914. On narcissism: An introduction, standard ed. 14: 67–102. London: Hogarth Press, 1957.

———. 1915a. Repression, standard ed. 14: 146–58. London: Hogarth Press, 1957.

———. 1915b. The unconscious, standard ed. 14: 159–216. London: Hogarth Press, 1957.

———. 1915c. Instincts and their vicissitudes, standard ed. 14: 109–17. London: Hogarth Press, 1957.

———. 1916–17. The common neurotic state, standard ed. 16: 378–91. London: Hogarth Press, 1963.

———. 1918. From the history of an infantile neurosis, standard ed. 17: 13–122. London: Hogarth Press, 1955.

———. 1919. A child is being beaten, standard ed. 17: 174–204. London: Hogarth Press, 1955.

———. 1920. Beyond the pleasure principle, standard ed. 18: 7–61. London: Hogarth Press, 1955.

———. 1924. The economic problem of masochism, standard ed. 19: 157–72. London: Hogarth Press, 1957.

———. 1926. Inhibition, symptom and anxiety, standard ed. 20: 77–128. London: Hogarth Press, 1957.

———. 1927. Fetishism, standard ed. 21: 149–58. London: Hogarth Press, 1957.

———. 1938a. Splitting of the ego in the process of defense, standard ed. 23: 271–78. London: Hogarth Press, 1957.

———. 1938b. An outline of psychoanalysis, standard ed. 23: 177. London: Hogarth Press, 1957.

Galenson, E., and H. Roiphe. 1981. *Infantile origins of sexual identity.* New York: International Universities Press.

Green, A. 1973. *Le discours vivant.* Paris: Presses Universitaires de France.

Grotstein, J. 1981. *Splitting and projective identification.* New York: Jason Aronson.

Hanly, C., and J. Masson. 1976. A critical examination of the new narcissism. *International Journal of Psycho-Analysis* 57: 49–66.

Kernberg, O. 1975. *Borderline conditions and pathological narcissism.* New York: Jason Aronson.

———. 1976. *Object relations theory and clinical psychoanalysis.* New York: Jason Aronson.

Klein, M. 1927. The importance of words in early analysis. In *Writings of Melanie Klein,* vol. 3: 215–26. London: Hogarth Press, 1975.

———. 1929. Personification in the play of children. In *Contributions to psychoanalysis* (1921–45), pp. 215–26. London: Hogarth Press, 1950.

———. 1932. *The psychoanalysis of children.* London: Hogarth Press, 1959.

———. 1935. A contribution to the psychogenesis of manic-depressive states. *Contributions to psychoanalysis* (1921–45), pp. 382–410. London: Hogarth Press, 1950.

———. 1945. 1945. The oedipus complex in the light of early anxieties. In *Contributions to psychoanalysis* (1921–45), pp. 339–90. London: Hogarth Press, 1950.

———. 1946. Notes on some schizoid mechanisms. In *Envy and gratitude and other works* (1946–63), pp. 1–24. London: Hogarth Press, 1975.

———. 1955. On identification. In *Envy and gratitude and other works* (1946–53), pp. 141–75. London: Hogarth Press, 1950.

———. 1957. *Envy and gratitude.* New York: Basic Books.

Kohut, H. 1971. *The analysis of the self.* New York: International Universities Press.

———. 1977. *The restoration of the self.* New York: International Universities Press.

Krystal, H. 1977. Aspects of affect theory. *Bulletin of the Menninger Clinic* 41: 1–26.

———. 1978a. Trauma and affects. *Psychoanalytic Study of the Child* 36: 81–116.

———. 1978b. Self-representation and the capacity for self-care. In *Annual of Psychoanalysis* 6: 206–46. New York: International Universities Press.

———. 1981. The hedonic element in affectivity. In *Annual of Psychoanalysis* 9: 93–113. New York: International Universities Press.

———. 1982. Alexithymia and the effectiveness of psychoanalytic treatment. *Journal of Psychoanalytic Psychotherapy* 9: 353–78.

Kuhn, T. 1962. *The structure of scientific revolution.* In *International Encyclopedia of Unified Science,* vol. 2, no. 2, 1976.

Lacan, J. 1966. *Ecrits.* Paris: Seuil.

Laplanche, J. 1970. *Vie et mort en psychanalyse.* Paris: Flammarion.

Laplanche, J., and J. B. Pontalis. 1967. *The language of psychoanalysis.* New York: Norton, 1973.

Lax, R. 1976. Some comments on the narcissistic aspects of self-righteousness. *International Journal of Psychoanalysis* 56: 283–92.

Lefebvre, P. 1980. The narcissistic impasse as a determinant of psychosomatic disorder. *Psychiatric Journal of University of Ottawa* 5: 5–11.

Lichtenstein, H. 1961. Identity and sexuality. *Journal of the American Psychoanalytic Association* 9: 179–260.

———. 1977. *The dilemma of human identity.* New York: Jason Aronson.

McDougall, J. 1964. Homosexuality in women. In *Female sexuality,* ed. J. Chasseguet. Ann Arbor: University of Michigan Press, 1974.

———. 1972. The anti-analysand in analysis. In *Ten years of psychoanalysis in France.* New York: International Universities Press, 1980.

———. 1978. *Plea for a measure of abnormality.* New York: International Universities Press, 1980.

———. 1982a. Alexithymia: A psychoanalytic viewpoint. *Psychotherapy and Psychosomatics* 38: 81–90.

———. 1982b. Alexithymia, psychosomatosis and psychosis. *International Journal of Psychoanalysis and Psychotherapy* 9: 379–88.

———. 1984. The dis-affected patient: Reflections on affect pathology. *Psychoanalytic Quarterly* 53: 386–409.

Mahler, M., A. Bergman, and F. Pine. 1975. *The psychological birth of the human infant.* New York: Basic Books.

Marty, P. 1976. *Les mouvements individuels de vie et de mort.* Paris: Payot.

Marty, P., and M. De M'Uzan. 1963. La pensée opératoire. *Revue Française de Psychanalyse* 27: 345–56.

Marty, P., M. De M'Uzan, and C. David. 1963. *L'investigation psychosomatique.* Paris: Presses Universitaires de France.

Meltzer, D. 1967. *The psychoanalytical process.* London: Heinemann.

————. 1977. *Sexual states of mind.* Perthshire: Clunie Press.

Meltzer, D., S. Hoxter, D. Weddell, and I. Wittenberg. 1975. *Explorations in autism.* Perthshire: Clunie Press.

Modell, A. 1969. *Object love and reality.* London: Hogarth Press.

————. 1971. The origin of certain forms of pre-oedipal guilt and the implications for a psychoanalytic theory of affects. *International Journal of Psychoanalysis* 52: 337–42.

————. 1973. Affects and psychoanalytic knowledge. In *Annual of Psychoanalysis,* vol. 1: 117–24. New York: Quadrangle.

Montgrain, N. 1983. On the vicissitudes of female sexuality. *International Journal of Psychoanalysis* 64: 169–86.

Nemiah, J. C. 1975. Denial revisited: Reflections on psychosomatic theory. *Psychotherapy and Psychosomatics* 26: 140.

————. 1978. Alexithymia and psychosomatic illness. *Journal of Continuing Education in Psychiatry* (1978): 25–37.

Nemiah, J. C., and P. Sifneos. 1970. Affect and fantasy in patients with psychosomatic disorders. *Modern trends in psychosomatic medicine,* vol. 2. London: Butterworth.

Ogden, T. 1980. The nature of schizophrenic conflict. In *Projective identification and psychotherapeutic technique,* pp. 135–71. New York: Jason Aronson, 1982.

————. 1985. On potential space. *International Journal of Psychoanalysis* (in press).

Pontalis, J. B. 1977. *Frontiers in psychoanalysis.* London: Hogarth Press, 1981.

Sartre, J-P. 1965. *Situation one.* Paris: Gallimard.

Rad, M. von, M. Drücke, W. Knauss, and F. Lolas. 1979. Alexithymia in a comparative study of verbal behaviour in psychosomatic and psychoneurotic patients. In *The content analysis of verbal behaviour,* ed. L. Gottschalk. New York: Spectrum Publications.

Rad, M. von, L. Lolucat, and F. Lolas. 1977. Differences of verbal behaviours in psychosomatic and psychoneurotic patients. *Psychotherapy and Psychosomatics* 28: 83–97.

Segal, H. 1964. *Introduction to the work of Melanie Klein.* New York: Basic Books.

Sifneos, P. E. 1973. The prevalence of "alexithymic" characteristics in psychosomatic patients. *Psychotherapy and Psychosomatics* 22: 255–62.

————. 1974. Reconsideration of psychodynamic mechanisms in psychosomatic symptom formation in view of recent clinical observations. *Psychotherapy and Psychosomatics* 24: 151–55.

————. 1975. Problems of psychotherapy in patients with alexithymic characteristics and physical disease. *Psychotherapy and Psychosomatics* 26: 65–70.

Smirnoff, V. 1977. Epreuve. *Nouvelle Revue de Psychanalyse* 16: 195–202.

Spitz, R. 1949. Autoerotism: Some empirical findings and hypotheses. *Psychoanalytic Study of the Child* 3–4: 85–120. New York: International Universities Press.

————. 1962. Autoerotism re-examined. In *Psychoanalytic Study of the Child* 17: 283–315. New York: International Universities Press.

BIBLIOGRAPHY

Stein, M. 1979. Review of *The restoration of the self,* by Heinz Kohut. *Psychoanalytic Quarterly* 49: 665–80.

Stewart, S. 1972. Quelques aspects théoriques du fétichisme. In *La sexualité perverse,* pp. 159–92. Paris: Payot.

Stoller, R. 1968. *Sex and gender.* New York: Science House.

———. 1975. *Perversion: The erotic form of hatred.* New York: Pantheon.

———. 1979. The gender disorders. In *Sexual deviations,* vol. 2, ed. I. Rosen, pp. 109–38. Oxford: Oxford University Press.

Stolorow, R. 1975. Toward a functional definition of narcissism. *International Journal of Psychoanalysis* 56: 179–86.

Strachey, J. 1934. The nature of the therapeutic action of psychoanalysis. *International Journal of Psychoanalysis* 15: 127–59.

Tausk, V. 1919. On the origin of the "influencing machine" in schizophrenia. *Psychoanalytic Quarterly* 2: 519–66, 1933.

Taylor, G. 1977. Alexithymia and the counter-transference. *Psychotherapy and Psychosomatics* 28: 141–47.

Warnes, H. 1982. The dream specimen in psychosomatic medicine in light of clinical observations. *Psychotherapy and Psychosomatics* 38.

Winnicott, D. 1951. Transitional objects and transitional phenomena. In *Collected papers,* pp. 229–42. New York: Basic Books, 1958.

———. 1960. True and false self. In *The maturational process and the facilitating environment.* London: Hogarth Press, 1965.

———. 1971. *Playing and reality.* New York: Basic Books.

Index

Index

Freud, Sigmund, 12, 19, 21, 24, 25, 43, 51, 52, 76, 78, 82, 85, 88, 96, 108, 110, 111, 111*n*, 116, 117, 124, 126, 148, 154, 181, 184, 187, 189, 193, 216, 219, 231, 249, 250, 278, 282; and concept of perversion, 247–249; and conceptualization of vicissitudes of affect, 151–154

genital play, 275
Grotstein, James, 78, 173

hallucinatory experience, psychoneurosis and, 207–209
hallucinatory wish fulfillment, 51
Hanly, Charles, 215, 220
homeostasis, libidinal, 24
homosexuality, 12, 32–33, 34, 36, 130–135, 212; role of partner in, 256–261; *see also* archaic sexuality; neosexualities; sexuality
humanity, basic dramas of, 63–64
humiliation, neosexualities and, 259
hypochondria, 85
hysteria, archaic, transformation of, 204–206; *see also* psychosomatic states

I: childhood and, 40; composition of, 286; concept of, 4, 5, 6, 7, 11, 13, 15; death and, 51; ego identity of, 43; narcissistic pathology and, 214; neurotic sector of, 44; play and, 56; psyche/soma disjunction and, 53; psychic survival and, 63–64; psychosoma drama and, 60; psychotic, neoreality of, 63; repetition compulsion of, 127, 128
I-World relationship, 76
ideas, affect and, 153–154

identity, maintenance of feeling of, 127–129
illusion, truth and, 284–287
impossible, notion of, 8, 10, 12, 14–15; as theater, 51–52
infant: autoerotism, 249–251; body of, 225–226; mother and, 162
Interiors (Woody Allen), 103, 104
irrepresentable, staging of, 81–106; chasmic mother and cork child, 99–102; neurotic symptom, first glimpse of, 90–93; phobia, birth of, 94–99; psychosoma and the mother, 84–87; somatic to psychological symptoms, 102–106; terrors and smother love, 87–90

Kernberg, Otto, 217
Klein, Melanie, 19, 78, 173, 184, 204, 219, 259, 274
Kohut, Heinz, 217, 222, 223, 225, 227, 231; and theory of narcissism, 219–221
Krystal, Henry, 112*n*, 121, 122, 160, 166, 280; and affects, research into, 157–158
Kuhn, Thomas, 220

Lacan, Jacques, 21, 44, 249
language, psychoanalysis and, 149–150
lateral transference, 203
Lax, Ruth, 72*n*
Lefebvre, Paul, 115
libidinal conflict, 116–118
libidinal stasis, 24
Lichtenstein, H., 126, 191, 271

McDougall, Joyce, 26, 36, 69, 82, 101, 103, 107, 110, 113, 114, 116, 123,

Index

parental images, neosexualities and, 264–265

parent(s): "double-bind," 58; neosexuality and, 277; unconscious of, 13

Paris School of analyst-psychosomaticists, 159

partner, role of: in neosexualities, 255–261; in homosexuality, 256–261

pathological transitional objects, 67

penis, *see* phallus

people, as addictive substances, 68

perversion, 245–247; as "character perversion," 69; as deviation, 246; Freud's concepts of, 247–249; meaning of, 246; perverse vs. psychosomatic organizations of, 119–123

phallic-genital vs. primitive Oedipal organization, 209–213

phallus, 44, 45; as dangerous, in neosexualities, 267–270; as symbol, 44

phobia, birth of, 94–99

phobic object, 45–46

phobic scenario, 41–46, 50

Picasso, Pablo, 191

Pirandello, Luigi *(Six Characters in Search of an Author)*, 68, 286

"play areas" (Winnicott), 56, 57; *see also* addictive play

Plea for a Measure of Abnormality (McDougall), 11*n*

Polanski, Roman, 210

Pontalis, Jean-Bertrand, 21, 249

preconscious functioning, 124

preverbal symbolism, 108

primitive communication, 171

projective identification, and alexithymia, 173–174

prostitutes, in masturbation fantasy, 101

pseudonormality, 156

psyche/soma split, 53, 123–124; in alexithymia, 177–179

psychic bisexuality, 44

psychic economy, 109–110; affect, role of in, 147–149

psychic elaboration, *see* psychic repertory, elaboration and transformation of

psychic rejection, 185

psychic repertory, elaboration and transformation of, 125–146; and anxiety neurosis, return of, 135–136; and homosexuality, 130–135; and identity, maintenance of feeling of, 127–129; nirvana, struggling against, 142–146; and rage and psychosoma, 139–142; and religious teachings, 136–139; repetition compulsion and antilife force in, 125–127

psychic states, static and ec-static, 24–26; analyst's experience of, 36–39; psyche/soma split, 25; stasis in analyst, 26

psychoanalysis, work of, 21–24; psychic elaborations, by analyst, 23–24; working out and working through, 21–22

Psychoanalysis of Children, The (Klein), 19

psychoanalytical theories of affect pathology, 160–165

psychoanalytic stage, 17–21; with analysis of children (Klein), 19–20; and free-floating associations and theorizations, 20–21

psychoneurosis from psychosomatosis, 180–213; and body-image, consolidation of, and sexual functions, 198–201; and dreams and visions, 184–189; and ego, failure of, hallucinatory experience and, 207–209; and eyes, role of, 181–184, 201–204; and hysteria, archaic, transformation of, 204–206; and Oedipal elements, archaic, 189–198; and phallic-genital vs. primitive Oedipal organization, 209–213; and sexuality, 186–187

psychosis, with psychosomatosis and alexithymia, 167–170

psychosoma, 53–63; death and, 60; delusion and, 61–63; mother and, 84–87; normality and, 92; psychosomatic communication and, 59; rage and, 139–142

psychosomatic personality, 185, 204

Index